"FASCINATING . . . reads like fiction." – *Ottawa Citizen*

"COMPELLING." – *Edmonton Journal*

"By the time the jury files in to deliver its verdict . . . readers would be forgiven if they have found Deverell guilty of writing A WELL-CRAFTED, GRIPPING STORY."
– Halifax *Mail-Star*

"For trial junkies, this is AS GOOD AS IT GETS, the real goods from an ultimate insider. And it helps that the book is gorgeously written." – Jack Batten, *Books in Canada*

"A warts-and-all picture of the courts . . . by the end of the book we find ourselves liking the pathetic Robert Frisbee."
– Frank Jones, *Toronto Star*

"Up to [Deverell's] usual high standards." – *Sunday Daily News* (Halifax)

"The narrative seldom flags; **Fatal Cruise** offers a rare insider's glimpse of the anatomy of a murder trial." – *London Free Press*

"Deverell succeeds admirably in relating the sorry saga of one Robert William Dion Frisbee, a 'glorified poodle' of a man."
– *Vancouver Sun*

"This is no whodunit. This is a howinhell." – Wilder Penfield III, *Toronto Sun*

WILLIAM DEVERELL

Fatal Cruise

The Trial of Robert Frisbee

M&S

An M&S Paperback from
McClelland & Stewart Inc.
The Canadian Publishers

An M&S Paperback from McClelland & Stewart Inc.

First printing November 1992
Cloth edition printed 1991

Canadian Cataloguing in Publication Data

Deverell, William, 1937-
Fatal cruise: the trial of Robert Frisbee

"An M&S paperback."
ISBN 0-7710-2668-4

1. Frisbee, Robert, 1927-   - Trials, litigation, etc. 2. Barnett, Muriel,
1905?-1985. 3. Barnett, Philip, d. 1984. 4. Trials (Murder) - British
Columbia - Victoria. 5. Murder - Juan de Fuca Strait (B.C. and Wash.).
I. Title.

KE229.F75D48 1992   345.71'02523'0971128
KF224F7D48 1992   C92-094753-0

Cover photograph by Peter Paterson

Printed and bound in Canada

McClelland & Stewart Inc.
The Canadian Publishers
481 University Avenue
Toronto, Ontario
M5G 2E9

Foreword

PORTIONS OF THIS BOOK HAVE BEEN CULLED FROM THE TRANSCRIPTS of the trial of Robert Frisbee and from his recorded pre-trial interviews. I have doctored the quotes only to excise, for the reader's comfort, most of the ums and aws and ers and other superfluous effusions that litter normal human speech. I have also weeded out most of the space-fillers lawyers love (in my respectful submission, with deference, may it please the court) and other excess verbal baggage, and I have reworked some phrasing for clarity.

In an effort to offer a more orderly account, the testimony of a few witnesses is reproduced in a sequence that differs from the order in which they gave evidence at the trial.

Although the story can be read as an anatomy of a murder trial, the reader must bear in mind that I have told much of it from the subjective viewpoint of both the accused and his advocate. Neither was a neutral observer.

I thank Jeffrey Green, John Conroy, and of course Robert Frisbee for their ideas and assistance, and my long-time editor, Ellen Seligman, for her untiring devotion to her work. I thank Richard Peck for making available transcripts I misplaced.

I dedicate this book to those who strive for a humane system of justice.

William Deverell

PART ONE
Pre-trial

THE BLUNT INSTRUMENT WAS A CHAMPAGNE BOTTLE. THE victim was a rich widow. Her manservant stood to gain several million dollars from her will. His name was Mr. Frisbee, and he was charged with Murder One: first degree. The foul deed had been committed on board an Alaska cruise ship, in an $18,000 penthouse suite.

Mr. Frisbee, incidentally, had been her husband's lover.

The narrator of this exotic set of facts was Jeffry Glenn, a friend and criminal attorney in San Francisco, and I was looking at the calendar: no, it was not April Fool's Day. We were into the merry month of May in the year of our Lord 1986.

Jeffry was at the other end of a long-distance line. I was unable to observe his condition.

I asked, "How many bottles of Chardonnay did you have for lunch?"

"I swear to God."

Who bludgeoned the wealthy widow to death with a champagne bottle in the cruise ship's penthouse suite? Surely this was the script for one of those ludicrous mystery weekend dinners. Agatha Christie would never have stooped so low.

"It's been on the front pages," Jeffry said. "'Murder on the *Royal Viking Star*.'"

"The accused is a Mr. *Frisbee*? Come on."

Yes, he insisted, this Frisbee was not a spinning plastic missile but an alcoholic fifty-nine-year-old gentleman who had been the dowager widow's chauffeur, secretary, housemaid, and all-purpose flunky. And Mr. Frisbee was likely to be extradited to Canada.

"Case of a lifetime," he said.

A fuller recounting of the events would wait. But Mr. Robert William Dion Frisbee, as it turned out, was indeed a living, breathing person. He existed – in the cells of the San Francisco County Jail. And the facts Jeffry gave me turned out to be substantially correct, although the weapon that felled poor Mrs. Muriel Collins Barnett was likely either a quart of Famous Grouse scotch whiskey or a bottle of white Demestica wine. The newspapers had preferred that it be champagne.

Why, I asked Jeffry, was Frisbee coming to Canada for his trial?

Because originally he was to have been tried in San Francisco, where he'd been arrested the previous August upon the *Viking Star*'s return from Alaska. An American prosecutor had just made the bold discovery that the ship was in Canadian waters when the murder took place.

The writ of the United States of America does not extend to foreign lands or foreign waters in cases of murder. (If you happen to be the president of Panama and you're a dope pusher, the law is different.)

The San Francisco attorneys who'd been preparing for trial were about to lose their client, no doubt remorsefully, to a Canadian lawyer. The reason for Jeffry's phone call: these attorneys had inquired of him about such a lawyer, and he had recommended me to them. Apparently money was available for a defense (a factor which lawyers must take into account if they wish to run a strong trial, not to mention dine occasionally in their favorite French restaurants).

Until Jeffry called, I was uncertain in that summer of 1986 that I wanted to commit myself to a big trial. I was researching a novel, and had recently spent more time writing than lawyering – and one's edge can quickly become dulled in the criminal trial business. On the other hand, one can't do justice, as it were, to all one's clients when juggling a dozen criminal files at once, as I used to do in full-time practice. And with the luxury of a second career writing novels, I'd been able to pick and choose my recent trials, interesting cases I could get my hooks into. I'd been on a winning streak.

And since I was going to San Francisco anyway, to research my next book . . .

"Any self-respecting lawyer would kill to get a trial like this," Jeffry said.

I said I'd think it over. It took me about ten seconds to do that. How could a lawyer *not* take this case? Most lay people, I am afraid, have little understanding of the animal known as the criminal counsel. They're bred to salivate when a juicy set of facts is dished up to them, with a side salad of interesting legal issues.

Almost before I put the phone down, I was thinking about possible defenses, the ones the public call "technical." I remember thinking, what jurisdiction does Canada have to try a U.S. citizen for the murder of a U.S. citizen aboard a Norwegian flagship?

Frisbee's lawyer in San Francisco was a young, vigorous ex-public defender named V. Roy Lefcourt. (I'm afraid I didn't get his name correct for a long time, and insisted on calling him Leroy.) His office was then on toney Union Street, an area which the middle-aged yuppies a couple of decades from now will think back on with the same fondness we from the sixties remember the Haight.

I parked my slightly bunged-up Mazda 2000 long-box pickup out of sight of Lefcourt's office for fear it would not properly impress him: if I'm a capable lawyer why am I not driving a BMW 325ix? But I was planning to travel some northern California back roads, scouting locations for my book, mental snapshots for my word processor.

Upon entering Lefcourt's office a client would know immediately he's not retaining some bucket-shop lawyer. The office was tastefully and expensively furnished, the desk organized. (That must be comforting to clients. My clients always looked with suspicion at the piles of file folders and unanswered correspondence that littered my desk.)

Associated with Lefcourt in the defense was Stephen Scherr, his research specialist, an amiable attorney who seemed to enjoy the disbelief that played upon my face as he narrated the story.

Mr. Frisbee, he said, had been secretary and travelling companion for seventeen years to the late and respected San Francisco attorney, Philip Barnett, who had died of heart failure two years earlier. Frisbee continued to carry on in similar capacity for his wife, Muriel, a more than merry widow who seemed bent on spending the family fortune.

The gist of the prosecution's case was that Frisbee had conspired to hoodwink Mrs. Barnett into altering her last will and testament in his favor. He knew her lawyer was drawing up a new will to be signed on her return from the cruise, a will which would largely disinherit him. To prevent this, as the ship was steaming back to San Francisco, he murdered her. The People rest.

The events aboard ship, as recounted by Lefcourt and Scherr:

Mr. Frisbee and Mrs. Barnett were sharing a cabin on the penthouse deck, with twin beds. The steward, a young Cypriot with the unlikely name of Michael Michael, came to the door about 6:45 with Mrs. Barnett's evening tray of caviar. Frisbee answered his knock. Michael Michael saw a body on the bed, blood on walls and ceiling. Frisbee told everyone he didn't know what happened.

There was a suggestion, said Scherr, that he'd blacked out, and suffered an amnesia.

The case didn't exactly seem like a walk in the park. But there was worse to come:

A couple of bottles were found in the bar area with blood smears on them. Police would testify it looked as if somebody tried to wipe them.

On the ship's return to San Francisco, police searched Frisbee and found two checks in his wallet drawn on Muriel Barnett's account. One was made out to Frisbee to the cheery tune of $300,000. Another was for $20,000, made out to Jerry Kazakes, the son of his lover – a certain Reverend Daniel Kazakes, a Greek Orthodox minister. And self-proclaimed psychic.

"This is the guy he lives with?" I was still playing with the thought it was all an elaborate hoax. But they had stacks of files, photographs, court documents.

Stephen Scherr didn't think Rev. Kazakes was going to be a positive factor for the defense. "He came to court one day wearing a robe as big as a blanket and a cross around his neck you could crucify someone on. He said he was going to blow the case wide open."

And how was Frisbee's defense to be paid for?

Well, apparently, just before Frisbee left San Francisco on the Alaska cruise, he made out yet another check on Mrs. Barnett's account, for $100,000, to Dan Kazakes. After his lover's arrest, Kazakes turned the check over to Lefcourt to pay for Frisbee's defense.

V. Roy had done a lot of work. He regretted that only $20,000 of that sum would be available to pay for Frisbee's Canadian trial.

I think I may have blanched.

Not to worry, said V. Roy. Mrs. Barnett would pay the rest. Her last will and testament contained a generous bequest to Frisbee.

Muriel Collins Barnett might not be pleased to know, from wherever on high she was now surveying our earthly domain, that she would be paying for the defense of the man charged with her murder.

◇　　◇　　◇

I took copies of some of the files and arranged to meet Frisbee the next day at the San Francisco County Jail. It would be up to him, of course, to retain me. I wondered if he would be a difficult client, this improbable Mr. Frisbee.

The files' cast of characters included names that seemed too absurd for any novel: Robert William Dion Frisbee, Concerta DeLuca, Michael Michael, Milagro Dearnaley, Inspector Klotz, the Reverend Dan Kazakes.

Lacking eye witnesses, this seemed the classic circumstantial case. That, despite what many think, is not just another term for a weak case. It really means that no direct, observed, evidence of the crime is available. The trial of a circumstantial murder is usually lengthy; the prosecution instinctively, in the manner of a spider, tries to spread a large, all-encompassing web. And the web in this case, with such strong evidence of motive, promised to be very sticky.

No witness saw Frisbee wield a weapon. And even were the evidence to point unquestionably to him as the assailant, several defenses reduce murder to manslaughter: provocation, drunkenness, assault without intent to kill. And a defense that could raise doubts whether Frisbee was acting with a conscious, rational mind could win an acquittal. Lefcourt and Scherr, realizing this, had been preparing a medical defense. Among the files were various reports from doctors of the mind, and the force of their views startled me.

Psychiatrist Joseph Satten:

"Clinically the amnesia does appear genuine. It does not appear to be a case of premeditated homicide."

Psychiatrist Fred Rosenthal:

"It is difficult to accept the possibility that Mr. Frisbee could have committed the violent act of killing Mrs. Barnett. To argue that Robert Frisbee was able to engage in this excessively violent action while in a completely rational state of mind is inconsistent with everything in his history and past behavior."

Psychologist Jonathon French:

"He is almost pathologically unassertive. I am unaware of one single instance of violent or socially negative behavior in his background. Test data are simply devoid of pent-up resentment, hostility or predispositions to violence. . . . The crime of which he is charged would seem to be quite out of character."

The reports were peppered with phrases like these: "Intensely needy . . . emotionally inadequate . . . subservient go-fer for a wealthy family . . . a glorified poodle . . . a court jester." Even the doctors who examined Frisbee on behalf of the U.S. Attorney-General seemed to share a view that acts of violence would be abhorrent to the almost pathologically unassertive Mr. Frisbee.

What manner of creature was this? What forces warped and shaped him? How does such a timid mouse gain the strength to batter in someone's head? I searched the files for answers.

My first peek at Frisbee came from a file of news clippings: a front-page photograph in *The San Jose Mercury News* beside a feature story by Kathy Holub: "MURDER on the *Royal Viking Star.*" The caption read: "Muriel Barnett and Robert Frisbee donned party hats while traveling on a cruise about five years ago."

I later learned the picture had been sold to Frisbee by the ship's photographer and given to the newspaper by his roommate, Dan Kazakes. It shows Muriel Collins Barnett to the left, short, perky, bold, smiling at the camera with lips ablaze and shining, wearing

14

a flowerprint dress and a hat that looks like, well, a cable car full of elves. Beside her, Frisbee shows a sly, happy expression. He has the look of one who is enjoying a secret joke. Spare, almost elfin, long of nose and little of chin, but not unhandsome. On his head is a peaked cap topped with ... possibly a spread fan of many colors. God knows what it is.

With both hands he holds a glass ... of gin or vodka? The hands seem to be caressing that glass.

Above the picture in bold type across three columns, Holub's first paragraph hooks you:

"She was a vivacious, wealthy woman who didn't like to cook or handle cash. He made her life easy, whisking her out to dinner and offering his arm. He kept her accounts, danced with her at parties, drove her through San Francisco in her Cadillac, and toted her luggage around the world. When she died on a cruise ship last summer, her skull split open by a bottle of champagne, he was bewildered and aghast."

On another page, another photo: "Philip and Muriel Barnett with their secretary and companion Robert Frisbee, right, on a different cruise several years ago."

The three of them stand facing the camera dressed as if for the captain's party. The late Philip Barnett is tall and dapper, probably in his seventies, carrying his weight well. White hair, a ruddy, strong face. One senses power; he's proud of being establishment. He has his arm around his wife, in rather proprietary fashion, and seems to be listing to his left. Resplendent in black tie, he more than vaguely conjures up the image of a distinguished penguin.

Muriel Barnett stands between and a little in front of her escorts, too close to the camera, which turns her white and ghost-like. Her fur-collared gown, like the flowerprint dress in the other picture, seems to suggest a fondness for ostentatious dress. (I later found out Frisbee often called her – affectionately – a "bird of paradise.")

Robert Frisbee seems unsure just how close he should get to Mrs. Barnett. He stands almost timidly apart from her, but his right arm is extended; his hand might be delicately upon the back of her waist. His dress shirt has frills: decorous, not showy. Again he has that look, as if savoring a little secret.

I went back to Holub's story: "Frisbee, who is openly gay, also stands behind the startling claim he made upon his arrest – that he'd carried on a ten-year sexual affair with Muriel's late husband, Philip. Muriel, he said, was like a mother to him and had been too much of a lady to protest the affair.

"In the interview room at the San Francisco jail recently, Frisbee refused to discuss the case, saying his lawyer would 'kill' him if he talked to any more reporters."

Reporters, psychologists, vague acquaintances, Inspector Klotz of the San Francisco Police Department, agents Wong and Zavala of the FBI, Frisbee had talked to them all. He'd been a gushing, babbling brook until Lefcourt tried, without complete success, to dam him up. (Later, I saw this note in some memoirs Frisbee had been writing: "After my arrest my attorney told me not to talk to anyone, and I did not, except the press.")

Clearly, with his claim to amnesia, he had talked himself out of a defense usually hard to refute: provocation. If a man reacts to a vile insult on the sudden, without time for his temper to cool, he may be convicted only of the lesser charge of manslaughter. The prosecution often cannot negative such a defense, because invariably its sole witness resides in the hereafter – a jurisdiction where no subpoena can be served. But Frisbee professed to recall nothing of the events that led to Mrs. Barnett's death. He had amnesia.

I don't like amnesia. To a jury, amnesia always seem too convenient, a coward's lie.

Chapter 2

WHILE HE WAS IN THE SAN FRANCISCO JAIL, ROBERT DECIDED he would write a book about himself. It begins: "In the gay life there is no future, only the past happening over and over again." Which sort of says it all. Maybe he should have ended the book right there.

Robert was no longer sure why he tried to write an autobiography. He'd told himself it was for the money – a best-seller about a life lived by an average gay gentleman of meager beginnings who was tossed on the shores of luxury. With a frightening murder at the end.

But later a psychiatrist asked Robert if writing about himself wasn't a way of seeking his past, of seeking himself. He learned a lot from the psychiatrists who examined him for court, especially Dr. James Tyhurst.

TYHURST INTERVIEWS

Mr. Frisbee, I'm going to record our conversation.

All right.

It is easier for me that way. Do you know my name?

Tyroost, Dr. Tyroost.

Tyhurst. And do you know why I am here?

You're a psychiatrist, I believe.

That's correct.

To interview me on the reason I'm here. On the order of my attorney.

At his request. All right, I'm not going to start with that particular matter. I am going to start a little further back in time, okay?
All right.
I want you to tell me where you were born.

Robert was born, for the record, in West Springfield, Massachusetts, in 1927, on the 5th day of May, under the sign of Taurus. The bull. (Patience, persistence, ardor, gallantry, sincerity, sensualism.) Anyway, he was fifty-nine now. Going on a hundred.

His roots are New England working class. Irish, with a little injection of French-Canadian Indian blood (so he's been told). And Catholic: although one must never suspect Robert of overindulgence in the homely comforts of formal religion. He'd never found many useful answers there, frankly. But each to his own.

His father was a trucking dispatcher for a company that made cardboard boxes. He'd been a radio operator in one of those two-seater aircraft of the First World War, and his plane had been struck by lightning during a reconnaissance, and he lost 85 per cent of his hearing.

TYHURST INTERVIEWS

How did your mother and father get along?
Silently.
What kind of man was he?
I never knew him well. We couldn't communicate with him, so we didn't talk . . . I guess he must have been a dual person because he was very stern and severe at home and when I become older I found out that he was one of the most charming men people wanted to meet. He had many friends. He had a mistress he kept.
And at home?
He had very definitely strong ideas about how the children should be brought up. A good provider, not a lot of luxuries because of the depression, but, um, he was the master of the house. My mother was terrified of him.
Why was she terrified of him?
He would get violent with her.

In his childhood Robert was visited by a recurring dream. He would be walking toward the edge of a cliff, although sometimes it was a roof. He would be pulled toward the edge as if by a magnet. And he would wake up in tears and sweat. Robert never used to question that dream; he accepted it. Part of life's continuing trauma. But now he has started wondering about it. He has been thinking: what was beyond that cliff? What jagged rocks of fear and self-debasement?

He had other nightmares. A cold and violent man attacking him. Sometimes that man became his father. And sometimes the victim became his mother. And Robert often wonders if he became his mother in some odd way, in the way of flesh and blood.

His daylight hours had also been filled with dreams. He used to imagine himself as a person of gentle birth in a gentle era, at ease in the drawing rooms of fine houses, a favorite guest of famous hostesses, a master of idle witty chatter. And at the climax of such a dream – the setting a gala ball – Cinderella would be swept off his feet by a noble hero. Someone like Douglas Fairbanks. Or Clark Gable in *Gone with the Wind*. Robert liked the book, loved the movie.

He found inspiration for his dreams in the local library, among the worn pages of romances and histories and biographies. He lived in the Court of the Bourbons in France, and shared sup with Henry the Eighth. He would don the sumptuous gowns of the heroine, he would become her, and share her glory as she was crowned Queen of the Gauls.

Another reason he liked the library was because they couldn't taunt him there . . .

TYHURST INTERVIEWS

I went to a girl's school, a girl's high school.

Why?

That was the only school in town that had training for short-hand and typing. It was ninety-five per cent girls.

How did you get along at school? Did you play sports at all?

Not very well.

What was the problem?

I didn't go for sports. The five per cent that were boys didn't want . . . I was rather feminine-looking, I guess, and acting.

19

Feminine-looking?
And acting, you know.
Were you?
Um-hm. Just right for the type of teasing people went in for.
Did they tease you?
Um-hm. (Inaudible) They teased me.

The way he walked. The way he talked. In that little false
soprano voice. They called him a pansy, a momma's boy. They
played ghastly jokes on him, tripped him on the playground,
pulled his pants down. He never fought back. He should have. But
who had heard of Gay Lib in West Springfield, Mass., in those
cruel years of the Great Depression? Had he been decades
younger, Robert knows now, he might have stood up for the right
to be what he is. But the fact is back then he didn't know he was
gay. He had no understanding of the *concept*. They didn't talk
about such things at home.

He must have known he was different. None of the other boys in
school enrolled in ballroom dancing or joined the girls' choir.
While it's true he didn't go out for sports much, he did more than
capable duty as a majorette. His school teams didn't win many
games, but Robert recalls its cheering squads consistently out-
shining the opposition.

The older neighbors didn't torment him as much as their children did, but Robert was always an oddball to them, an outsider.
He was known as the funny kid who knitted as he strolled to the
butcher's to get a couple of fifteen-cent center-piece cuts.

The thing is, Robert has always knitted. If there was nothing
else to do, he'd just take out the needles and the yarn. He used to
knit at home with his adoptive father. And with his lover, Dan. He
knitted when he was serving the Barnetts. He knitted while awaiting trial. He knitted scarves and sweaters for almost everyone in
the lawyers' office. He wanted to knit in court, but his guards
wouldn't let him have needles. Too dangerous. He might kill
someone.

How he started his knitting was like this: in his sixth year of
school his teacher, who was very progressive for the times,
announced that an hour of each week would be put aside so the

students could express themselves – by performing a favorite handicraft. Robert wasn't sure why, but he chose knitting.

His first creation was a scarf that would have fit an elephant. His teacher had shown him how to start the process, but not how to stop.

Knitting seemed to help quell the terrors within. And it kept him away from his fingers.

TYHURST INTERVIEWS

Did you bite your fingernails?

Yes, I did.

For how long?

I have always wondered about that. It was a terror in my mother's life for years.

Your mother was concerned about it?

Yes, she put iodine on my fingertips and, uh, lectured me about biting my nails and disfiguring them.

How did you get along with your mother?

We were very, very close. She considered me her baby, her pet, her adorable, and I loved her.

What was your mother like?

Very nice person. Very quiet, reserved. She had an inferiority complex, very easily dominated.

Mother didn't like him to play outside, and maybe she was right, because one day his brother and his pals dared him to make a Tarzan-like jump from one branch of a cherry tree to another. He closed his eyes. He fell. He broke an arm. This was after Mother had told Robert he should wear clean clothes in case he ever got run over by a car. He wasn't wearing clean clothes when he broke his arm, so she had to get him dressed for the hospital. After scrubbing him from top to bottom.

Sometimes when she saw him outside, she would call, "Get out of that sun or the neighbors will think we have a nigger staying with us." Mother often worried about what people would think. People like the neighbors. Like the nurses at the hospital.

The weight of silence that hung over the dinner table was partly due to Father's deafness – it just wasn't worth the effort to express

21

one's desires without screaming – but also to Mother's lace-curtain Irishness. She was always closing those curtains, always just *so* afraid the neighbors would hear. Their dinner conversations were usually limited to three words and an index finger: "Can I have...?" and point.

Dear, dear Mother. How Robert would like to speak to you now. Somehow he became you, didn't he? Right down to the migraine headaches. But clothed in another skin, a badly fitting skin. Why, when he cries for you, does he feel like he's crying for himself?

You lived with her after they separated?

Yes, I did. The three of us, my brother and sister.

Were they divorced?

Yes, they had a formal divorce.

And she didn't remarry?

Yes, she did, but it was a tragic –

How long did that marriage last?

I think maybe about fourteen months.

Why do you call it tragic?

I think, doctor, it goes right down to sex.

What do you mean?

Mother was so very completely, um, non-educated about sex. I think she married a man that was very aggressive and, uh, adventuresome.

What do you mean?

By doing things she would have thought were just not very natural.

But now Robert thinks, maybe Mother learned to associate sex with brutality; her trauma was a ... conditioned response, they call it. Sex is hate. That's what she felt about sex. You have to submit to it.

Robert remembered the nights when the beatings would come: first his father's brooding, silent rage, then cursing, then the battering – controlled, methodical – until she submitted. Robert still has a picture of Mother curled up like a helpless animal on the floor, her clothes being ripped from her, his own voice choking

22

back unheard sobs and words: "Run away, Mother, run away!" And take me with you . . .

(And yet . . . and yet, how could he deny it, he did admire his father, so charming, so forceful, so manly.)

The day his father finally left is darkly etched in his memory. Mother had been home all day, in the kitchen, in a mood rather dangerously close to happiness. Aunt Mildred's marriage had been announced; there was to be a celebration of food. When his father came home he found Mother laughing in the kitchen and he raped her in the bedroom.

The next day, Robert's father took his belongings to his mistress's house and moved in.

When it gets right down to it, Robert doesn't enjoy sex any more than his mother did. It's the sort of thing you have to do.

TYHURST INTERVIEWS

What is your role there?

Well, in fact, I suppose you would say, the female role. I seem to get involved with bisexual men, if there is such a thing. My relationship has always been more or less one-sided with the other partner.

It has. How about your satisfaction with a man?

I have had a love affair going with my right hand for the last forty years.

I see. With what ideas in mind when you are masturbating?

Oh, fantasies. I fantasize a lot.

What sort of fantasies?

I really don't fantasize very much about sex . . . my main object is pleasing the other person.

Yes. Are you masturbating at that moment?

I give up. My main thought is just pleasing the person I am with.

All right. How many children were there?

I had a brother and a sister. She is four years my senior . . . she is a little annoyed with me right now.

Yes. About what?

Just personal.

What is she annoyed about?

I have told her I don't want her to come up here for the trial.

I see.

She is rather upset about that.

I see. All right. Is she married?

She is married to a policeman.

The next child?

Francis. My brother Francis. He passed away, he was around forty years old.

What did he die of?

The autopsy report came in pneumonia. Do people die of pneumonia nowadays?

Well, they may. It depends on the nature of the pneumonia.

He was a heavy drinker also.

How heavy?

He was a bartender.

How close were you to Francis?

We weren't very close in our later life. He was the one that turned me into a homosexual.

What do you mean by that?

Well, when I was five years old – that is my earliest recollection.

How did he turn you into a homosexual?

I couldn't have done it myself. I just remember him putting his penis in my mouth for some reason when I was five. It went on until I was around fourteen or so. My brother and I always shared the same bed.

You did?

He used to use it as a threat over my head, if I didn't do what he wanted to do in the daytime he wouldn't let me snuggle up to him at night.

Was he a homosexual?

No. When it came to the point of our teens, he went just the opposite, he became overtly anti-homosexual. If there is such a word or description.

What brought it to an end?

We never talked about it, but he just stopped annoying me after I was about fourteen.

Did the two of you ever talk about it subsequently?

Never once.

Thus went his days. From school or the library, back home, home to the angry silences of his father, to his explosions at dear Mother, Robert retreating in fear into the night, running, running, up the unlit back stairway that led from the basement to the tenements upstairs, to the bed where his brother impatiently waited.

Dr. Tyhurst had asked him: "Were you afraid of the dark?"

Robert had evaded: "I think I did have suspicions about the dark."

The child Robert had been absolutely terrified of the dark. Riven by an almost manic fear. Yes, Dr. Tyhurst, Robert has *always* been afraid of the dark. Dark hallways and dark streets and dark moments. It is only now as he has started to see himself, to learn how the clay of Robert Dion Frisbee became molded to this peculiar shape, that a dawning light has begun to soften his darkness, and the fear begun to ebb.

Chapter 3

FROM EXHIBIT 58, ROBERT FRISBEE'S MANUSCRIPT

Tossed in a cave-like jail with ten other strangers. Life is a blur. Everywhere just faces without character. Why are people talking to me and about me? "Oh, you're the one on TV, a real celebrity."

Sailing in a boat, experiencing moments on the ocean of motion . . . Where am I, what am I doing adrift like this?

There is a daily routine you have to conform to. Orders given to a deaf ear. A name is called – but that's you, you, Robert, come out for an interview. How many times have I made this journey down a hall . . . Suddenly a flashing of lights and questions fired at you. Unable to think clearly, and adjust to something that has you engulfed, surrounding you as in a nightmare – oh, to sleep from this impossible dream.

You are on a bed of iron, with no pillow – a gruff call for breakfast, the sensation of handcuffs scraping against your wrists, trying to remember a series of events, forcing you to account for a happening you are involved with . . .

Here are the blunt facts: you are in jail, accused of a nefarious crime, and awaiting trial for murder! They are accusing me of murdering dear Muriel! . . . The how and where I do not fathom.

The judge had a commanding voice. "I will not consider bail, you can bring forward a hundred witnesses and I will not grant bail, because this man will run." The judge said, "If I were on this case I would see this man stays in prison for the rest of his life." More handcuffs, and back to a familiar place you have been before. It is a jail! You are a prisoner! Do not think of that today. Think of that tomorrow . . .

I remember meeting a psychiatrist the day before, and requesting the gay cell. I look for the first time at my surroundings and the people I will be forced to live with from this time on. Quiet people seen through an elusive blur. There is the boy who had been kind to me. His name is Patrick. The other prisoners are considerate to me, and kindly offer to share their treasured possessions. One boy makes me a pillow, one offers candy, another covers me with a blanket, as I am cold, and a pill to help me sleep.

What utter dejection. I get a feeling of abandonment.

I prefer to just stay alone in bed and try to lose myself once again . . . Another dreamless sleep . . .

On my third day I have another talk with Robert – here are the blunt facts: you are in jail, accused of a nefarious crime, and awaiting trial for murder! I have to somehow adjust myself, and get out of this feeling of complete helplessness.

I force Robert to get up to breakfast and become involved with these people who have been kind to me . . . just a bit cautious, as my shoes have disappeared. And also a clerk who signed me in gave me a five-dollar bill and four ones, now I have only a five-dollar bill. So forcing myself I agree to play a game of cards with Pat and two others. Soon I adjust a little, and only the haunting questions in my mind come creeping into my shocked consciousness at night.

I am trying to lift myself out of this state of self-pity when Pat sits on my bed and asks if I would like to talk to someone. So I just listen for an hour about the circumstances which brought him here. As he talks I realize that all of these boys are between 19 and 30, and are here mostly because of their devotion to cocaine. Pat keeps me mesmerized in the tales he tells . . . We share a soft drink, and Pat very bluntly asks me if I fool around. Such a direct approach sets me back very much, and without thinking, I thank him and say no.

Later, alone, I again realize this is my future way of life, and mentally kick myself for not realizing that a few moments of just plain desire should be welcome to me. Someone to reach out to, to reassure you; after all, you are not just another vegetable. I will be selfish from now on, think of Robert. Feelings of guilt at these words and thoughts of selfish pleasure revolt me...

My first thoughts on awakening are the same thoughts in my mind before dozing off ... a feeling of complete rejection, remorse and wonder as the tears come from my eyes, realizing I will not be going home.

A young man comes to my bed and offers me a pill to calm me back to reality, and speaks to me, trying to help me adjust to this world of the nothing, people bereft of any identity. He puts me to bed and tries to soothe some of the frightened pictures I see in my mind. Then to a fitful sleep, dreamless sublime existence in cool waters.

In the morning after breakfast I have a long talk to myself, forcing my brain to recapture the events of the last few days – they are still not clear to me... After a few minutes I am distraught, and pick up my body as it is time for lunch, but I am not hungry. The boy that helped me last night is sitting next to me trying to be kind. He offers me a book to read, and I try to absorb myself in it, fighting the idea that this will be my new environment.

Then an interview with a lawyer who tells me Dan has hired him as my lawyer. A very practical talk discussing my complex motives, movements, brings out the unwelcome thoughts I refuse to believe. They are accusing me of murdering dear Muriel! The full shocking truth is unveiled to me. The how and why I do not fathom. Mr. Lefcourt listens to me recite most of my movements on the Star, and tells me not to talk to anyone. No one I can talk to anyway, as the fourth estate hung me last night to sell their filthy headlines. Too dismal to imagine.

It was in those cheerless cells of the San Francisco Hall of Justice that I first met Robert Frisbee. It's a full-facility institution, providing criminal courts and ancillary services, a police office, and cells for prisoners awaiting trial. It's south of Market, not in the plastic upscale section near the Moscone Center, but down at the corner of Bryant and Seventh, below the Tenderloin. Above and behind the building are freeway ramps: the 101 and the Interstate 80 clasp their fingers together here in a net of one-way arteries, and resonate with a numbing rumble of traffic. Across from the Hall of Justice the bail-bond offices of Bryant Street are lined up shoulder to shoulder, homely signs pitching their all-day, all-night services. This is San Francisco: the City Ugly within the City Beautiful.

Inside and out, the seven-storey building is bleak, square, functional, architecturally depressing. The lobby is a human potpourri; pin-striped lawyers scurry to and from courtrooms, uniformed police officers chainsmoke and gulp coffee as they wait for their call to court. Crooks, court marshals, prosecutors, court clerks, court reporters, and victims of crime: the Great Zoo of Justice.

In H-1, the homosexual wing, most of the guards are gay. Frisbee was sharing, with eighteen others, a sleeping room and what was called a day room (iron bed and a shower). He later described the facility to me: "Everything was open, and the toilets were open, and the shower was open, and sex was open, and dope was open." Bunk-jumping, he said, was the main recreation. Frisbee didn't partake in it.

They were locked behind doors for twenty-four hours a day. The lights were left on day and night. "The vermin and the cockroaches came out so heavily that we had to plug our ears up to keep them out of our ears."

Robert Frisbee lived here for exactly a year, among the desperate, the destitute, and the drugged out, while awaiting trial in San Francisco – a trial which was ultimately aborted – and then waiting while his attorneys fought his extradition to Canada. It was much later that I read in his manuscript this wistful note, apparently made in passing, about his unhappy time here:

"To live here in this ghastly atmosphere of the underdog is an experience every juror or person involved in law should live at least one day. Some of these people are really desperately in need of help..."

At our first meeting, Robert seemed distressed not so much about being in jail as about his appearance, and he apologized for it, ashamed that I had encountered him in a condition ungroomed, underdressed for the occasion of meeting a Canadian

29

barrister and solicitor. He was clothed in regulation inmate orange. (On visiting him here, his sister's first words were, "Orange is not your color, Robert." "It's no one's color," he responded dourly.)

"Oh, my goodness, I really wasn't expecting anyone..." he stammered. "I must look terrible. I didn't shave ..."

I might have told him that in my sportsjacket I felt rather overdressed. (I live on a rustic little island where to be seen wearing something more dressy than patched bluejeans seems a fussy pretension. Mr. Frisbee wouldn't have understood.)

His handshake was limp and not a little shaky. He somehow reminded me of Farmer Brown's frightened rabbit, but more obsequious, desperate to please. He was as much concerned, I suspect, with being well-respected as well-defended. He was lonely with isolation and fear.

He was slight of build, about five-foot-six, leaner, more haggard, than in the newspaper photos I saw. But I also observed laugh wrinkles at the corners of his eyes.

After I returned home, a letter arrived from him that began: "Thank you for coming down to S.F. It was a pleasure to meet you. You impressed me as a man of confection who will stand up and proudly stick to his arguments. You are one of the few people I feel I can trust." (A tendency to malapropism is among Frisbee's many self-confessed failings; among his varied saving graces, however, is an elfish but stiletto-pointed sense of humor. I hoped that it was not his sense of humor but a form of verbal confusion which inspired his description of me as a man of confection.)

I told him it would be entirely his choice whether he wanted to retain me.

"If Mr. Lefcourt recommends you, then that's good enough for me." V. Roy Lefcourt was also a man he could trust. Frisbee was a client hungry to believe in his lawyers, prepared to be eagerly submissive to them. I gave a silent thankful prayer for that: no client is more vexing than one who wishes to conduct his own trial.

I didn't ask Frisbee for his version of the facts. Too early in the process. (Yes, I know, those lawyers on TV shows always say something like, "I want to know everything that happened, Miss

Jones." Reality differs: a good defense can become badly compromised if an unprepared client blurts out unhelpful truths – because a lawyer may not, in good ethics, call evidence from a witness who he knows will give perjured testimony. I don't want to hear from a person charged with impaired driving that he drank a case of beer before the accident; on the other hand, I don't want to hear from a murder client that he had only one beer before he began waving his gun around. It is only after I explain how drunkenness reduces murder to manslaughter that I, or any self-respecting criminal lawyer, will ask a client how much he had to drink.) I recited the standard litany: Don't talk to *anyone* about your case, to social worker or psychologist, to policeman or prisoner; jail cells have ears. Don't write letters except to your lawyers. Don't write anything and don't sign anything.

He nodded. Of course. He wouldn't dream of it. My wish was his command.

But I sensed a holding back. I remember thinking: Have I sufficiently made that clear? Submissive Mr. Frisbee seemed like a person who might sign a confession just to be liked.

He asked, "If you don't mind – you don't have to tell me if you don't want to – do you think I've got a chance?"

A fact of the business: not a few criminal lawyers will fill clients with false hopes for their prospects, exuding a robust optimism until the pre-trial retainer has been fully paid. Such lawyers often tend, once the fees are in, to recommend a guilty plea. This practice is said to be justified by the far greater number of cases in which clients in their turn fill lawyers with false hopes, promising retainers that are never paid. I try not to buoy a client's spirits up too much if chances are good, and try not to discourage them from a feisty defense if the case is risky.

I told Frisbee I needed more facts, and time to study them, before offering an opinion. I told him that although it might not be an easy case to win, other verdicts than murder were possible.

Frisbee nodded. He understood. He was sure I would do my best. He felt he was in good hands. He would try to be a good client. He hoped I wouldn't be disappointed in him.

Before I got up to leave, he picked some lint off my jacket.

I felt bowed with an extra weight as I left the prison. He didn't seem an evil person. The evil are easier to defend. You don't worry so much about the result.

I drove from San Francisco to California's north coast, where I wanted to imbibe the sights and sounds and smells of a small coastal town for a mythical community called Foolsgold for my novel, *Platinum Blues*. The ghosts of Frisbee's complex cast of characters wandered across the Redwood Highway, taking form among the ocean mists that billowed from the forests. I would await his arrival in Canada.

Chapter 4

THE FIRST MATURE MAN IN ROBERT'S LIFE WAS THE MANAGER of the neighborhood movie house. Robert is still a little embarrassed about the whole thing, even though he was just a boy of twelve, which sort of makes the man a child molester, when you get down to it. Robert had learned, of course, from his brother the appropriate way to respond to this gentleman's requests, and that gave him entry, so to speak, into the theater. As a guest of management.

Later, when young Robert was working in the local soda pop ice cream parlour candy shop, he entered into a more meaningful relationship. His name was Jim Fitzsimmons, and he worked for the post office as a clerk. He was thirty-seven.

TYHURST INTERVIEWS

We would meet on weekends, and –

What age are we speaking of?

I was 14, 15, 16. He was the first man I was really serious with.

You were quite young. Did you travel with him at that age?

Yes. We wouldn't see each other very much. I would meet him at movies sometimes. Once a month, once every two months, and on occasion we would have an affair. But the actual sex thing was not, um, primary... I was not very active in sex at that time. I was a little frightened, I didn't know what to do.

It was occasional?

Even when we went to New York, I stayed at one hotel and he stayed at another.

But he was paying for it all?

No.

Who did?

I did. When we went to New York I was working.

How old were you?

About 15 or 16.

Where were you working at the age of 16?

Soda jerker.

All right.

Well, he gave me little gifts, too, little cash gifts. Anyway, when we got to New York, I usually had enough of my own.

What happened to Mr. Fitzsimmons?

Well, he and I passed the stage of being lovers. We became very good friends and . . . he played with other flowers.

Jim Fitzsimmons was a kind man, comforting to be with – although their sexual relationship did not exactly throw lightning into blue stars. But as Robert moved into his late teens he simply got too old for Jim's taste.

Their relationship formally ended when Robert's mother found his friend's collected naughty letters (addressed to a Mrs. Fitzsimmons in care of one of Robert's brief places of employment), and discovered that Jim Fitzsimmons had been arrested for stealing wartime gasoline stamps. But Fitzsimmons continued a correspondence with Robert in later years – a friendship by mail that continued until the older man's death. ("Your first love is the one you always remember," he wrote in one of his last letters.)

When Jim used to take Robert to New York, the older man would stay at his favorite YMCA and Robert in a separate hotel. One afternoon, while Jim presumably was cultivating his other flowers, Robert, then sixteen, wandered down to Times Square, and it was in a drugstore there that Robert met the second important man in his life – a merchant seaman from the West Coast by the name of Tom Leary: tall, husky, blond, and Irish. He coaxed Robert up to his room. Robert was really quite awed by him, overpowered by his confidence.

Robert soon found out Leary was a piece of rough trade, a hustler. At some point in their evening, Leary proposed that his new friend go into business with him. The business was shaking down closet gays.

These were the war years, times of bravery and masculinity. To be openly gay was almost traitorous – and downright dangerous. Tom Leary, it turned out, ran a whole team of boys. How it worked was Leary would go with them to the bars of the better hotels, where the boys would sit and smile at single gentlemen. When a man of apparent means would return the smile and engage the boy, Leary would follow them to the man's home, flash a five-and-dime police badge, and threaten to arrest his prey. But he always let him know he could be bought.

Tom Leary offered Robert a cut.

But Robert, with his puritanical New England upbringing, had a sense of correctness. He turned down Tom Leary's offer of this job.

They did continue to see each other, though, until Robert was inducted into the army.

He was drafted in August 1945. The reactions of family and friends were unanimous and predictable: "Maybe it will make a man out of him."

He tried. Tried to straighten out his life. No more homosexuality. No more loose and dangerous living. No more Tom Leary.

FRISBEE'S MANUSCRIPT

They started me off with something odoriferously called Basic Training. They gave me a rifle, but I lasted only one day on the target range – a long day, because I continually closed my eyes when I pulled the trigger.

Then I was exposed to the delicate maneuver of throwing hand grenades. My instructor, Sergeant Knight, a man with little sense of humor, felt I had placed him in a ridiculous light by throwing the hand grenade with an underhand technique, like a softball pitcher. He ripped off my stripe, but it was returned the next day when I was assigned to the Adjutant-General's office. I wasn't capable of firing a gun, but I could hit the hell out of a typewriter. I was in charge of personnel files for a while, and while I was there Sgt. Knight's file happened to slip behind a file cabinet. It was misplaced until spring cleaning.

Later I became a court reporter with the Judge Advocate's office. Robert would sit in on court martials and cases of discharge without honor: dreamers and bed wetters who could not adapt to army life. Many of our clients were homosexuals disillusioned by the adventures lurking behind the posters, the unfortunate shy ones who did not have the courage to display a nyloned leg to the indoctrination board.

TYHURST INTERVIEWS

You were drafted at what age?

Eighteen.

Okay. What was your rank on discharge?

Corporal Robert William Dion.

Why do you mention the names?

Because at the time that was my name. As you go along you'll realize my name changes because I was adopted later on.

Then what did you do?

I had married while I was in the army. She was a girl in the typing pool, next typewriter to mine.

And how old was she?

She was about four years older than I. Pauline Hazzar.

And how old were you when you were married?

Nineteen, or just approaching nineteen.

And how was your sexual relationship with her?

Well, we were both . . . both virgins. We didn't know what to do about it. In fact, she was still a virgin six months later. Neither one of us knew what to do.

Yes.

I shipped out right away so I didn't see her. And then she came to visit me, and we became truly united.

You mean you had intercourse?

Um-hmm. Successful intercourse. After the army I took advantage of the G.I. Bill of Rights and went to school to become a hairdresser.

And where was that?

I was living in Lawrence, Mass., at this time with my wife. I had a child in December of '47.

That would be after the discharge, eh?

Yes. He died in infancy.

Of what?

Congenital heart disease. My wife was a severe congenital diabetic.

Robert Paul Dion, who survived only long enough to be loved. And passed away of congenital heart disease. It was the first of many deaths of those whom Robert Frisbee loved, deaths that brought pain into his life.

Then what happened?

After my son died, I suggested we go back to Washington, D.C., where she had worked prior to the war, and we both took exams for secretary work. I worked for the Navy Hydrographic office. And then around the first part of 1949, I believe, my wife and I separated.

Why did you separate?

I don't know, really. I was already a confirmed homosexual, doctor. I tried to make it as a straight, and it just didn't seem to be working out the way I hoped to.

I see. All right.

My wife was getting more ill, and eventually she died of diabetes. Horrible way, and ...

I see.

She died of gangrene poisoning. She contracted that, and they just started operating on her limbs, and when they got to the ... where there wasn't anything left, she died during the last operation.

But before Pauline died, while Robert was still searching for the right place in the universe to fit the round peg in the square hole, Tom Leary worked his way back into his life, and brought the marriage to its foredoomed end.

What happened?

In 1949 ... he called Mother, and Mother gave him my

telephone number, and he came down [to Washington] to see me, and that ended my marriage. He turned my whole personality around again.

What do you mean?

I was trying to be normal and straight, and, um, he just pointed out the disadvantages of it, and how I was wasting my time, and he wanted me to come back to New York.

Did you at that point make any decisions as to what preference – I knew I was going to go only for men.

You did?

Yes, I knew by then. This man was very much into the scene, and he taught me more or less what I should do and not do. So I left Pauline and I moved to New York and went back into the hairdressing.

The fact is that Tom Leary asked Robert to return to New York and be his wife.

Tom Leary needed a wife because a union collective agreement required his employer to send regular bonus checks to any grieving, lonesome spouse whose husband was at sea. So Robert became Mrs. Leary, collected the checks for her sailor man, and enrolled again in beauty school.

Pauline phoned several times, hysterical, hurt at his desertion. But what could he have done? He didn't know.

Chapter 5

AMONG THE FILES V. ROY LEFCOURT COPIED FOR ME WERE A
dozen witness interviews by his private investigator, Russell
Stetler, and some alarmingly long transcripts of police interviews
with Frisbee which I almost didn't want to read. What defenses
had my loquacious client forced me to abandon? What costly
admissions had he made?

Most accused persons hang themselves with their own tongue –
I'd say 90 per cent of all convictions result at least in part from a
confession. I don't know why: people *know* they have the right to
remain silent. And police officers always (almost always) recite the
standard caution. But with some persons you can scream it in their
ears and set it in front of them in neon lights and they'll helplessly
rattle on, vocal cords functioning independently of the mind.

Even denials of guilt can incriminate. Especially if replete with
contradictions and absurd alibis.

Frisbee had been kept under loose ship arrest after the murder,
but San Francisco authorities had been alerted by phone and were
at the scene when the *Royal Viking Star* – 28,222 tons, 504 feet,
420 crew, 750 passengers – slid into its berth at the Embarcadero.

The San Francisco Police talked to crew members before they
interviewed Frisbee, and I put his interview aside until I gained
the strength for it. The first of the crew staff to see Mrs. Barnett's
bludgeoned body was Michael Georgiou Michael, the butler on
the penthouse deck. An energetic Cypriot, he seemed to be the
epitome of the cooperating witness, eager to please.

This is Inspector Ora Guinther, Star Number 693 of the homicide detail along with Inspector Klotz of the homicide detail. Today's date is Wednesday, August the 21st, 1985, time now is approximately 11:41 hours. About to conduct an interview on the *Royal Viking Star*, which is docked at Pier 35 in San Francisco, relative to the death of one Muriel Barnett. That's spelled B-A-R-N-E-T-T. The party being interviewed, and would you state your name, please, for the record, sir?

My name is Michael Georgiou Michael and I am the butler for the penthouse suites on the *Royal Viking Star*.

Okay.

In other words I take care all the people concerning service, food, in all the suites.

All right. One of your duties was to take care of, um . . .

Penthouse Six.

Mr., ah, or Miss Muriel Barnett and Mr. Robert Frisbee were, ah, housed in, ah, penthouse suite number six, is that correct?

Yes, sir.

All right. Could you relate for us, when was the last time you saw both these individuals together and alive in good physical condition?

Well, in the morning about 8:00, I served them breakfast.

Okay. Ah, for the record, that would have been August the 19th.

All right.

And that day, you, ah, made a port of call at what city?

Victoria.

That's Victoria, British Columbia.

Right.

Okay, did anything unusual occur on that particular morning?

No. Everything was calm, and they didn't have no arguments between them, and . . . they were calm.

All right. What other contacts during the day did you have with these individuals?

During the day, I didn't go to their room, only until 6:45 in the evening.

Okay.

I working.

And, ah, were you summoned to the cabin, or was this just a normal routine?

In the evening I normally go in with some cannabis or caviar, and Mrs. Barnett she used to like the caviar. So, I came that evening to work as usual at 6:30. I knock the door of Penthouse Six to ask them for the cannabis and the door was open, and I heard an answer from inside, "Who is it?" and I said, "Michael."

English was clearly not Michael's first tongue, and probably as a result of that, the transcriber heard "cannabis" for "canapés." (It took a minute to figure out that Michael was not Mrs. Barnett's marijuana connection.)

Suite six was on the ship's Sky Deck, one of nine penthouse suites on this luxury liner. It was the largest of the staterooms, with floor-to-ceiling windows and private balcony. The bedroom had twin beds – Frisbee had slept several feet from his employer – and was partitioned from the living room, with its bar, refrigerator, and lounge chairs. Access to the suites of the Sky Deck was by a hallway running between them.

Although Michael Michael said the door to suite six was "open" when he arrived with his canapés and caviar, by that, I later discovered, he merely meant "unlocked." Still, it was an important piece of evidence for the defense. If Frisbee were planning to beat his employer's head in, would he do so behind unlocked doors? Especially when he knew the butler would soon be showing up with the caviar.

Did you know whose voice it was you heard?

It was Mr. Fris...

Mr. Frisbee?

Fris ... Frisbee, that was it. He said, "Wait. I coming," or, "Wait a minute," something like that. And the passenger from next door, they came out, Penthouse Eight next door, and they start talking about, how was your day, did you have a nice day, and suddenly the door was opened.

Okay –

Number six.

And the door was opened by Mr. Frisbee?

By Mr. Frisbee, yes, sir.

And what occurred at that point?

He was holding his head.

You're indicating, for the record, ah, both hands to the side of your head...

Yeah, and he was start to say, "She's dead," and she was looking sad ... *he* was looking sad.

He was looking what?

Sad. Sadded.

Sad?

Yeah, and I walk in because the door he open it, and I saw the lady with all the blood, and –

Okay.

– I call right away, I went outside, I run outside, I told both stewardesses.

You walked in, took a quick glimpse –

Quick look, I, I...

Saw a large amount of blood –

I saw her lying on the bed like this or like this. I'm ... I don't remember exactly, like this or like this –

Now you indicate she might have been lying on her side, or some way –

I don't –

– Different, you're not quite sure.

I'm not, not quite sure.

Fine.

Because it was confuse that time –

Sure –

You know, the blood...

Michael Michael seemed to have found the whole episode not a little traumatic. Two nights after the murder, his memory clouded by blood, he could recall few details of the murder scene, was unsure how Mrs. Barnett's body was positioned on her bed. Unfortunately, in the reverse order by which one would presume such things happen naturally, the memory of many witnesses tends to improve with age. This process of course is never assisted by the prosecutor during his pre-trial interviews.

We would wait to see whether time and careful handling would sharpen Michael's memory.

Messrs. Guinther and Klotz met with Frisbee five hours later in the city cells. It was obvious they didn't quite know what they had on their hands.

The time now is approximately 14:58 hours. We're conducting an investigation into the death of Muriel Barnett –

"C.," does that matter?

Pardon me?

Muriel C. Barnett. Does that matter?

That's, ah, fine, ah, who was a passenger aboard the *Royal Viking Star* with, ah, Mr. Frisbee, when some time on August the 19th, 1985, she sustained injuries causing her death. Now, ah, Mr. Frisbee do you understand each of the rights I've explained to you?

Yes, sir.

Awright. Having these rights in mind do you wish to talk to us now?

Yes, I do.

Okay, and, ah, this year you had an occasion to take a cruise with Mrs. Barnett?

Yes, I did.

Can you describe the circumstances that day, ah, say from the time you made a port of call to Victoria, British Columbia?

Yes, we arose around 9:00, I believe, and had coffee and breakfast, and then we departed the ship, we had made arrangements for a driver to meet us, and he drove us around to see the sights of Victoria. Then we came back to the ship around 4:30, and Mrs. Barnett and I went back to our stateroom. We had a cocktail and I took a bath and she took a bath, and as usual we just took a nap in the afternoon. And sometime later, I don't know when, I woke and started to get dressed, and put on my pants, and turned around to raise Mrs. Barnett, and, ah, the wall and her pillow were full of blood. I tried to turn her over, and I went to the door and called the stewardess.

Ah, okay. That day, ah, when you were visiting British Columbia, what areas did you view?

We saw a castle, and we saw the famous gardens, had lunch –

Famous gardens. Which gardens are you referring to?

Ah, I can't think of the name of them . . . Butch?

Busch Gardens?

Something like that, yes.

The, ah, like the beer manufacturing . . .

Might have been. I don't know the background.

It had been a long day, and the inspector may have been thinking of a cold lager but the gardens, a standard stop on Victoria's tourist treadmill, are famous neither for being Butch or Busche, but Butchart, after green-fingered Jenny Butchart who, in 1915, decided to tone up her husband's abandoned lime rock quarry.

They also visited Victoria's cloyingly pretty Fable Cottage.

Did you visit any other places in Victoria?

We did visit another little landmark with a little cottage of some kind with gnomes all over it, and then we just drove back to the ship.

Okay. Um, excuse me, I just lost my train of thought. Okay, you entered the cabin . . . you secured the door?

I'm not sure of that, but I probably did not. When we were in the cabin I did not lock the door as a rule.

The position of Mrs. Barnett when you woke up. How was she located?

Well, she was at the edge of the bed with . . . I believe her head was on the pillow and she had her face turned, and, ah, she was kneeling down, I think. She was kneeling down.

What kind of relationship did you have with Mrs. Barnett?

Son and mother.

Did you have an argument that day?

No, never. Never have argued with her at all.

What was your opinion of her?

I loved her.

Like a mother or like a wife?

Like a mother, naturally.

Okay. Ah, how much had you had to drink that day?

I can't say volume-wise, we had drinks before breakfast, and cocktails at lunch, and some . . . one cocktail when we came back to the ship.

How would you classify your condition as to your sobriety?

Well, not sober.

Not sober?

No.

Was . . . you in full control of your capacities at that time?

Yes, I was.

So I mean you wasn't drunk then, you just maybe feeling a little high –

Very merry.

Pardon me?

Very merry.

Our very merry Mr. Frisbee was scuttling his own boat, and the intoxication defense was fast receding under the waves. Later I discovered other strong evidence to the contrary – the ship's doctor had been called to the scene and observed Frisbee to be drunk. So did the captain.

Everyone with experience of alcoholics knows how it works – you minimize, deny. Never admit to how much you've had to drink. Only gets you in trouble.

But the admission that he was in full control of his capacities – for which read capabilities, presumably – would clearly compromise our defense, and somehow we would have to keep these statements from the jury. The rule is that statements made by an accused to police are inadmissible unless the judge, hearing the evidence in the absence of the jury, is satisfied they were made voluntarily. And although the inspectors threw a lot of leading questions at Frisbee, I doubted a judge would on that basis deny a jury the chance to hear such evidence.

But the rules of the game would require the Crown to produce for cross-examination all persons in authority who had contact with Frisbee prior to his giving any statement. Otherwise a judge could not be satisfied that no threats or promises were made. Collecting the whole array of police, ship's officers, and officials of the Norwegian consulate who briefly boarded the vessel could prove too onerous a task for the prosecutors.

Among the most damaging items of evidence found in the suite were the bottles of scotch and Demestica wine, both sitting on the bar. They bore blood stains that appeared to have been wiped.

Do you recall you woke up before puttin' on your pants, do you recall washin' the bottle off?

Bottle?

Um-hmm. A wine bottle. Do you recall washin' the wine bottle?

No, I don't.

You think it's funny that we're askin' . . . the right questions?

I'm not being humorous at all, sir. It's the last thing I thought that could have happened in my mind. No, I don't remember a wine bottle. No.

Frisbee's reaction to being told about a bottle had been one of unfeigned surprise: a smile. I think it caught the inspectors off guard. There was an odd ring of truth here, an unmannered openness.

Inspectors Guinther and Klotz turned up the temperature.

Mr. Frisbee, everything you told us is true?

Yes, sir (inaudible) sorry. That's all I recall.

She was laying no more than two and a half feet away from you. That's true.

Maybe if she would have fell you would have woke up.

I probably would have. I don't know when she fell.

So you should have woken up, right?

I should have . . . Maybe I did. I don't know . . . I may have but I don't recall waking up.

What you're tellin' us, Mr. Frisbee, just doesn't wash with, ah, what Inspector Klotz and I observed.

(Inaudible) much I can say about that, I guess.

You've indicated to us that you are a problem drinker.

Yes, sir. I'm also a homosexual if that makes any difference.

It . . . doesn't. Ah, Inspector Klotz and myself are of the opinion right now, and what we're hearing you say, ah, doesn't add up.

Yes, sir.

And we can't see you sleepin' through what occurred. We think you're being less than truthful with us.

I'm sorry.

Well, you want to tell Inspector Guinther and myself what really happened.

This . . . it's hard.

I know it's hard, I know it's hard.

Yes, sir. I'm scared out of my wits, but I'm afraid that's all, uh, that I can tell you. I don't know anything else that happened. I can't recall another word, another thought or deed.

What are you scared of, Robert?

Well, I don't know, the future, I guess. I've been locked up for a day and a half, and I'm just a little bit emotionally disturbed.

We're not . . . you're not tellin' us the truth, the whole story. There's more, there's more, you know more.

(Inaudible)

Well, I wanna tell you something, Bob, we're gonna take you upstairs and we're gonna book you in. Charge you with murder. We have no alternative. Your story that you gave us right now –

– nothing I can do about that, is there?

We're not looking for you to fabricate anything.

No, I couldn't do that.

We was not there that day. You were and Mrs. Barnett was. When something happened and you killed her.

I won't deny I did it, or I won't say I did. I just don't know what happened. She's dead.

Are you thinking it's possible you could have killed her and not recall it?

It most certainly is possible, sir.

Why do you say that? Have you had violent episodes before when you have not recalled it?

Never before. No. Never had a violent moment in my life that I know of.

But you in your mind think that you possibly could have killed Mrs. Barnett and do not recall it?

Well, of course, I'm the only suspect. I have to think that.

At this point, ah, we're gonna take you upstairs and book you in on a charge of homicide.

Yes, sir.

Do you have any questions of us before we end the tape?

No ... I was just wondering if I could donate any money that came into me while I was here to the San Francisco Police Department.

Well, why would you wanna donate money to the San Francisco Police Department?

I think they're just a wonderful organization.

Okay. We'll end the interview now.

I picture them solemnly shaking their heads as they led Frisbee into the booking room.

By the next day the FBI was involved in the case. The bureau claimed jurisdiction because the murder occurred on the high seas, not in the State of California. By the time Special Agents Zavala and Wong started afresh on Frisbee, the authorities had learned that Frisbee, just before the cruise ship sailed, had signed a $100,000 check on Muriel Barnett's account in favor of his lover, Dan Kazakes.

He's a reverend?

Yes, retired reverend.

Oh, a retired minister.

Reverend.

What association do you have with Mr. Kazakes?

Normal homosexual relationship of thirty-two years.

Thirty-two years. Would there be any reason for you to be writing Mr. Kazakes out checks from the fund that Mrs. Barnett –

Yes, there could be. Yes, there probably were.

Was Mrs. Barnett aware of these checks?

Oh, yes. She asked me to make them out. We talked about them.

To Mr. Kazakes?

While given the check, he thanked her, but, uh, he also worked for her part time.

What amount of money are we talking about as far as you writing checks to Mr. Kazakes?

One specific check was $100,000.

Can you tell me what that was for?

No, we just explained it was a gift.

You gave him a gift of $100,000.

No, she did.

Through you.

Yes, I signed the check and gave it to him. I'm not sure if I made it out to myself or to him, but it was for him.

Mr. Frisbee, so basically you are telling us that not only do you write out checks to pay expenses for Mrs. Barnett, but you also write out checks, say, to someone like your roommate out of her account. And all of these are done with Mrs. Barnett's knowledge?

Of course, yes.

Did you and Mrs. Barnett ever have any arguments regarding the balancing of the accounts or where the money was going or anything like that?

No, nothing like that, no.

So she concurred completely with your decisions –

Her decisions.

One more thing, Mr. Frisbee, would you be willing to take a polygraph examination?

Yes, sir.

Have you ever been put under hypnosis before?

(Inaudible)

To get to the bottom of this matter, would you be willing –

Anything you desire to be done, I will be happy to comply with. Castration.

I don't think that will be necessary.

(Inaudible) . . . Not important any more.

Mr. Frisbee's generous offer was never acted upon.

49

ROBERT WAS TWENTY-ONE YEARS OLD WHEN HE MADE HIS
grand entrance into San Francisco in 1948. Tom Leary put him on
an airplane in New York after giving him careful instructions
about how to run the West Coast end of Leary's current business –
selling forged work papers to unemployed sailors. Leary promised
he'd be along soon to supervise.

Frankly, Robert felt uncomfortable about this. Selling false
papers to out-of-work merchant mariners posed certain risks to
the vendor's limb and body. And it was *wrong* – it was like that gay
blackmail swindle: Robert just felt it was . . . improper.

Instead, he used the trip to the West Coast to further his major
work ambition, that of becoming a hairdresser. A couple whom
he'd met in New York owned a San Francisco hair salon, and had
offered him a job.

And the job was indeed waiting for him (in what he disdainfully
regarded as a hair-burning sweatshop). But when he applied for a
hairdressing license, the regulators of California's hair-salon
industry – it's licensed in that state, just like law, medicine, and
engineering – turned him down: Robert, they said, you have
insufficient hours of formal training.

So Robert resigned himself to the furtive future of a life of
crime with Tom Leary, who was on his way west.

But Leary never joined him. He was arrested in New Orleans on
a charge of counterfeiting merchant marine working papers.

Living with an impecunious friend of Tom Leary, broke himself, stranded in the wilds of San Francisco, Robert contemplated

returning east, but was suddenly dealt a new hand of cards. It was one of life's happily wrenching turns of fate.

The friend of Leary's with whom he'd been staying, a cow-lipped workingman (which is to say, he worked the streets) by the name of Holly, took Robert to a party one night where he met William Dwight Frisbee, an amiable gentleman of means whose chauffeur had just walked off the job – drove off it, actually, in Dwight Frisbee's Cadillac. Dwight was enchanted to meet what he called a real live lady from Boston. He asked Robert to be his new chauffeur.

Dwight was a lawyer – degreed, but he'd never practised – and the scion of a wealthy lumber king. He'd been brought up spoiled in a home of women – if Mother refused to indulge his wishes, there was always Grandmother, and if not her, Auntie Anne.

After Dwight's mother passed away he felt he lacked women in his life, and married a lady of genteel birth, whose first name, like Mrs. Barnett's, was Muriel. In fact she was a girlhood friend of Muriel Barnett's.

The marriage quickly foundered – bisexual Dwight didn't seem to know which side of the road to walk on – but he and Muriel remained social companions even as Dwight was paying her a handsome monthly alimony. They visited, they gossiped, and shared their problems; he was a regular at her table.

Often Dwight would ask her permission to bring a friend to that table – he enjoyed parading before her the various street tramps and other oddities with whom he had replaced her – and on one such occasion, Robert was the proposed guest. She wasn't expecting much – Dwight tended to be rather tasteless in his choice of companions – but after she looked Robert over she announced her assent to her ex-husband's most recent liaison.

Armed with this approval, Dwight swept Robert into his life. Dwight was forty-eight, twenty-seven years older than Robert, but they shared the same birth date, and somehow that made the relationship seem pre-ordained. The stars were in their favor. The older man won Robert's heart with an extravagant display of affection, buying him twenty-one presents, one for every birthday Dwight had missed.

In San Francisco, Robert and his new lover haunted the grand hotels of Nob Hill and Union Square, the Mark, the Huntingdon, the St. Francis. It was while so deporting themselves that Dwight, an experienced voyager to the mysterious inner world of the perfect martini, introduced Robert to the pleasures of drink, an acquaintance that for Robert ultimately grew into intimate friendship.

The older man seemed to make few demands of Robert, in play or in work. Robert carried on happily, as companion, secretary, and chauffeur, helping Dwight maintain the family business and spend the family trust fund.

Ultimately they moved into a three-bathroom, one-swimming-pool home that Dwight built in Atherton, an exclusive township south of San Francisco. They would wander, hand in hand, through the half-acre of formal gardens surrounding the house. They would sit by the pool and gossip or read to each other.

The only thing that ever seemed to annoy Dwight was Robert's constant knitting – the clicking of the needles, he said, disturbed his naps. Robert's accomplishments with needle and yarn became the talk of the Frisbee social set – he liked to do fun packages, particularly in holiday times: yarn decorated with Scotch tape, ribbons, glitter, and furs. One Christmas he knitted some mink-decorated ornaments for their tree.

Dwight was a gastronome, and under his tutelage Robert became an accomplished chef. Shrimp cocktails with rémoulade sauce, noisettes of lamb with truffles, strawberries Romanoff for dessert – Robert learned all his master's secrets.

Dwight had always wanted a family, and that is why Robert agreed to become his son. And since Dwight did not want his inheritance to lapse – his mother's trust fund could pass to only his son or daughter – he took Robert to a lawyer, and made application under a new state law permitting the adoption of an adult. Robert went to court one day to give himself – legally – to Dwight Frisbee.

Robert remembers the judge shaking his head, saying, "I hope you two know what you are doing."

Upon leaving the courthouse, Dwight said, "Well, that's the

end of that." At that point – Robert was twenty-two – their sexual relationship ended. One does not commit incest with one's father.

Dwight became Daddy – Dwight wanted him to call him that. And Muriel, Dwight's not-quite-estranged spouse, became a kind of mother. They shared a joke: she was the wicked stepmother, Robert the wicked stepson.

Robert remembers the years until Dwight passed away as the happiest of his life. They lived indulgently, attended upon by maids and gardeners and mechanics, enjoying countless martinis beside the swimming pool.

Following the adoption, Robert remained celibate until he met Daniel Kazakes. Their first social encounter was at a restaurant party. Dan, six years older than Robert, was there with his current lover. A housing contractor, Dan began a serious courtship of Robert, who ultimately invited him to the Frisbee house for dinner.

That night, Dan Kazakes, after calling his wife to tell her he was drunk and couldn't drive, ended up staying overnight at the Frisbee house. Dwight, himself rather taken by the gruff, blustering Greek-American, didn't notice the secret glances between his new son and his dinner guest, and after they dined, Dan, pleading ill, went to the guest bedroom. Robert nervously slinked down to see him, and was in the midst of an embrace when Dwight came calling (with amorous intentions of his own). Robert scrambled out of the bed and hid in the closet as Dwight entered, found Dan feigning slumber, then left. Robert crawled back in with Dan and composed his shattered nerves. It was one of the most fearful events of his life.

Dan continued to visit, and finally Dwight took Robert aside for a paternal conversation, learned the two were quite serious about each other, and stamped the relationship with his approval. Dan Kazakes and Robert Frisbee became lovers. And remained so, for the following thirty-two years. It was an odd ménage: Dan's wife, of liberal views, accepted it. Robert grew fond of their only child, Jerry, then eight. Frequently Dwight and Muriel Frisbee exchanged family visits.

Dwight's ceaseless imbibing of martinis began to take its toll, and he frequently became ill: the alcoholic complications included a severe bout of pneumonia. Dan and Robert began taking him to the doctor every day for vitamin shots, and those became his only sorties from the house.

As Dwight's periods of sickness, invalidism, and alcoholic incoherence became more frequent, Robert would often have to clean him up – in the tub. Robert remembers one frightening night when – alone, without Dan to guide him through the trying time – he just couldn't get Dwight out of the tub. He remembers his tearful frustration, remembers how his portly father, maddened with drink, refused to give an inch. He decided that henceforth he would never clean Daddy in the tub, only the shower. Robert ultimately established a routine of carrying him up the three stone steps leading to the bedroom, then sitting him on a small rug and pulling him to the shower, later returning with rug and cargo down the hall to the bedroom, where he would lift Dwight into bed and tuck him in for the night.

Dwight died May 3, 1958, at the age of fifty-eight. The end was terrible – he choked to death on his own vomit. He was interred in the family crypt in Cyprus Lawn beside his beloved mother and aunt. Robert cried a short lifetime of tears – he'd loved this gentle alcoholic.

Robert was to receive a generous bequest from the estate, but not before one of the deceased's cousins attacked the will, maliciously – and hurtfully – claiming that Dwight bequeathed the money to Robert in return for illicit sexual favors.

He inherited an estate of $160,000, including the house in Atherton. But he was unable to maintain that expensive home, and bought a smaller house in nearby Menlo Park, where he lived for a while. Dwight's family broker advised Robert to invest in growth stocks (so-called). In eight years he lost $45,000 in an unsteady market, and $5,000 in bank and lawyer fees.

His small fortune fast dwindling, he placed an advertisement in the classifieds – experienced secretary, salary no object – and accepted a position at Stanford University, $200 a month, secretary to the professor running the law school's fund drive.

In 1963, he sold the house and put the balance of his savings into the construction of a six-suite apartment building – Dan did the contracting – and moved into its penthouse, and tried to retire into the life of a landlord. But within months, he realized he did not enjoy being always at the beck and call of tenants. The interruptions impaired his solitude: his days and nights were busy with missing light bulbs, stuffed disposals, burned-out fuses, and noisome dogs and cats.

Chapter 7

As of 1986 I HAD QUIT AS A SENIOR PARTNER OF DEVERELL, Harrop and Company in Vancouver, and joined the Victoria firm of Turnham, Green as associate counsel, defending occasionally in court, but mostly writing. The staff of that firm celebrated the turning of the season in June with what we announced as the first annual Summer Solstice Frisbee Golf Tourney.

"At approximately 12 noon the games will commence at the internationally acclaimed Frisbee Golf Course on North Pender Island," read the inter-office memo. North Pender, one of the Gulf Islands, is where my wife and I try to hide out in the summer, and the small island (two thousand mostly city-weary souls) does boast a disc golf course known widely among aficionados of that arcane sport. The holes are really large tin cans that the frisbee must clang against. It is usual to equip oneself for the ordeal with a six-pack.

After completing the course, the lawyers and secretaries met at my house to toast our new client (champagne, of course), and a few days after that I packed my still incomplete novel away and wrenched my head from writing mode to courtroom mode, moved from the world of imagination into the world of . . . well, reality.

During the summer I read recent case law, catching up on the latest attempts by the British Columbia Court of Appeal to lay waste the rights of the accused, and preparing affidavits for V. Roy Lefcourt in San Francisco, who was fighting a hard-nosed federal judge in a losing cause: Frisbee was clearly going to be extradited.

Jeffery Green, a partner in the Victoria firm, had agreed to serve as co-counsel on the case, whenever it meandered its way to Canada.

Then in his late thirties, Jeff had become one of the West Coast's pre-eminent criminal counsel. He'd earned his spurs defending impaired drivers – no mean chore (an impaired involves more intricate turns of law than a murder case, probably because it's a crime which the respectable and the elite, people such as lawyers and judges, tend to commit with the same alacrity as do the unemployed.)

I had met Jeff several years earlier during a joint, no pun intended, defense of a thirty-five-ton marijuana smuggle (a successful defense, as it turned out, for all twenty-three accused) and was impressed by his aggressiveness and vocal disrespect for abusers of authority, an essential attribute of the successful criminal lawyer. He is also a digger – strong in the library. And strong in the courtroom corridors where deals are made with prosecutors. He was married to the poet Susan Musgrave when I first met him. (Now he's not. Now she's married to a retired bank robber, the writer Stephen Reid.)

Jeff had recently won an acquittal of a fratricide murder – his young client stabbed his brother in the heart – by invoking the automatism defense. His jury reasonably doubted whether the accused's actions were those of a mind acting voluntarily. We planned a similar defense for Frisbee, and Jeff Green agreed to run it, along with other medical aspects of the case.

The one medical defense we agreed not to raise was insanity.

A Canadian jury may render two kinds of not guilty verdicts. Not guilty period. Or not guilty by reason of insanity. Only in exceptional cases does a defending lawyer consider the latter verdict a win, because the result can be the client's consignment to a hospital for the criminally ill (a Dickensian prison in most cases) for the rest of his natural years. Prosecutors have been known to vigorously urge such verdicts.

Because of the risk of opening up a possible insanity verdict, an automatism defense is prickly with danger. And it gives judges indigestion: it's vague in meaning, not easy to explain to juries without risking appealable error. But the defense exists in law, and if Jeff could build up a factual basis for it, our judge, however unwillingly, would have to place it before the jury.

The defense – as it has recently evolved in Canada – is this: a

57

person commits no offense if the mind was not with the body when the crime was committed. The act is then said to be involuntary, unwilled. The classic case is an act done by a sleepwalker, or one injured by a blow to the head, unconscious but still capable of action. He or she could be acquitted totally.

◊   ◊   ◊

MEMO
TO: JEFF   RE: FRISBEE
FROM: BILL   JULY 9, 1986

1. Jeff, I think it is worthwhile your looking at the psychiatric and psychological reports in the file that Lefcourt gave us. Some of them are actually excellent and might well support a finding of manslaughter.
2. I notice from the file that all of the defense psychiatric material will be in the Crown's possession. Sounds like it will be a trial with no secrets.

Under U.S. Federal Court rules, defense and prosecution must make discovery to each other of their psychiatric reports before trial. This offensive practice undermines three of the cardinal principles of criminal law: the presumption of innocence, the right to be silent, and the principle that the state must carry the burden of proof. The Canadian rule is that defense reports need never be shown to the Crown, although it is proper to alert the Crown to the nature of the defenses that will be raised.

We intended to obtain further medical reports from Canadian experts which would not have to be shared with the Attorney-General, but those of Dr. French and Dr. Rosenfeld, who had been retained by V. Roy Lefcourt, were already in their hands.

Fred Rosenthal, who holds double-barreled doctorate degrees in psychology and psychiatry, was of the view that Frisbee – if he committed the crime at all – did so as an act of uncontrolled violence while in an intoxicated blackout. His report was straight-forward and emphatic.

Jonathon French's report was both more exhaustive and more troublesome.

Dr. French runs a private practice as a clinical psychologist, and is an expert used often in the California courts. He specializes in working with adolescents, usually victims of physical, sexual, and substance abuse. An obviously caring person, who has helped many ghetto youths, he studied for his masters in English literature before taking his Ph.D. from Berkeley in clinical psychology.

There exists an unfortunate tendency shared by prosecutors and judges, and often by the lay people who make up our juries, to downgrade the opinions of psychologists, who may have spent many more years in the study of the mind than those darlings of the criminal courtroom, the forensic psychiatrists. And I could see a prosecutor making hay with Dr. French as an adolescence expert. ("Your speciality is treating children between what ages?" "Twelve to seventeen." "And how old is Mr. Frisbee?")

Dr. French's report was excellent in all respects – but it didn't afford a legal defense. One of his conclusions was that Frisbee – who had a history of alcoholic blackouts – was prone to suffering a "pathological intoxication."

So far, so good.

"This condition refers to a grossly exaggerated response to small quantities of alcohol, accompanied by moderate to extreme disinhibition and amnesia. Individuals thus afflicted have been known to experience rage reactions to fairly mild and even innocent social or physical stimuli."

We felt handcuffed by this opinion. "Moderate to extreme disinhibition and amnesia": what was the jury to make of that? It could sound as if drink and drugs made Frisbee less inhibited, and because of amnesia was unable to recall that he killed Mrs. Barnett. The expression "rage reaction" was simply one we didn't wish the jury to hear.

And if Dr. French told a jury, as he wrote in his report, that Frisbee suffered from a "partial lack of control" at the time of the crime, we would be stranded oarless on troubled waters. It is no defense to a murder charge that the accused merely lost control.

Frisbee, as a result of over-indulgence in spirits, had suffered an "impaired capacity for rational behavior." Dr. French added, "Simply put, not all the brain cells are there any more."

Simply put, however, no argument may be raised – at least in

Canada – that a person's capacity to think was merely impaired. We have no concept in Canadian law, as exists in other jurisdictions, of diminished responsibility.

Dr. French found it doubtful that a normally acting mind would choose a penthouse suite of a cruise ship as the locus of a murder. "One must wonder why he chose a setting of almost theatrical proportions to commit the offense... Mr. Frisbee doubtless had innumerable prior opportunities to dispatch his benefactress."

I had kept asking myself that obvious question: Why would a clever murderer not simply have doped the victim up in the blackness of the night and tossed her in the sea?

Dr. French described Frisbee as a fussy and demanding person who "probably argued in a snippy fashion with close friends." But he was not the kind of person "who smoldered with resentment or sullen anger.

"It is my impression that intense emotion, especially anger, may be especially unsettling to Mr. Frisbee, requiring a measure of behavior restraint which he was unaccustomed to utilizing."

He speculated that Frisbee had reacted to "a neuropsychological event of tragic proportions," and added:

"Mr. Frisbee had virtually no personal resources for dealing with such an event once it began to unfold. In my opinion something must have transpired between Mr. Frisbee and Mrs. Barnett which provoked an over-reaction in the former. I don't suppose we will ever know what this was – it might have been something innocuous which Mr. Frisbee merely interpreted as an insult or rejection."

That opinion would be helpful only if we could call evidence of such a precipitating event. But we would never know if anything had occurred between Frisbee and Mrs. Barnett before the murder. His unpremeditated reaction to an insult could have helped us build a provocation defense, but Frisbee's amnesia had denied us the tools.

Generally, Dr. French gave our client poor marks for memory.

"Short-term memory functions were clearly impaired and there was some evidence of mental confabulation," Dr. French wrote.

This wonderful word in its more familiar sense refers to a friendly chat. (My *Webster's* quotes Elinor Wylie: " . . . drew close in whispered confabulation.") *Webster's* also gives the more technical meaning: "a filling in of gaps in memory by free fabrication," or, as Dr. French put it, making up "bland filler material to compensate for significant lapses in memory."

Mr. Frisbee, he said, "seems moderately adept at this procedure." This augured poorly for Frisbee's ability to withstand a tough cross-examination, and I knew we would have to prepare him carefully for the witness stand.

The pages of the standardized Weschler test Dr. French administered were decorated with the psychologist's jottings: "A bit shaky in the hands," "gives up easily," "laughter," "overly abstract."

The word comprehension test involved defining a number of simple words. Two points if you're right on, one point if you're vaguely right, zero if you miss.

Frisbee was asked to define "swallow."

"Means a bird – I was thinking of a drink," Frisbee wrote. He won the maximum two points for that answer. He got zero for this one: "Matchless: a matchless person would not be desirable for another."

Another test commands: "Complete these sentences to express your real feelings."

I like "good food served perfectly and also a joy to see as well as eat."

The happiest time "is at home with Dan, enjoying our first cocktail of the evening."

I want to know "more about myself and what makes me tick."

I can't "eat carrots."

The future "is rather bleak."

I wish "I were home and today's life just a memory forgotten."

I hate "carrots again."

Dr. French made these notes as Frisbee studied drawings: "This is sex. No, not sex. A man has the remains of an erection. He's attacked this voluptuous virgin. Now he feels remorse and she's mystified."

Another: "Oooh, this is a little more gruesome . . . This man is laying down from a gunshot wound."

Ink blots: "Reminds me of an elephant with big floppy ears, trunk coming down the middle. I have a bad sense of perception, distances and depths confuse me. I can't tell an inch from a yard."

It was hard to see the murderer in all of this.

Chapter 8

Now at some point Philip and Muriel Barnett arrived in the picture. When was that?

They were friends of Muriel – the former wife of my Dad. I'd known about them but hadn't really met them.

It's through Mrs. Frisbee that you met Muriel Barnett and Philip Barnett?

Yes, I gave a dinner party for her, and I sent them invitations.

Remember when that was, the date?

I think that would be . . . say around '65, '64. Would have been Christmas time.

And how did the relationship then proceed with the Barnetts?

Slowly. We liked each other and of course we'd been wondering about each other all these years. Mrs. Barnett put me on her list of eligible bachelors and she invited me to several of her parties.

Eligible bachelors to meet whom?

Extra men are always welcome at a big dinner party or a gala or a ball.

And so did you see them more frequently as time progressed?

Yes, I did. We exchanged dinners, and we just liked each other, and I think the breakthrough came when Mrs. Barnett fell down and broke her hip, and I visited her quite a bit in the hospital, and I had some dinners with Philip while she was there.

Now Mr. Barnett did some work for you as an attorney?

That's where we got a little more involved. There was a lawsuit involving my little apartment house, and I asked Philip to represent me. The people buying it would not pay the amount of money they owed me.

And what did he do for you?

He presented my case in court, um, brilliantly.

Did he win it for you?

Yes, he did.

All right. Now Mr. Barnett was, I take it, a very influential and powerful attorney in San Francisco?

Yes, they were very social-minded, um, when I got to know them I was mesmerized with all of these balls and galas and the talk of the parties they had. And Mrs. Barnett always dressed beautifully, all of her furs, jewelry. And her friends were charming and important people in the city. Is that what you asked, Mr. Deverell?

That's not what I asked but that's okay.

I'm sorry.

You ultimately came to work for Mr. Barnett?

Philip in one of our lunches told me that he was going to semi-retire, he wanted to close the office down. And his partner was getting married, and his secretary was getting married, and he wanted to put his office right inside his own home.

Which was where?

One Thousand Chestnut Street, that was an apartment that they had built, and they had two apartments, and the rear one he would convert into more or less a semi-office.

What were the circumstances of his hiring you?

Well, he knew I wasn't doing anything, and probably to keep Robert out of trouble he offered me a position. I think probably he thought I might fit in in, um, several ways.

What . . . what do you mean by keep Robert out of trouble?

Well, keep him busy. All I did was knit and look at television at the time.

Yeah, okay. And so what was his proposition to you?

He asked me – I'm trying to think of his exact words – "I hate to insult you, Robert, but would you consider coming to work for me for $50 a month?" I thought about it and I said yes, I would.

Now you've given evidence that you sold your apartment building. What did you do after you moved out?

I moved to a smaller apartment very close to the Barnetts, about eight blocks away. I was almost in walking distance if it weren't for the hills.

Tell us how your relationship progressed with Mr. and Mrs. Barnett on a social basis.

It became very friendly. They were two very caring people, lovely people. They . . . Mrs. Barnett loved to dance, I was a good dancer, and we –

Mr. Barnett, did he dance?

Yes, but he liked to shuffle along the floor. He wasn't very happy doing it but he would contribute.

All right.

We just got along very well, very happy. It was a different kind of life than anything I'd experienced. I helped her plan her parties, her guest lists, and Philip thought I had an artistic flair with the decor, so we got along very famously, became close. They accepted me as I was.

Robert was in awe of Philip, a domineering male, a brilliant lawyer and businessman, a handsome, imposing man with flowing white hair that Robert just loved to touch. Philip had risen from a poor San Francisco household, one of several children of a deserted single mother who ran a little corner store. He worked during the day and studied at night at the law school of the University of San Francisco.

He married up. Muriel was bourgeois upper class. Her father, who owned a candy-making business, had sent her to private school. She was petite and bouncy and constantly, energetically happy. A social butterfly flirting and flitting about, with whom Philip was ecstatically in love.

He put her on a pedestal. He was the poor little boy from the corner store who married the rich girl up the street. Their marriage lasted sixty years, and through all those years he called her "the bride." Robert thought they were just a perfect couple.

Robert made their marriage even happier. Muriel finally had someone to dance with; Philip could concentrate on a more amiable pursuit, which in common with all Robert's mentors, was the consumption of vast amounts of alcohol. The threesome began to be seen in public with predictable regularity. Robert felt grateful to them. Shy, effete Robert with his homosexual lifestyle had been allowed in the front door, had been accepted by Nob Hill society.

Dinners, parties, balls. Opening nights at the opera. Excursions to the casinos of Reno. Traveling and chauffeurs and limousines and champagne and caviar. He moved in a crowd to whom a cocktail was like a lollipop, and under Philip's and Muriel's tutelage, Robert became by his early forties, an alcoholic – although perhaps he didn't yet know it.

TYHURST INTERVIEWS

How do you see your alcoholic problem now?

I know if I start drinking I will be dead in a month.

Why do you say that?

Well, my liver is in such a condition that it just couldn't tolerate another bout of excessive drinking. That will be the end of Robert.

Frequently, Mr. Frisbee, you speak of yourself in the third person.

That is a terrible habit I have had all my life.

Why do you do that?

I don't know . . . I am fond of my name.

You were quite dependent on alcohol, obviously, to get along?

I am afraid that's something I am going to have to face when I get out.

What do you mean by that?

Whether I am going to be able to lead a life without some kind of an artificial help. I am very anti-dope, I don't want to go into anything that is as repulsive as that. I am going to live a very plain, simple life. I am going to go to the desert. I have a house down there, and–

Down where?

In Palm Springs. Dan lives there now. He bought a mobile home. I expect to retire there.

Enchanted, drawn like a magnet, Robert slid closer into their lives. Although his job description was never discussed, he became much more than a secretary, and after a few years was serving them in a myriad of ways, chauffeur, bartender, valet, masseur, hairdresser, dancing partner. Except for weekends, when he escaped to the bosom of Dan Kazakes's family, he worked for the Barnetts from 7:45 in the morning, when he made them breakfast, until midnight when he put them to bed.

He mixed a lot of drinks in the process. On a typical day, Robert would start them off with their morning cocktail. He would fill Muriel's tub. He would take a little dictation, then drive Philip to the World Trade Club or Jack's for a luncheon date. They would have cocktails with lunch. Later, they would have cocktails with dinner. They would have brandy before Robert tucked them in.

His grateful benefactors gradually raised his salary to $200 a month.

Philip and Muriel spent with gusto – childless except for three godchildren, they had no one to leave their fortune to. But little of the coin that Philip threw around rolled in the direction of Robert. In fact he always insisted Robert pay his full third share of the threesome's awesome hotel and restaurant bills when they traveled. Which they frequently did, usually to Europe in first-class cabins on the Cunard Line, followed by chauffeured odysseys through England and the French wine country, boat trips down the Rhine, tours of the Holy Land. Australia. The Soviet Union. Hong Kong.

Keeping up with the Barnetts meant Robert was dipping ever deeper into his remaining inheritance. So he finally gathered together what little fragments of courage resided within him, and, hoping he wasn't being too much of a bother, explained – by letter – that he was unable to afford the Ritz in Paris or Claridge's in London. The thought of putting his feelings in spoken words to the overpowering, godlike figure of Philip Barnett was simply inconceivable.

In equally indirect response – Robert and the Barnetts talked to each other incessantly, but not *about* anything – Philip quietly increased his salary to $400 a month, and thereafter paid for the pleasure of Robert's company on their subsequent pilgrimages to Europe.

He also picked up Robert's share of the check at Jack's, where Philip had his own table; at Trader Vic's, Muriel's favorite restaurant; at the Mark Hopkins and the other Nob Hill retreats to which they commonly repaired, and at the World Trade Club in the old Ferry Building, an international businessmen's club of which Philip was a founding member.

But Philip found a way to ensure that most of what he spent on Robert came back to him. Regularly he would give Robert a bonus of $5,000 or $12,000, up to $16,000. Just as regularly, a week after receipt, Robert would return the check to Philip. Robert liked to call it not a bonus check but a bogus check: Philip deducted the amount from his taxes. His professional advice to Robert was to claim the uncashed check as income. Robert, of course, had to pay taxes on it, sometimes $3,000 or $4,000.

He didn't think it was a very nice thing to do, but he said nothing.

TYHURST INTERVIEWS

Why did you put up with that?

He did things like that to me, I don't know why. I just put up with it.

All right.

He was very powerful, persuasive, and naturally being an attorney he had great presence and a very clever mind.

Yes?

Not to put him down, Mr. Barnett was a very demanding person. He was, um, vocally sadistic and he would sometimes like to put me down for some reason.

How would he do that?

Oh, he would be at a bar and for no reason he would say, "Robert as a secretary you're the shits."

I see.

He would be at a cocktail party and he would introduce me and say, this is Mr. Frisbee, he is like a monkey on a string, um, he doesn't talk unless I pull the string.

I see.

I was never allowed to let my true personality come through. Philip used to like me to keep my certain place.

Yes.

We never got over the fact I was hired help.

You never got over that?

No.

What do you mean by your true personality, what was being kept back?

Well, what was being kept back was my sense of humor. He didn't like that at all, and I think I have a little sense of humor of my own.

Yes.

And as I say I didn't speak freely, but when I did, he would say, "That's enough of that, Robert."

I see.

He did not want me to be in the forefront. He wouldn't use the word servant, but that's what he implied, the hired help.

How did you react to that?

Well, I would just go into complete despair and depression.

You wouldn't react to it?

No, I would just keep it inside.

Would you feel angry?

Not anger, but just complete desolation, and try to recuperate.

How would you recuperate?

Probably take a pill.

I see.

And then wait for cocktail hour and have a cocktail.

Yes. What was Mrs. Barnett's attitude?

She never heard any of these remarks. They were always done while we were at lunch, or in a group.

And when you were with her, was she ever rather peremptory?

Nothing to be alarming. She never wanted anyone to know her business. She used to kick me under the table if I was saying something she didn't approve of.

I see.

She is what we call a Mrs. Full Charge.

I don't know what that means.

It is a woman that will come into a room and no matter what you are planning, she will take over and tell you a better way to do it.

How did you feel when Mrs. Barnett did that?

I would just back down and say, "Yes, I think so, too."

How did that leave you feeling?

I felt most of her suggestions were very good and approved.

I see.

Sometimes I would get artistic and a little bit flighty and she would calm me down.

How would you characterize the difference in your relationships between Mr. and Mrs. Barnett?

Well, Mrs. Barnett was a more gentle person. She accomplished what she wanted using a little subtlety. Mr. Barnett would just prowl into the lion's den and just roar.

I see. You never pushed back, so to speak, at Mr. Barnett?

Never in any kind of word or deed.

Why not?

I don't know . . . respect, or fear. He did terrify me at times. He was so overwhelming.

About the worst thing that Philip Barnett did was order vanity plates for Robert's car. The plates read, "STINKY," which was Philip's pet name for Robert.

Despite it all, Robert felt . . . enraptured with him.

But Dr. Tyhurst called it a sado-masochistic bonding. That's what he said in court. A "morbid dependency" on others, a bondage that began with his brother, was transferred to other protectors, Tom Leary and Dwight Frisbee and Philip Barnett. The doctor called it a "personality disorder," a neurosis. But it felt like love to Robert. It still feels that way.

Robert had underlined a passage in the report Dr. Tyhurst filed with the court, quoting an expert on neurotic dependency: "By submerging his own identity entirely and merging with the partner, the masochistic person gains a certain reassurance. His reassurance is to be compared with that achieved by a small endangered nation which surrenders its rights and its independence to a powerful and aggressive nation and thereby wins protection. One of the differences is that the small nation knows it does not take this step because of its love for the bigger nation, while in the neurotic's mind the process often takes on the appearance of loyalty, devotion, or great love."

That was Robert: a small nation, a little Estonia under the

thumb of the Czar of Russia. Except Robert loved his czar. And Mrs. Barnett, too. Dear Muriel. They were the cream of society, and Robert was allowed to lap from the bowl.

Did you ever cook for them?

Yes, that's a hobby of mine. Mrs. Barnett never liked to put me in the cook category because secretaries have dinner with family, but cooks don't.

You also indicated something about her dressing for dinner.

Well, that was one of the things that he was most proud about. He told me his wife would be ready to meet any guest he wanted to bring home at cocktail hour. She'd have full makeup on, jewelry, even down to the shoes which would match the gown.

Did you have to dress up for dinner?

Mr. Barnett would not allow you to come to the table ever without an ascot. I changed sometimes two or three times a day. I was never allowed to appear without complete tie, even for breakfast. No naked skin was ever to show.

Yes.

We always ate very formally.

And talked happy talk. They liked to look at the positive side; the Barnetts didn't abide melancholy.

The Barnetts let Robert know early what the rules were: they didn't want to hear depressing thoughts of any kind. No sad news dared enter their home. If Robert was ill, they didn't want to know about it. If Robert had woes, they must not be set on the table with the cutlery.

Nor would personal questions be asked or angry words spoken; they bickered of course, as married couples do ("You're a lousy lay," Philip would say to his wife, "and you always have been"), but they never did so in public. Robert, of course, was not considered a part of the public, more like a fly on the wall.

The rule book also demanded that when company was present, no family business should be discussed. Muriel was almost fanatical about not wanting anyone outside their little extended family to know their personal affairs. If Robert transgressed, there'd come another little sharp kick under the table.

Barnett was a man of some vanity. Although lacking an honorary degree, he enjoyed being addressed as "Doctor," in the manner of the European lawyers he hobnobbed with, and he insisted that Frisbee so address him when in dignified company. When his servant would page Dr. Barnett at the Presidio Golf Club, his fellow U.S. attorneys would often erupt in a chant of "Quack, quack, quack."

His vanity was not outdone by Muriel's, who suffered from acute astigmatism but refused to wear glasses in public. (Except for a pair of prescription lenses which were dark-tinted and which she pretended were for the sun.)

Also, Robert believed she had taken five years off her age. She claimed 1905 as her birth year, but Robert knew she'd gone to school with Dwight Frisbee's wife, who was born in 1901. Her birth records were destroyed in the San Francisco quake of 1906 – an event which she once told Robert she recalled vividly. This was patently impossible, Robert believed, if she had been only one year old. She wasn't seventy-nine when she died. More like eighty-four.

Chapter 9

JEFF AND I RECEIVED WORD IN MID-JULY THAT A JUDGE OF THE U.S. Federal Court had ordered the extradition of Frisbee, and shortly after that a letter from our new client arrived at the office. On the face of the envelope he had drawn with colored pencils a lovely bouquet of yellow roses adorned by a spray of baby's breath. (I received other letters from Frisbee similarly decorated. One from Wilkinson Road jail, his Canadian address until his trial, seemed a little funereal with its two perfect lilies.)

July 12, 1986

Dear Mr. Deverell:

I hope this letter is clear and concise and not a mistake, confusing issues. I thought you might like to know a little about me. You will have to present an unknown quantity and correct it into a product acceptable to the Establishment.

Robert is a slightly introverted quiet person with average intelligence. He is sincere and tries to live up to the logo of his high school: Industry, Integrity, and Honesty. He has a kind of personality that blends in with the nearest wallpaper. Once you peel off that veneer of Yankee puritanical background he is most gracious and charming – a trustworthy and steadfast friend.

He longs for graduation from this insufferable institution. The degradation is indescribable, and he has been subjected to experiences too horrible to relate. They even have an occasional O.D. here, dope is so rampant. With my reputation as a jet setter they would just not believe I did not even know what one of those stupid cigarettes looks like. The live-in psycho and a few others here wondered at my ability to adjust and slip from life in a penthouse to one of a prisoner.

On the subject of psychos, the psychiatrists seem to agree that Robert suffered brain damage when he had a seizure in London in May 1984. I have closely watched my mental process to look for a clue to such deficiency. . . .

This letter will in no way help you in understanding Robert, but perhaps may be a basis for some of your groundwork. I will try wholeheartedly to cooperate with you, so you can be sure I am the type of person you want to be associated with, and stand up proudly in court with.

Thank you for your time and patience in reading this.

V. Roy abandoned his appeal against the extradition, and Frisbee arrived unannounced in Canada on August 19, 1986, one year to the day from Muriel Barnett's murder.

MEMO
TO: FILE   RE: FRISBEE
FROM: JEFF   AUGUST 21, 1986

1. At approximately 3:30 on August 19th, I spoke to Robert Frisbee who phoned me from the Colwood cells. He told me that two police officers, Sergeant Rehman and one other, wanted to talk to him about the case. He wanted my advice. I told him that he ought not to talk to the police at all.

2. I spoke to Sergeant Rehman and told him the same thing. He told me I could trust him to honor Mr. Frisbee's wishes not to discuss the matter.

3. I then spoke to Frisbee and told him to muster all of his inner resources not to discuss the case with any police and that I would see him in court tomorrow morning.

4. Bill and I appeared on the morning of August 20th, 1986, and the matter was put over to September 5th.

5. At 1:30 in the afternoon on August 20th, we saw Frisbee in

cells. Frisbee is a self-described passive individual and he is going to have to get more oomph to have some input into this case. He doesn't seem too interested in getting out on bail and seems very happy where he is.

Happy, that is, until his first experience with Canadian hospitality. Upon a second court appearance, he passed me this note: "They are spitting on me in the holding tank: what kind of animals do you have in Canada?"

I said I'd look into it, but learned later he was treated even more egregiously while being transported in the sheriff's wagon to the Wilkinson Road remand cells. They'd put him in the back of the bus in the P.C. (protective custody) section, behind a metal mesh. (Corrections authorities tend to put gay persons in P.C., along with the molesters and the pederasts, though for a good reason: to protect them from the manly non-deviates in the prison's general population.)

When Frisbee told us of the episode, we asked him to record it in writing:

"Someone called me and as I turned, five men let out a spurt of filthy, phlegm-filled spit, hitting me in the face. I turned my back but they continued the attack for fifteen minutes, trying to break down the screening to get to me, shouting, 'Rapist, if I had a gun I'd kill you, etc.' They wanted to urinate on me but no one had any ammunition. I mentioned it to the guard inside the building who hands out the clothes, and his remark was, 'That's what you get for being in P.C.'"

That happened only once. The sheriff's office obliged us by henceforth having Frisbee escorted to and from court alone, in his own chauffeured van, and they settled him in the Wilkinson Road P.C. unit, which is rather more comfortable than the San Francisco jail. There he managed to avoid contact with the animals, and enjoyed a cell to himself with a pleasant pastoral view through the bars.

Wilkinson Road jail (Wilkie, they call it) is in the Victoria suburbs, northwest of the city, once a pretty countryside, now giving way to encroaching development. The style of the prison building is early twentieth-century B.C. institutional. It's a morose, forbidding structure of red brick and stone arches and turrets. Inside, around the yard, the walls are hung with fearsome decoration – many coils of razor wire. But the Protective Custody unit, apart from the other buildings, is new and bright and clean. It is there, at a table in the prisoners' common room – and occasionally in his cell – that Jeff and I most often met with Frisbee.

Assured he would no longer have to endure the taunts of the prison bullies, Frisbee did not press us about being released on bail. In any event, in Canada persons accused of murder don't win bail unless of unparalleled repute and blameless past. (I represented the adopted son of an Ontario Appeal Court judge on an attempted murder. Even he didn't get bail. My client's case was prejudiced, however, by the fact that the alleged murder attempt was upon the person of a uniformed police officer, and happened just after his alleged robbery of a bank.)

Still, if we got the right judge for a bail application, and if we found quarters for Frisbee in Victoria – he had but a microscopic chance of being allowed outside Canada – we might not get laughed out of court. I knew my guy was the world's finest candidate for bail, but how to persuade a judge of that? Passive Robert Frisbee would not dream of disobeying a court order – were he dying of cirrhosis he'd show up for a parking ticket in his wheelchair if firmly told to do so.

Jeff and I decided not to make a too-hasty application for what the Criminal Code calls Judicial Interim Release. Often a criminal trial of complexity – especially if it involves subpoenaing witnesses flung far across the world – takes several months, and often years, to assemble. If the Attorney-General's office could not quickly get its tackle in order, and if it looked as if a timely trial date could not be set, Frisbee's chance of bail was enlarged.

MEMO
TO: FILE   RE: FRISBEE
FROM: BILL
1. The Crown estimates that it will not be possible to get a date for the trial until the end of February and suggests that a special assize might have to be convened. The client is not very happy

about that long delay and I indicated that we may have something to say about that when it comes before the court.
2. The Crown is directly indicting and will file the indictment on Monday so it will not be necessary for the accused to appear in Provincial Court again.

The Crown's decision to file an indictment directly with the Supreme Court of British Columbia, the province's high court for criminal trials, meant we'd be going straight to trial, without a rest stop for a preliminary inquiry before a Provincial Court judge.

There was no other reason for a direct indictment in this case other than cost – the case promised to be expensive enough to the Crown without its having to pay two return air fares and pay double the hotel bill for dozens of out-of-town witnesses.

A preliminary hearing is often vital for lawyers fighting a complex case; it lets them know clearly what evidence must be met, and allows them to test the veracity of witnesses. But my experience (I learned this while prosecuting) has been that such a hearing prepares the Crown almost as much as the defense – inexperienced counsel tend toward windy cross-examinations, and give away more than they get. Anyway, pressing as we were for an early trial date, we couldn't be heard to complain too strongly about the direct indictment. At all events, our courts, everprotective of the Crown's prerogatives, refuse to tamper with such decisions.

We mustered some indignation anyway, and exacted a promise from the Crown for full disclosure throughout the trial, and Jeff and I were guaranteed the right to interview all their witnesses. But we know prosecutors like to keep little secrets in their back pockets, and, without a dress rehearsal, we would risk playing much of the trial by ear.

Chapter 10

MEMO
TO: BILL   RE: FRISBEE
FROM: NANCY

1. I talked to Mr. Frisbee after I spoke with you and apparently Mr. Frisbee asked Dan Kazakes to send him some money to buy a TV.
2. Mr. Frisbee wants a TV desperately and if he has to wait through the normal channels (whatever they are), it could take up to another two or three weeks.
3. He wants to know if the firm will advance him about $300 (on his word to pay us) for a TV set.

Robert wanted the TV so he could follow the game shows and the travel documentaries. Escapism, he called it. Escapism from the Protective Custody unit of Wilkinson Road. He didn't much care for the soaps. They were about lives he couldn't relate to.

A friendly corrections officer at Wilkinson Road cut the red tape for me. He told me I could get the best deal in town at Crazy Mike's, where I delivered a personal check for $300 and a bit for a fifteen-inch color TV. Then the amiable jailer picked up the set for Frisbee on the way to work. All screws aren't Hollywood-version pathological misfits.

I knew I might not get my money back. We'd advised Frisbee the fee for the trial would be $60,000 (Canadian), and $10,000 a week more if it dragged out longer than a month. He'd found that perfectly all right and signed a letter of agreement. But to date we'd received only a $20,000 retainer from V. Roy Lefcourt. The rest of the fee was a gamble: V. Roy had assured us another $250,000 (U.S.) was coming to our client from Mrs. Barnett's will.

Yes, there does seem something vaguely immoral about profiting from your alleged murder victim's will. But some negotiations were going on in San Francisco which might allow Frisbee to do just that.

Mrs. Barnett had drawn her will in March 1984, and, following her deceased husband's wishes, named as chief beneficiary of her $4-million estate the law school of the University of San Francisco, Philip Barnett's alma mater. But she also directed a $250,000 cash bequest to Robert Frisbee.

In October of the same year, Mrs. Barnett signed a codicil to her will (an addendum, as it were, legally binding) directing that the lion's share of the $4 million be left to Frisbee. The law school had contested the validity of the codicil in California Probate Court, claiming that it had been signed by Mrs. Barnett as a result of chicanery on Frisbee's part.

But settlement talks proceeded, and by the time the Frisbee file got to me, a handshake agreement had been reached. Frisbee, at the time still in custody in San Francisco, had accepted his lawyer's advice and signed a waiver of claim to the disputed codicil on the promise of the executor to honor the $250,000 gift in the original will. The University of San Francisco's law school decided, on doubtless good advice, to swallow its pride and kiss goodbye a quarter of a million dollars.

Otherwise, they would risk Robert Frisbee being found not guilty of murder, in which case the codicil might be probated and they could lose the whole bundle. The wise law professors of U.S.F. agreed not to raise the judicial maxim that a person who feloniously kills another cannot take a benefit under that person's will.

But at the time I agreed to accept Frisbee's retainer, the settlement had yet to be reduced to writing or approved by the probate judge. There could still be slips between cup and lip, and Jeff and I knew that putting our names on record for Robert Frisbee could mean we could get stuck for the bill.

I don't remember losing much sleep over it. As I've said, it's the kind of case most criminal lawyers would trade their eye teeth for. It meant ink. Show me a criminal lawyer who doesn't like ink.

Still, we were prepared to forgo a month of seeing our names in the papers if we could avoid exposing Mr. Frisbee to undue risk. His chances – although we were shy about telling him – seemed bleak with a Victoria jury.

The City of Victoria is the tidy, pretty, tourist-ridden capital of British Columbia. It likes to be thought of as a little bit of old England. It's no metropolis; maybe 300,000 inhabit the metropolitan area, many of them pensioners, escapees from the merciless winters of the grain belt. Like much of B.C., Victoria claims a share of drifters, oddballs, artists, writers, and various other fringe elements, but our chance of impaneling twelve Victorians of ultra-liberal view seemed remote. Victorians hold rather strictly to the virtues of, well, the Victorian era.

We hoped for, of course, a jury that would feel no prejudice against homosexuals, but despite a boastful claim to being among the most tolerant of nations, Canada harbours its proportionate share of those of narrow mind, many of whom hide their thoughts behind a mask of all-too-Canadian politeness.

Many such polite people, who wouldn't dream of referring to Frisbee as a queer or faggot, especially in a jury room, might be prepared nonetheless to punish him for a lifetime of inappropriate conduct. There are those, too, who might resent him having lived too indulgently off the table scraps of the rich.

With that in mind, and aware of the risk of Frisbee going down for the full count, we decided to sound out the Crown about a possible plea of guilty to the lesser offense of manslaughter.

If Frisbee were convicted of first-degree murder he would not be eligible for parole for twenty-five years, and would doubtless live out his remaining years in prison. If convicted of second-degree murder – and that seemed the most likely result – he could win parole in as little as ten years.

If Frisbee were convicted only of manslaughter, however, sentencing would be solely a matter for the judge, who might send him to the penitentiary for only five or six years, depending on the warmth of the judge's heart, and Frisbee could expect parole after serving no more than half his time. A conviction for manslaughter, in this case, would be a clear win.

Crown counsel routinely deny that cost factors enter into decisions to accept lesser pleas, but we had a feeling that the several hundred thousand dollars required to put the Frisbee prosecution together might (unconsciously, of course) make the prosecution more amenable to a manslaughter plea.

One carries on such discussions, if possible, over lunch with a little wine, and a few days after Frisbee's first apparance in a Canadian court, I met with Dirk Ryneveldt, an easy-going young man on the staff of the Regional Crown Counsel's office, in a yuppily popular Victoria cafe.

And that's where the Frisbee case took a decided turn for the trickier. After a few formal pleasantries over a glass of red, Dirk, a benign expression on his face, laid a fat envelope in front of me with 221 pages of sweating TNT: Mr. Frisbee, I learned, had composed an "autobiography."

When I looked at the ingloriously self-deprecating title, I almost choked up my Beaujolais: "A Demented Parasite."

"How'd you get hold of this?" I asked Dirk, who seemed to be enjoying my discomfort.

"RCMP seized it when they booked your guy in. He told them he wrote it in jail in San Francisco."

Maybe, I thought, insanity is indeed the correct verdict for Robert Frisbee. Writing his life story for all the world and the Royal Canadian Mounted Police to read. . . . Then I remembered: in the San Francisco cells Frisbee seemed to be holding something from me when I cautioned him about keeping his words to himself. He'd had a naughty-little-boy expression on his face.

I looked at the proposed subtitle: The Day-to-Day Account of the Notorious Facts of the Life of the Author. After that, a couple of pages of chapter titles: "Tiptoe Through the Pansies," "The Army and Other Privates," "Only a Queen in a Gilded Cage," "Open Up Those Golden Gates."

I tried to quell tremors of panic as I flipped through the pages. Yes, here is Robert Frisbee in full adolescent trauma. Here is his adopting father, Dwight. And here Dan Kazakes. And Philip Barnett. And dear, dear Muriel, too.

Much of the manuscript was in shorthand: Frisbee had studied the Gregg method in secretarial school. I turned to the last few pages, fighting a sudden weariness.

A sentence on page 219 seemed somberly evocative of human passage into death: "The dark silhouettes over your shoulder are here in the guise of fortune tellers, guiding your hand for the final thrust that says goodbye to the past."

But whatever philosophical musings Frisbee was immersed in weren't given elaboration, and his mood suddenly lightened:

"On to Victoria and its charming salute to times past. With charming chit-chat we tour this small English paradise. We must return by 4:30. As indeed we do. What Madam declares, Madam gets results. First, Bloody Marys, vodka, and French 75s. Only the best with Dom Pérignon and Stolichnaya vodka. A cocktail fit for the mood of a pleasant captain's goodbye dinner."

A French 75, I later learned, was a favorite drink of Mrs. Barnett's. Toss a few ounces of gin or vodka over ice and fill the glass with champagne. I liked these French 75s: strong tonic for our intoxication defense.

But in the next paragraph, a heavier, ominous note sounded. It was if another side of Frisbee had taken the pen:

"In the distance the calliope is releasing strains of forgotten melodies . . ."

Calliope? Such steam-driven instruments were once common in circuses and riverboats – but on board the *Royal Viking Star*?

". . . a calumnious act to perform as promised in a faithful meeting in his conscious of the early morning. Today is the DAY."

A chill went through me.

The final paragraph of that page was liberally sprinkled with shorthand and barely readable:

"A canonical hour to be revered. (Shorthand.) The shocking realization a startling battle of his wits. The dull day only heightens conviction, giving false strength. A happy (shorthand) very hearty drink to ease the senses and induce a purple cast over a sky of blue. One could be happy always. She (shorthand) first (shorthand)."

I was relieved the story seemed to end here.

But it didn't. Dirk showed me three additional pages, handwritten on long sheets, titled "Ending."

"We decided to have a French 75 while changing for a nap. While Muriel was in the bath I made myself another 75 and took a tranquilizer, as I wanted to make sure there would be no more incidents. We got along very well, but we were straining our relationship progressively. I really will go all out for a private room. Her reasoning was with two first-class tickets, just a few more dollars and we could have a suite. She felt, and with reason, she wanted absolute control over my waking hours. She was not well, and had the same vague symptoms as she had previously when the doctor said, 'Cancer.' She just did not want to be alone any more."

Frisbee obviously was feeling tightly squeezed by Mrs. Barnett, but that didn't seem much of a motive for murder. He implies a growing resentment, sounding of truth but not menace:

"In passing she told me we would be going to England in April for her birthday and we would look for a suitable flat in Mayfair. This had all the earmarks of interrupting my personal mode of life ... It looked to me this may be the beginning of the end! I'd like to retire with Dan soon."

"Beginning of the end": that could seem an unfortunate choice of phrasing – easily taken out of context by a suspicious prosecutor – but clearly he was contemplating leaving Mrs. Barnett to retire with his lover. That is not an offense under the Criminal Code.

"When she came out she commented, 'I love these French 75s – they will be the death of me yet!'"

That seemed improbable. I wondered if Frisbee was trying to dress up his memoirs with a little fiction.

"I followed her into the bedroom and kissed her happy-nap. This was also getting to be a habit. We retired and I thought of the many questions Dan would ask. Dreams and fantasies came into my mind – maybe she would hire Dan also! Would not please him, he loved Muriel but from a distance.

"In my reverie, I thought I heard someone at the door. The door closed and the impression of footsteps on the carpet were getting closer. I barely opened my eyes and saw him ... an indeterminate shadow of a man, my height, coming closer ... He picked up her jewelry and put it in his pocket. Muriel stirred – was she sensing his intentions also? I was unable to break the bonds that held me so tightly ... when did he tie me to the bed and stuff my mouth with a soiled sock? She was stirring, and she let out a cry! He has a bottle in his hand. 'Robert ... he is hitting me!' Bam! 'God let me die.' Bam. 'God let me die.' Bam. With every bam was an outcry until she stopped moving. He ran to the bath and came back with a towel. He held it to her mouth.

"He is turning toward me – what is he reaching for? I feel myself levitating, my spirit spiraling me up to his mobile body, and I look down to see my body as if in a dream ... was he now me?"

There was more of the like, surrealistic and schizoid. The last line read: "I somehow have become a horrible monster. A call for help."

I raised my eyes from the end of the page.

"What do you make of that?" Dirk asked.

"Strong evidence of automatism. That makes him not guilty."

There was some reality beneath the bluster. Probably this was Frisbee's idea of a blockbuster ending for his best-seller, heavily fictionalized. On the other hand, all the indicia were present here of someone not acting in a voluntary state of mind. At worst, so drunk he didn't know what he was doing.

Or perhaps he was suffering a full-blown psychosis if and when he killed Mrs. Barnett. A verdict that Frisbee was insane at the time of the offense was a distinct threat now, and our expert medical witnesses would have to be made aware of the thin line the defense would have to walk.

Dirk said he would like to have a Crown psychiatrist examine Mr. Frisbee. Over coffee, we haggled.

MEMO

TO: FILE   RE: FRISBEE

FROM: BILL   SEPTEMBER 9, 1986

1. Lunch with Dirk Ryneveldt, for the Crown. He is prepared to consider a plea of manslaughter and suggests that in order for him to justify it, because he has no facts on the file which would so do, that I prepare a letter setting out in my view what the difficulties are the Crown faces.

2. He wants the request to come formally from this side but my

reading of it is that he will go along with such a plea if we make a case for it.

3. His second request was to have a Crown psychiatrist examine Frisbee, particularly in view of the three-page ending of Frisbee's autobiography, which he gave me a photostat of and which is in the file, and which suggests some schizophrenic mind at work. I said I would be very reluctant to have that done unless some agreement as to plea is reached in advance.

4. I think we should consider having Jim Tyhurst examine him but I would want to talk very carefully with Jim before that happens, so that he will appreciate the nature of the case and the possible defenses. I don't think we want an insanity defense here.

I later confronted Frisbee about the manuscript, and I think he was cowed by my anger. In apology, he said he didn't think his innocent scratchings were important enough to bother me with.

Was it possible, I asked him, that somewhere in the dark recesses of his mind he recalled an intruder in the penthouse suite, that the ending of his story might not be fiction? No, he invented his ending – because he couldn't remember the real one. I believed him. I didn't want to. I didn't want Frisbee to be a killer.

Chapter 11

FEDERAL BUREAU OF INVESTIGATION
Date of transcription: September 6, 1985
File SF 45A-1773, Special Agent Hugh W. Galyean

Daniel Kazakes, 2055 Sacramento Street, Apartment 404, San Francisco, was contacted at his residence and was advised of the identity of the interviewing agent by display of credentials, at which time Kazakes voluntarily supplied the following information:

Kazakes stated that he feels devastated by the arrest of Robert Frisbee who has been his close friend for the past 32 years. Kazakes also apologized to Special Agent Galyean for his "condition" having had a "couple of drinks" this morning due to his being upset at Frisbee's arrest.

Galyean asked Kazakes if Robert Frisbee had ever made any comments about doing away with Mrs. Barnett. Kazakes replied that Frisbee would not kill Mrs. Barnett because he was Barnett's heir and what would be the point in that. Kazakes continued by saying that Frisbee was gentle and would not kill a fly.

Kazakes recalled that Frisbee telephoned Kazakes in an apparent hysterical condition while on board the ship and told Kazakes "she is on the floor again. There is blood all over her."

9/25/85

At 2:50 p.m., instant date, Daniel Kazakes was contacted at his residence. Present was V. Roy Lefcourt, attorney for Robert Frisbee.

Kazakes was advised that a request was being made for consent for a search of the Kazakes/Frisbee residence. Kazakes replied,

"There is nothing here." Mr. Lefcourt then requested a few minutes for a private consultation with Kazakes. Following the consultation Lefcourt stated that if Galyean would state the items desired by the FBI from the Kazakes residence, Mr. Kazakes would be willing to turn over such items if they existed.

Galyean then advised Lefcourt that Kazakes certainly had the right to refuse consent for a search of his residence but that the FBI had no desire to merely stand by and accept any items Kazakes might wish to furnish.

11/21/85

Galyean attempted to interview Kazakes in his apartment, but Kazakes failed to respond to several knocks on his door by Galyean. Outside the security gate there is a telephone which accesses each apartment. The interviewing agent dialed the number for Kazakes's apartment. Kazakes advised us he was too sick to have any visitors.

Kazakes was asked if he could think of any reason why Mrs. Barnett would have made out a codicil dramatically changing her will. Kazakes could offer no explanation. Kazakes advised that although he was a medium, he would not be able to call Barnett back from the dead because she was deceased for only a short time. Kazakes said she was somewhere in the "ether."

11/30/85

Daniel Kazakes was contacted at his residence by way of the house intercom phone. Kazakes stated that he was not feeling well and therefore did not want to see anyone in person.

12/06/85

Daniel Kazakes was telephonically contacted at his request. Kazakes asked Galyean if his residence phone was bugged. Kazakes was informed that his phone was not bugged.

Kazakes stated that he would be at Frisbee's trial whether he was subpoenaed or not, and that he would be the one person to "turn the trial around."

TYHURST INTERVIEWS

Dan is not completely absolutely a hundred per cent homosexual, I don't think. He doesn't do the regular things that a homosexual does in bed.

Yes, all right.

Uh, I am a good partner for him and that has always been satisfactory to him. We have great rapport.

Yes.

And we love each other very much.

The object of Robert's untiring devotion was born in Omaha, Nebraska, of devout Greek Orthodox parents. When he was eighteen he moved to San Francisco where a marriage was arranged for him, in old-country fashion – he'd met her only twice – with a young woman of Greek background, sweet, ever-uncomplaining Irene. Seven years later they conceived Jerry, their only child.

The marriage lasted thirty-seven years until Irene's death in 1977, the last years of it a triangular affair – Robert was not merely a regular visitor but a sort of member of the household. Robert took Irene's place in Kazakes's bed on weekends, when he escaped from the Barnetts.

Robert loved Irene, she loved him. He was Uncle Bob to Jerry, a somber little boy who, influenced by his father, seemed destined to seek a spiritual life. (When Jerry grew up he moved to Australia and joined a cult. He referred to it as "The Family" in his letters to Robert.)

Robert used to help Dan with some of the secretarial and bookkeeping chores of his contracting business. For a while Dan specialized in large houses for the well-off, but went bankrupt during a recession. He recovered and began building apartments in San Francisco, and built one for Robert with what remained of the inheritance from Dwight. For a while Dan also ran a few Greek import shops near San Francisco, but they didn't do very well, and he closed them up.

Dan hadn't gone past the seventh grade, but he always wanted to have some kind of degree after his name, and one day he saw an advertisement in the paper and sent off a check and got a certificate in the mail that allowed him to be called a reverend. It was like Philip's doctorate in law, sort of imaginary, but it gave him standing.

Dan had what he called a religious mission – sometimes he referred to it as a calling, sometimes as an avocation – but Robert never quite understood its nature, how it worked. Frankly, he never asked about it. He regarded Dan's religion as his hobby, in a way. Dan liked to wear clerical garb and the backwards collar and hang a big crucifix around his neck – Robert thought he looked very imposing – and in San Francisco he used to counsel young men in trouble, and also AIDS patients, although he told Robert he found this task depressing, and he quit it after a while.

Dan had psychic powers. He said they were in his genes, and that many of his forbears were psychics. He liked "reading people." His favorite word was "vibrations." He assured Robert he could levitate any time he wanted to. Robert never actually saw him put this power to work, but Dan said he didn't want to perform like he was in some kind of circus.

Another thing he could do was contact voyagers to the great beyond. He was a medium. Robert was never present for a seance, though. In fact, he was a little skeptical of Dan's claims to psychic prowess, but of course he never mentioned that. Being a psychic and a medium made Dan happy. And really, what's wrong with that?

After Robert introduced Dan to Philip and Muriel Barnett, the Kazakeses were often invited to dinner at the Barnetts, and the families regularly came together for Christmas and Easter holidays. Muriel, of course, just loved Irene and also the little Kazakes boy, Jerry, but Philip never found much to talk about with Dan. They didn't hit it off.

There was a jealousy.

There was?

Oh, yes. Philip was very jealous of Dan. He knew about Dan and our association. He was jealous. And Dan resented all the time I spent with them. I think . . . I hate to put Dan down, but I don't think he was in Philip's stratosphere. I think Philip [regarded him] as just another little garbage street cleaner or something. Dan is not the most intelligent person in the world, not in the classification that Philip would be. Philip was nasty. He would come up to Dan and say, oh, have you been to Italy, and knowing Dan, he's never been out of the States except for once. Philip liked to corner him if he could, and Dan felt resentment.

What sort of things do you think I should discuss with Mr. Kazakes?

Well, Daniel. I will tell you about Daniel. He is on the defensive about alcoholism.

What do you mean?

Most alcoholics are. He's very sensitive about his position as minister. I don't think he could stand a four-hour intercourse . . . conversation. He would have to be in the witness stand for quite a few hours.

Why wouldn't he be able to deal with that?

Because he is also very secretive about his homosexual tendencies, and he doesn't like criticism. No one does, but he has less tolerance for it than I do, I think.

Chapter 12

MEMO
TO: FILE   RE: FRISBEE
FROM: JEFF

1. I phoned Dan Kazakes in Palm Springs. He will be cooperative.
   He is going to come up here in a couple of weeks to see Frisbee
   to give him some moral support.
2. He also told me that Frisbee had telephoned him from the boat
   in hysterics, telling him that Mrs. Barnett had hurt herself again
   and that he had come out of the bathroom and there she was on
   the floor.
3. Kazakes said there were a number of incidents of Mrs. Barnett
   drunkenly falling and hurting herself. He described her as a
   very pushy Jew.
4. He then asked if I was Jewish because my name was Green. He
   said some of them use that name. I said no, I wasn't, and
   imagined it would have been embarrassing to him if I had been.

Dan Kazakes rarely visited Frisbee in the San Francisco jail. It was
like working with the AIDS sufferers – he found it burdensome. But
he summoned the effort to travel to Canada to meet us, bringing
with him a hacking smoker's cough and a catalogue of ailments
from emphysema to anemia, arthritis, cataracts, and herpes,
along with some typical indicia of severe alcoholism. Our interviews were punctuated by the incessant clacking of his ill-fitting
dentures.

He was a wiry, stooped man, then sixty-five years old. What
Frisbee saw in him, frankly, was the subject of much speculation

on the part of Jeff and me. But our client was indeed fond of this wizened, ornery, over-defensive bigot, and had remained his partner for thirty-two years.

Kazakes's memory of some critical events was unclear, and with respect to others he evaded, launching into petulant non sequiturs about the insolent and overweening behavior of Philip Barnett. Several times, he promised us he would "blow the case wide open." When we asked to see his ammunition, he changed the subject.

A loose cannon, we decided, without powder or shot. We hoped we wouldn't have to call him as our witness. We feared, though, the Crown might do so: putting him through the grinder as a hostile prosecution witness. It appeared from police reports the authorities felt Kazakes had played a dubious role in the events leading to Mrs. Barnett's death.

He was, for starters, one of two witnesses who signed the codicil giving the main part of Mrs. Barnett's estate to Frisbee. And shortly before the *Viking Star* sailed from San Francisco he had received that curious check – signed by Frisbee on her trust account – for $100,000.

Still, the Reverend Kazakes seemed too dim-witted to have been a part of some grand conspiracy. We didn't let the Crown know he was visiting Canada.

◇   ◇   ◇

My discussions with Dirk Ryneveldt were never rewarded with a plea agreement. In fact he mysteriously disappeared into the prosecutorial void, and the file was turned over to a private lawyer on retainer to the Attorney-General, Peter Firestone, a friendly unpretentious bustler popularly known as Peter Fireplug. He'd won half a dozen murder trials, lost only one, and we knew his self-deprecating manner often teased a jury into liking him. That wasn't good, but he'd be fun to be in a courtroom with, and would play fair.

We were unaware at the time that Dennis Murray, assistant deputy Attorney-General in charge of criminal law, had agreed to lead the prosecution if the case went to trial, with Peter as his junior. Had we known that, we might have been uneasy. Dennis is as skilled as Peter, but often prefers to play hardball.

Peter quickly advised us that the Crown had decided it would not accept a plea to manslaughter – only to second-degree murder. Otherwise the prosecution would take its chances on whatever verdict the jury might bring.

Frisbee, just shy of sixty years old and not in the pink of health, knew he might not survive the minimum ten years before parole on a second-degree murder conviction. He agreed to take the gamble. We also told him there'd be little point now in applying for bail: the registrar of the criminal trial division, through some mysterious form of legerdemain, had found us an early trial date, December 1 next. Two and a half months away.

Peter then announced he would apply to take commission evidence in San Francisco from witnesses either unwilling to testify in Canada or unable to.

Since no foreign resident may be subpoenaed into a Canadian court it is permissible by international treaty to take evidence outside the realm. In former practice, the evidence was sworn before an appointed commissioner, transcribed, then read aloud to the jury. (An unsatisfactory procedure – the monotonous reading of transcripts turns juries somnolent.) Now it's done with video cameras, and Peter planned to fly down to San Francisco with an RCMP technical crew to tape the evidence.

The Attorney-General's ministry balked at paying the defense's full expenses for San Francisco, so we had to ask a chambers judge to make them to cough up. Which he did. He also approved Peter's shopping list of witnesses: mostly medical men and a few police officers – plus, unhappily, the loose cannon Dan Kazakes, who had become in Peter's mind the embodiment of great and utter evil.

Kazakes was the key, he felt. He had conspired with Frisbee to do the woman in. Kazakes may not have been aboard the *Royal Viking Star*, but his evil presence lurked there. Sorcery, psychic powers, a post-hypnotic trance: by some means or other, the hand of the mastermind had directed Frisbee in the wielding of that blood-smeared bottle of . . . yes, Greek Demestica wine.

Peter talked with us incessantly about his black theories; he speculated, too, about the motive and the mind of Robert Frisbee. I couldn't blame him – he suddenly had the most important trial of his career. Doing the early spadework for the trial was helping to take his mind off a sudden marriage breakdown. He talked openly with Jeff and me about it, and we felt empathy for him.

But Peter Firestone never got to go to San Francisco with us. He was relieved of his responsibilities by Dennis Murray, who replaced Peter as his junior with his Vancouver Island regional director, Ernie Quantz.

The public was not made aware of the circumstances of Peter's removal until the Frisbee case, long over, resurfaced in the headlines in July of 1990, after B.C.'s Social Credit Attorney-General, Bud Smith, made the mistake of talking into a car phone, unaware a Victoria radio reporter was taping his calls (car phone conversations that are transmitted over radio waves can be legally tapped with a scanner.)

The background was this: the opposition New Democratic Party had begun a prosecution – the Attorney-General having refused to do so – of the ex-tourism minister, who had resigned over a lottery scandal. The NDP retained Peter Firestone to handle its private prosecution.

One of the taped calls was with Bill Stewart, Smith's assistant deputy in charge of criminal law, and was about Peter:

Smith: Who is this guy?

Stewart: A nobody . . . Murray fired him off a case 'cause he wasn't any good. That was, uh, that Frisbee case, that was that murder on a cruise ship.

Smith: Yeah?

Stewart: And he couldn't handle the pressure, didn't do any work and so, uh, Dennis fired him and . . . the guy almost had a nervous breakdown.

Smith: How can we get that out?

[Peals of laughter.]

Smith: We could do anything we want now.

Stewart: He's got no, well I shouldn't say no respect, I mean he's a likeable, likeable-enough guy, I guess . . .

Smith: Yeah.

Stewart: I can hardly wait to talk to Quantz . . . he'll wet himself when he hears it's Firestone.

Smith: Who will?

Stewart: Ernie Quantz.

Smith: Oh, I see, yeah.

Stewart: Yeah. He couldn't carry Ernie's bags or anyone else's bags around here.

I phoned Peter after I read that transcript in one of the local papers, and said I'd be happy to carry his bags to court for his slander suit. The truth is that so far Peter had done everything right – under difficult personal circumstances.

Bud Smith later car-phoned his favorite legislative reporter, Margot (Rocky) Sinclair, who worked for a Vancouver television station, CKVU:

Smith: The, uh, gentleman who's doing the, uh, prosecution.

Sinclair: Mm-hmm.

Smith: Was, um, retained to do the prosecution on the Frisbee matter . . . the lady on the boat.

Sinclair: On the boat, right.

Smith: And was fired because, uh, he crumbles under pressure.

Sinclair: Oh, oh.

Smith: And he, uh, simply did not get himself prepared . . . so Dennis Murray fired him. 'Cause he was just, uh, wasn't up to it. The pressure got to him.

In discrediting Peter Firestone, the highest law officer of the province had been caught attempting to undermine his own justice system. Later, tapes were discovered which, suffice it to say, showed the Attorney-General and Ms. Sinclair engaged in less than a hands-off relationship. Bud Smith resigned his post the day after the tapes were tabled in the legislature. Bill Stewart was reassigned within the department. After consulting with her boss, Margot Sinclair announced she was ending her employ.

Bill Stewart's predecessor as assistant deputy in charge of criminal law was Dennis Murray. As such, in 1986, Dennis was the highest-ranking prosecutor on the public payroll. Ernie Quantz, who would be assisting him, was just a step below.

We knew Ernie Quantz would be doing the library stuff. He's a methodical researcher, a terrier who never lets go the pant leg of whatever evidentiary problem he's arguing. He would bring to the trial a deadpan sense of humor, the kind that doesn't let you know you've been cut until you notice the bloodstains.

I'd known Dennis Murray for a dozen years – from the days when he did a lot of legal aid in the Vancouver criminal courts. Back then I frequently prosecuted on retainer to the Attorney-General, mostly murders and rapes, and Dennis was once against me, defending a slimy piece of business who'd abducted, tortured, and raped a teenage girl. I'm afraid, in my address to the jury, I ran away with myself, characterizing the accused as human garbage not fit to be free on the streets. Dennis had taken emphatic objection to my comments, but didn't get far with the judge, and his man was duly convicted.

I always worried that Dennis might still be holding this episode against me. (And he was, I think. He insisted on regularly reminding me of my intemperate language in that earlier trial – in a tone only vaguely jocular.)

Dennis later tried to beat the lawyer burn-out syndrome by retreating to a small Vancouver Island practice, but soon began doing a few ad hoc prosecutions. He became good at this, and was quickly grabbed up by the provincial government. He made the right moves and rose through the ranks with uncommon speed, heading up the A.-G.'s criminal side while in his late thirties.

But when I first met him he was running with a pack of fairly radical guys who'd graduated together and were going to change the world from within the courtroom. Most of them mellowed into good lawyers, but kept the faith, and were surprised at Dennis joining the Crown. He was considered to have jumped ship, gone establishment.

Jeff Green considered Dennis a friend. With his extensive Vancouver Island criminal practice, Jeff had fought Dennis across numerous courtroom floors, had found him fair to deal with, generous in manner, and a man who like Jeff enjoyed a few hard drinks after a hard day in court and could hold them well.

My last dealing with Dennis involved the defense of a prominent lawyer who was a long-time Member of the B.C. Legislative Assembly and former Speaker of the provincial House. He faced eleven counts of conspiracy to subvert justice, fabricating evidence and influence peddling (a bizarre tangle of facts involving a former aide to Howard Hughes and the body-pack taping of my lawyer-client's conversations with an imprisoned PLO commando). But the charges were spurious, and Dennis, as crown counsel, risked the wrath of the RCMP by agreeing to enter a stay of proceedings – in fact, a high-ranking RCMP officer issued a public statement decrying the decision. Many prosecutors are content to take their orders from the police, but Dennis proved himself capable of being his own man and no lackey to high police authority.

When Ernie phoned us to announce he and Dennis were taking over the prosecution he again offered second-degree murder. Again we declined. We said we would be honored to be in the same courtroom with them.

Ernie moved quick off the mark, applying for a pre-trial hearing before a Supreme Court judge, trying to cut off at the pass some of the jurisdictional arguments we were saving for the trial.

Our central argument was that even if the crime occurred in Canadian territorial waters – which was still in question – murder by a foreign national aboard a foreign ship was beyond the jurisdiction of a Canadian court. As unexcitingly esoteric as that concept may sound to a lay person, it kept Jeff and me in the library for two weeks and a weekend.

We drew our line of authority from an English decision of 1876 involving two ships in collision off the British coast. Seven law lords went one way and six the other, and their words are recorded in one of the longest decisions I have ever had the distinct discomfort to slog through: 174 pages of debate as to whether the Queen's sovereignty ends at low-water mark.

High seas jurisdiction was only one of a dozen equally difficult points of law we would prepare in advance of the trial. When a jury trial begins, it's too late to start looking up the law – and one over-prepares, readying arguments one will make only if the trial takes a certain turn, and anticipating arguments the other side will make.

This is a part of trial work the public mercifully never gets to observe. Some lawyers hate it; some oddballs (I number among them) obtain a fetishistic pleasure from musty law books, enjoy constructing from them an intellectual edifice with the plaster known as the Common Law. All that constant agonizing by judges about what other judges have said. The backward looks into the past. The cold, conservative logic of precedent.

I handed several kilos of such precedent, photocopied, to Mr. Justice Lloyd McKenzie and was on my feet for a day and a half, but His Lordship didn't share my enthusiasm for my jurisdictional arguments. He at least paid us the courtesy of reserving on it a week, and rendering a fourteen-page judgment. If Frisbee were convicted, the Court of Appeal would have a chance to rethink his decision.

Justice McKenzie also made a finding of fact I was unhappy with, relying on expert evidence to hold that the *Viking Star* was in Canadian waters at the time of the crime. This was, I believed, an issue for the jury, and he had misstepped. We were hoping later to argue that the accused should have the benefit of a reasonable doubt as to whether the ship was in waters controlled by Canada or the United States. It was on our list of arguments-to-be-made, but so far we lacked much helpful evidence. We hoped to find it at the hearing of commission evidence in San Francisco.

◊   ◊   ◊

While we prepared his defense, Frisbee kept up a busy – often light, sometimes philosophic – correspondence with us:

"The Postman Rings Twice. Robert promised he would not bug you with stupid letters, but he has been known to have pencil withdrawal sensations if he's separated for long from his eternal letter writing."

On Life with his Cellmates:

"I do not relate to these young people. I missed a couple of generations somewhere, and their language and lifestyle is foreign to me . . .

"I kept a detailed account of all [that happened] but at some time during my stay (S.F.) my bed was set on fire and all my personal property of every kind destroyed. This happened when I refused to finance the dope habit of my fellow inmates."

On Looking at the Future:

97

"Mr. Deverell, there was a look of questionable concern on your face when you asked me if I could survive a life of several years in the penitentiary. I do not know – there are some reservations of course. I will have to program my mind to that realization. If it is just 20 per cent as comfortable as it is here; and if they will leave me alone and not invade my territory; let me have books, TV, music, and do not take too much advantage of me, I think I will survive."

Looking at Oneself:

"I will fight desperately against the bastions of reality, and anyone who tries to break down my ever-present mental defenses... I do think, Mr. Deverell, that I feel remorse and dark Irish depression, but at times I do feel I am a puzzlement to myself."

Book Review:

"I have enjoyed your *Dance of Shiva* very much, an intriguing story carried out with evident skill, one to keep you up at nights. As it did last night. When I chastized myself for the lateness of the hour, I thought, what the hell, Robert, what date do you have to keep tomorrow?

Coming to Grips with a Drinking Problem:

"I'm in the middle of a three-day symposium on alcohol. And there are A.A. meetings. Have not gotten into the frame of mind to attend one of the church services yet. In S.F. each Monday evening we had a gay service conducted by a cherubic, epicurean, Episcopalian priest, who, with his taste for the delights, was progressing through the second stage of AIDS. It was a very relaxed affair – sort of a 'rap' session. Not sure I am ready to face the all-forgiving Lord – is He ready for Robert?"

Chapter 13

PHILIP BARNETT JUST COULDN'T RETIRE, AND IN 1972 – AT THE age of seventy-two – he took on the biggest case of his career. His client was the blushing youthful bride of a Los Angeles banker and philanthropist, who'd taken her to Europe where he was to receive an award for his generosity (reward, thought cynical Robert) in the form of a medal from the King of Denmark. Before this life ambition could be satisfied, he expired on a park bench in Brussels.

The banker intended his $40-million estate to be given to charity. But the banker's bereaved bride, who had signed a pre-nuptial agreement limiting her legacy to a meager $5 million, retained Philip to slice off a more generous piece of the pie.

He began a suit in Los Angeles probate court, and dutiful Robert had to work long and extra hours for the next year and a half, typing letters and court documents, handling the phone, and transcribing fearfully long memos on the law. (Robert called Philip the Great Dictator.) Philip journeyed almost weekly to Los Angeles, fighting the good fight against the charities, and ultimately settled the suit for $10 million. The case sapped him.

FRISBEE'S TESTIMONY AT TRIAL

He suffered a heart attack at some point?

Well, I consider 1974 a big year. He had a heart attack in 1974.

Where?

In Disneyland.

Was that during the course of getting ready for this trial?

I think we had just about finished it, the papers were signed, and this was to be the last trip to Los Angeles and Mrs. Barnett and I drove him down. It was the Fourth of July, and we made a holiday out of it.

And how was it you were in Disneyland?

They had never been there.

Tell us about this heart attack.

We lost him in the park in Disneyland, Mrs. Barnett and I. We went back to the hotel and he came back early in the evening exhausted, and said he was terribly cold, although it was ninety degrees outside, and we put him to bed and covered him up. I called the house doctor and he came up and he wanted to put him in hospital. And Mr. Barnett said, "Absolutely not," and [the doctor] said, "Can you get him home by tomorrow?" and I said, "Yes, we can drive home tomorrow and be home by night." And the doctor said just tell him to be careful and not have any stressful moments. And Mr. Barnett said, "Well, does that mean I can't have cocktails?" And the doctor said, "No cocktails."

Did he have a cocktail after that?

We stopped at a restaurant for lunch, and Philip was sitting there at the table, and he said, "Well, I guess the doctor said I can't join you and Robert for cocktails," and her response was, "The doctor said you couldn't have cocktails, he didn't say anything about Canadian Club." So he had one or two Canadian Clubs.

And you got him back home?

I got him back home, I put him in the hospital the next day.

Philip went into intensive care. Madame wasn't pleased with that at all. She phoned Philip's doctor demanding that her husband get well immediately – they had a dinner date soon, and she was also planning a ball for the weekend, and two dancing parties for the following week.

"I have to have my husband out of the hospital by tomorrow," she said. The doctor said, "Mrs. Barnett, your husband has suffered a near-fatal attack and will not be going out for at least six or eight weeks."

"This is ridiculous," said Muriel. "Goodbye." The doctor was exaggerating. It was unfair. He had ruined her social schedule for the next two months.

After Philip recuperated and gained release from the hospital, he sent his widowed client a statement for his services, and she rebelled at it, hired another lawyer, and took poor Philip to court.

It was an awkward irony of Philip's professional life that his final courtroom battle was in defense of his own fees. After a trial lasting several weeks the court awarded Philip only a quarter of the $800,000 he'd felt justified in charging.

While he was thus embroiled in his own noble cause his relationship with Robert altered in a way that caught his faithful servant a little by surprise.

FRISBEE'S TESTIMONY AT TRIAL

We were on trial for thirty days, and one Sunday after dinner we were sitting in the bar having a brandy, and apropos of nothing whatsoever he said, "Robert, do you think you can arouse me sexually?"

And what was your reaction to that?

As I say, '74 was a very heavy year. I was shocked. Been almost five, six years now, and he'd never made any advance. And, uh, I complied.

They proceeded – a little drunkenly, it must be admitted – to their hotel suite where he did his master's bidding.

The affair – the back door stuff, as Robert called it – continued for several years but diminished in intensity as Philip's health waned with his advancing years.

If Muriel ever became aware of it, she didn't let on. In fact, there was no one Robert could speak to about it. The affair, though, became obvious to some: the winking gay conspirators, the waiters and captains and maître d's who watched Philip, his inhibitions disabled by a cocktail too many, sneak kisses of Robert, or grab at him under the table. Certain members of the Barnett social circle also had their suspicions, and although they doubtless gossiped with unbridled gusto, nothing of course was ever said in the Barnetts' presence.

It was not that violent an affair because he was seventy something years old by then.

Yes.

But it was a closeness. He would come to my apartment for a massage, and I did his hair of course, he had beautiful leonine white hair, and . . . we were lovers.

Yes.

And he would go back and clap his hands and say to Mrs. Barnett, "This is my home and Robert's is my pad."

Yes.

That's as close as he ever got to making any kind of a verbal declaration of our relationship.

You seem to be upset talking about it. Why is that?

Well, because I was leading a double life.

You were?

I didn't tell Daniel.

You didn't tell him?

(No audible response)

It was hard for Robert to bear the strain of his disloyalty. He wondered if Dan suspected. Maybe that was why Dan never allowed Robert to say one nice thing about Philip, Dan just got so testy. Anyway, there was faithless Robert, sneaking around behind his partner's back just when Dan was going through a bad time: his wife, Irene, had developed a terrible throat cancer.

Robert spent his every spare moment with Irene after the cancer was diagnosed. He gave her the morphine shots because Dan couldn't even look at a needle. He bathed her, fed her, attended to her dying needs – poor Dan couldn't bring himself to look in on her much; the sight of her sick, thinning body was too utterly depressing.

Her illness lasted three months before she died in 1977. Soon after, Jerry Kazakes (he'd become involved with a young woman enamored of Eastern religion) went to Australia in the pursuit of God and his inner self, and Dan and Robert moved together into a mobile home north of San Francisco. Robert was fifty years old now, ready to settle into a life of comforting routine. He would make the coffee and the Bloody Marys for Dan every morning, then trundle off to work at the Barnetts, do their paperwork and make their drinks, drive them to their soirees, then back home, put them to bed, and kiss them happy-nap. And return to his own home to The Grouch and relate the stories of the day over a final glass or two. Or four.

The years seemed to go by in a soft alcoholic haze. Robert remembers those (he thinks) as happy years.

TYHURST INTERVIEWS

And by then, of course, my relationship with Philip was just a normal relationship. There were no more bedroom antics by this time. He was getting to be eighty years old.

Um-hum.

But he liked his massages, and certain areas he liked to ... sensitive areas he liked massaged.

I see.

Mrs. Barnett had – I hate to say the word but I think she was accident prone – she was always breaking something. Falling down. The three of us drank too much, much too much. And she would fall down and break her collar bone. And she also had a bout with cancer. I saw her through that.

Cancer of what?

Let's see. I'm not familiar with women's down there – could it be the uterus? – I'm not sure.

I don't know.

At that age ... it involved an operation in the pelvic area somewhere.

All right.

And then Philip had some kind of obstruction in his kidney tract and they operated on that and he couldn't control himself. So he carried a bag. I'd have to empty that for him.

Every morning and a couple of times a day until Philip's kidneys recovered. Robert didn't mind. You do things for people you love. And for serving the people he loved his salary was raised from $400 a month to $425. There were extra duties, though. Robert was now acting as the secretary to a company in Alaska,

Northern Machine and Marine Railways Inc. The company once repaired fishing boats and had an interest in a salmon packing plant. Although it had divested itself of these businesses, it still owned quite a bit of Ketchikan, where it was based. Philip was its secretary-treasurer. And its major stockholder.

Robert knew Philip had gained control over the company as a result of another of his self-enriching shenanigans. After Mrs. Schlothan, the previous owner, died, and while the estate was being settled according to her will, Philip suddenly produced, out of nowhere, a subsequent will, apparently signed by Mrs. Schlothan, a will which he had prepared himself and which made him her sole beneficiary. The will was challenged in court but the suit later dropped. Philip was reported to the California Bar Society but died before any action could be taken.

Robert suspected the will was a fraud. But it wasn't up to him, after all, to expose his master, his mentor, and his lover.

Robert's income of $425 a month wasn't enough for him to live on, but he still had his apartment rentals, and a little left in his savings from Dwight's estate. He was using it up, but he was sure Philip would look after him, even in death, which, with his declining health, seemed not far distant.

In 1979, while on a little trip to Reno, Muriel, who loved to gamble, lost a little, but Philip nearly lost it all: he was rushed into the hospital after a second heart attack. Again he recovered, but his heart problems persisted. Robert spent long periods at his bedside, eighteen days, twenty days, twenty-four days, and he watched him gobble those nitro pills like popcorn.

But once out of the hospital, Philip regularly returned to the cocktail treadmill. His constant devoted shadow had to do everything for him but lift his glass to his lips. At private dinners Philip would impudently change the place cards – causing no end of distress to the hostess – so Robert could be seated beside him. When he went to the washroom at a restaurant, Robert, his mobile walking stick, would take him by the arm, prop him against the urinal, and sort of lean against him to hold him in place.

Philip began to make plans for Robert after his departure. He started to call him the "Frisbee insurance policy."

Robert was insurance that Muriel would continue to be accepted into San Francisco society after Philip passed from it – into whatever eternal social whirl awaited him.

Effervescent Muriel would always be welcome at parties if accompanied. But when a hostess makes up her lists she usually decides first what widows to eliminate – there always seems to be such a regular influx of them in the city. Widows are in demand only if they have someone in tow, someone to entertain them. No one likes to stand around just talking to widows, trying to think of nice things to say. It puts such a damper on everything.

So when the Barnetts were invited to functions, Philip always insisted Robert be asked as well. It got so he simply wouldn't go unless Robert were included. Their hosts on the Hill became used to seeing him in their ballrooms, consuming their champagne and canapés, or gliding across the floor with Muriel. It became assumed that when Philip cashed in, he would not leave his beloved Muriel socially destitute – she would keep her name on the guest lists and could be counted upon to arrive at the party on the arm of her insurance policy.

Chapter 14

A CERTAIN PERVERSE THRILL IS ENJOYED BY MEMBERS OF THE criminal bar in winning a case on a technical defense. Especially if the Crown is thereby embarrassed. "My mouthpiece got me off on a technicality," boasts the miscreant who has beaten the system. The public, of course, finds such occurrences suspect, the result of disreputable behavior on the part of counsel, proof that the legal system is out of gear.

In my early exposures to the courtroom process, I sat at counsel table watching my principal, John Macey, in action (although inaction might seem the better term). If I had expected that winning lawyers invariably argued vigorous, passionate defenses I had a lot to learn. John, a lawyer with whom I as a newly graduated LL.B. served a year's apprenticeship, was a devotee of fast horses, and read a racing sheet through many of his trials, checking off the best bets as he checked off, on another sheet of paper, the various essential items of evidence the Crown was called upon to prove.

His cases were usually impaireds or motor vehicle offenses (our major client was a motorists' association whose slogan was, "We put a lawyer in your car"). John rarely asked a question in cross-examination, but at the end of the prosecution's case, he would calmly rise, point out that there was no evidence that the said stop sign was located in the City of Vancouver or no evidence of what year it was or no proof the breathalyzer machine was in working order.

The court reporter would be called upon to reread the evidence, following which the judge would make comment on the ineptitude of whatever young counsel was acting for the Crown, and throw out the charge. John would go back to his racing form while his next case was called – we used to pile them up, three or four in a day. Only way to make a dollar.

It's a little more difficult to win a technical defense on a serious charge: police witnesses and prosecutors tend to be more experienced, and judges are less than eager to let a bank robber walk because no evidence was called to show the New Westminster Credit Union is actually situated in the City of New Westminster.

In the case of Robert Frisbee, the location of the Norwegian cruise ship was very much more than a technicality. It was an issue which went to the very jurisdiction of a Canadian court to try him.

The vessel was a Norwegian flagship. None of the star performers in the case – certainly neither the accused nor the victim – was a Canadian, so the only basis for Canadian jursidiction was one which demanded exacting proof that the ship was in Canadian waters at the time of Mrs. Barnett's death.

The charge read that Frisbee committed murder aboard a ship in "Canadian territorial waters," and proof of that, I thought, like every other particular of the charge, had to be beyond a reasonable doubt. If a jury wasn't sure the Crown had proved the murder occurred in Canada, they would have to acquit.

On the other hand, I was never quite able to conjur the image of a jury collectively saying to itself, "Even though Frisbee murdered the deceased, we're not sure on which side of the international boundary he did it. So we have to find him not guilty." Juries don't think that way.

But a criminal trial is a process of casting doubt. And if the jury ever neared a point of uncertainty whether Frisbee was guilty, a little additional doubt as to whether the offense even occurred in Canada could tilt the scales.

Jeff and I wouldn't make a big deal of it – the jurors mustn't think we had our hopes pinned on a technicality – but we nonetheless prepared carefully, interviewing experts in marine navigation, analyzing with them the data the Crown would rely upon to isolate the ship's position at the time of death, 6:45 p.m. on the 19th of August 1985.

At that time the ship was somewhere in the Strait of Juan de Fuca, the fifteen-mile-wide passage south of Vancouver Island and north of Washington's Olympic Peninsula. It's a busy waterway: cruise ships and freighters and tankers pour through it into Puget Sound and Georgia Strait, into the megaport facilities of Seattle and Vancouver. During seasonal openings, fishing boats swarm into the area.

The Canada-United States boundary bisects the Strait of Juan de Fuca, taking a couple of zigs south of Victoria, and a long zag west out to sea. On either side of the international boundary are the shipping lanes: outbound to the Pacific on the Canadian side, inbound on the U.S. side.

The evidence to be tendered from the bridge of the *Royal Viking Star* was that the vessel left Victoria at 5:00 p.m. on August 19. The ship stayed in the outbound lane – the Canadian side – and never veered to the U.S. side.

But as against that, we had curious indications to the contrary. For one thing, Frisbee was originally arrested on a murder charge laid in the United States, alleging the offense took place in U.S. waters. That may have been due to a typical American assumption of sovereignty over parts of planet Earth that don't belong to them, or to an ignorance of international geography.

It was hard to accept that U.S. authorities would hold Frisbee in jail for eight months preparing a case for murder if they honestly believed they had no jursidiction. Surely the FBI, which had conduct of the case, had checked and rechecked the navigational data.

We were determined to ferret through FBI records to determine how this blunder had come about. Our chance came during the taking of commission evidence in San Francisco.

Four days in mid-November were set aside for the hearing. The commissioner appointed to preside was Tim Singh – now a judge of the Supreme Court of B.C. – a warm, robust barrister, audacious and outspoken. A refugee from South Africa, he'd practised in the rough and tumble mining town of Flin Flon, Manitoba, before going to the West Coast.

The hearing was held in the assembly room of Canada's San Francisco consulate in a downtown business tower, an austere space into which were crowded four lawyers, Commissioner

Singh, court reporter Anne Dyke, and the chief RCMP investigating officers and their video crew, whose stationary camera glared stolidly down upon the various occupants of a witness chair.

I had asked the FBI to produce their case files and was allowed to rummage through a box of them for several hours. I came up with a few nuggets, including an FBI press release of August 23, 1985, proudly announcing to the media the bureau was taking over the prosecution from the S.F.P.D.

"The FBI entered into the investigation," it said, "after it was determined that the incident took place while the ship was located 6.5 nautical miles off the coast of the State of Washington."

A nautical mile is less than a hundred yards shy of a linear mile. That would have put the ship on the American side of the boundary.

An affidavit from Special Agent Jan Smith deposed to the source of this information: Interviews with personnel of the Royal Viking Lines Agency.

A memo from Special Agent Hugh Galyean suggested he'd confirmed the position of the ship with Lieutenant Preston of the U.S. Coast Guard, whose office monitors ship traffic with land-based radar – somewhat in the manner of air traffic controllers. Preston had taken a radar fix on the vessel at 5:40 p.m. on the day of the murder. Galyean's report: "Based on that data, Lieutenant Preston advised that the ship would have entered U.S. waters at approximately 6:00 p.m."

The best evidence of the time of death was 6:45 p.m. Unless the Royal Viking Lines and the U.S. Coast Guard were both wrong, the case for Canadian jurisdiction appeared tenuous.

Yet the FBI was now arguing its information was incorrect.

The agent carrying the ball for the FBI in San Francisco was Jan Smith, a trim, young, no-nonsense investigator who had got straight A's in the FBI's how-to-survive-cross-examination class. Lesson one: Keep your answers short. Lesson two: Don't get into arguments with counsel.

She testified that as case agent she was in charge of marshaling the evidence against Frisbee (although her only real encounter with him was on the way to court when he complimented her on her choice of perfume). She was adamant that a mistake had been made: the FBI, on the basis of information from the Coast Guard, had erroneously believed the vessel was in U.S. waters, and had held to this belief for eight months after Frisbee's arrest.

I cross-examined her:

"You're saying, as I understand your evidence, there was an apparent error on the part of U.S. Coast Guard officials?"

"I don't know whom the error was with, but I am supposing so..."

"And you spent several months investigating the case with a team of seven or eight agents interviewing all sorts of people, traveling around the world?"

"Yes, sir."

"Never thought to doublecheck whether that vessel was in Canadian or American waters during all that time?"

"No, sir."

"Were you aware whether there was an international boundary going up the middle of that strait?"

"No, I was not."

"Did you check the map?"

"No, I did not."

"You never looked at the map to see where the vessel might have been?"

"No, sir, I didn't."

"Did anyone draw your attention to the possibility that this vessel might have been in Canadian waters?"

"Yes, we received a telephone call from the – I believe the coroner's office in Canada – stating that the ship was in Canadian jurisdiction."

"And what did you do about that?"

"I advised the attorney, Mr. Dondero."

"Yes?"

"And he said not to be bothered with that at this time, and to call the Coast Guard in Seattle."

"And to proceed full steam ahead?"

"Yes."

"Weren't you concerned about whether the vessel was on the Canadian side or the American side?"

"At that point, no, I was not."

"Why?"

"Because I was collecting evidence and talking to witnesses."

"Well, did you not think that all that effort might have gone completely to waste if the vessel were in Canadian waters?"

"No, I did not think so."

"You were happy to have Mr. Frisbee remain in custody here on American charges during all that time?"

"Yes."

"Yes?"

"Yes."

Throughout all this, Smith maintained a calm, almost machine-like temper. I guess she knew someone had to carry the ball for the fumble-prone team of the U.S. Attorney General, and she gamely accepted her role as fullback.

"You were not concerned that he may be charged in the wrong jurisdiction?"

"No."

"You weren't concerned about that whatsoever?"

"No, sir, I was not concerned."

"And were you alerted in any other way in the late days of August or early September that the vessel might have been in Canadian waters?"

"I believe I received two telephone calls from their [the coroner's] office."

"What about the second call, what did you do about that one?"

"I passed that information on to Mr. Dondero also."

"And Dondero said: Forget about it, we're carrying on?"

"Words to that effect. He said to proceed with our investigation."

One should not impute any improper motive into the gritty determination on the part of American authorities to carry on regardless, but while Robert Frisbee was languishing in the gay wing of the San Francisco Jail, various representatives of the U.S. Department of Justice were arduously traveling the world at taxpayers' expense: taking commission evidence in Hong Kong, interviewing ship's witnesses in Norway and Holland.

I showed Smith a newspaper clipping which quoted V. Roy Lefcourt. A few days after Frisbee's arrest, V. Roy had hinted the ship might have been in Canadian waters. She recalled seeing the story.

"You did not check it out at the time?"

"No, I did not."

"Why?"

"I was not directed to do so."

"In your capacity as case agent, do you just do what you are directed to do?"

"No, not entirely."

"Do you have some initiative?"

"Yes, sir."

I don't think Smith thought fondly of me after this. On the other hand, I don't recall seeing any FBI press releases announcing they'd made a botch of their case.

But embarrassing the authorities over a senseless miscue, however satisfying from an adversarial point of view, was not going to win Frisbee an acquittal. Unfortunately – for the defense – Canadian authorities had kept badgering the U.S. justice department, which finally interviewed officers of their Coast Guard. They confirmed that the *Viking Star*'s coordinates placed the ship in Canadian waters at the time of the murder.

What I was seeking was information that would leave the location of the ship still in doubt. I found only bits and scraps, including FBI notes of an interview with an officer of the Coast Guard's Vessel Traffic Service in Seattle: "Commander Bennett advised that ships might occasionally cut across the border line if there was no other ship traffic in the area, and might conceivably take a slight shortcut for a faster route into the Pacific Ocean and their travel south."

It wasn't much, but we hoped to turn it to advantage.

Chapter 15

RELUCTANTLY, I SUPPOSE, THE CROWN DECIDED NOT TO CALL, at the San Francisco hearing or at trial, evidence of Frisbee's interviews with the police. The effort of assembling the huge cast of characters required to prove the voluntariness of Frisbee's statements would be, Dennis told us, too burdensome to undertake.

We were relieved: Frisbee's statements to the police that he was feeling "very merry" from drink prior to Mrs. Barnett's death, and in control of his "capacities," were not calculated to assist an intoxication defense.

So only one officer of the S.F.P.D. was called at the San Francisco hearing – Inspector David Suyehiro, crime scene investigator for the detectives' division. Fingerprints and photographs were his specialty.

He introduced in evidence some fifty-three photographs taken in Penthouse Six. They portrayed the layout of the suite: it is rectangle-shaped; the hallway door leads into a small anteroom adjacent to a toilet and to a bathroom with tub and shower. At the opposite end the glass door opens onto a private balcony, protected by a railing and accessible to an intruder only if he were to scramble to it over some lifeboats. A wall separates a living-room area (two sofas, two armchairs, a high-back swivel chair, tables, cabinets, clothes closets, half-size refrigerator, and bar) from a large bedroom area with separate access to the bathroom. Facings are all wood and formica and brass.

One would hesitate to say there is much in the way of artistic designer touches here – it's all very functional and square-angled.

Suyehiro's photographs were taken shortly after the vessel berthed in San Francisco. The victim's body had been removed to a cold storage facility on the vessel, but otherwise, he said, the scene remained untouched.

The photos showed a few articles of male apparel that seemed to have been carelessly tossed about the living room. On the floor near the front entrance was a blue bathrobe. It was caught under a closed closet door. The witness said the robe's sleeves were "turned almost inside out, as if someone were taking the robe off."

Suyehiro had spread the robe out before taking a closeup of it. It was Frisbee's robe – we knew we would be unable to argue otherwise – and a highly incriminating garment. Several small blood spatters showed on the front of it, and a smudge of blood on the sleeve. But, significantly, on the left sleeve – Frisbee was right-handed.

On a table nearby was a black suit jacket, a carnation in the lapel. On a chair in front of the bar a white dress shirt was draped. On the swivel chair, another white garment of some kind – Inspector Suyehiro didn't know what it was; it wasn't seized.

On an end table beside the bar were a telephone and a wine glass half filled with what appeared to be champagne. In a waste-basket near the bedroom wall was a discarded, empty half-sized bottle of champagne – a piccolo bottle, as it is known among the champers crowd.

Frisbee had brought his emergency supply of liquor with him, a portable bar with a handle and a snap fastener which was open on top of the fridge, and in it were four quart (mostly full) bottles: a Stolichnaya vodka, a Canadian Club, a Johnnie Walker red, and a Beefeater gin.

Nearby, three more bottles on the shelf: a Moët champagne, open and half full; a corked bottle of white Demestica wine, its label showing a few small red stains, and the infamous bottle of Famous Grouse scotch, still sealed, the label torn at the edges and bearing blood stains.

Suyehiro tendered that bottle as an exhibit. "When I saw it originally it looked as if there was a residue of blood and that it had been wiped or washed off with liquid." Exhibit Sixteen.

The bottle of Greek wine, he said, had a single strand of hair fiber stuck to a splotch of blood. It wasn't established where the hair came from. The bottle became Exhibit Seventeen.

This bottle was not the only manifestation of the ancient Republic of Greece in evidence in this room: stuck in the greenery of a vase on a table was that country's national flag, white stripes and cross against blue background. A bon voyage adornment from the redoubtable Reverend Daniel Kazakes.

Scattered near these bottles were several items that seemed anxious to tell us a story: a champagne cork lay on its side near its gold foil wrapping; an ice bucket sat near a tray bearing three glasses that were clean, one that was dirty and containing an orange slice. A large tumbler was beside it with a quarter-inch of fluid still in it.

Also on the shelf were a red bowtie, a red silk handkerchief, and a frilly sleeve garter – Frisbee's formal attire which he had laid out for the captain's party that night. Nearby was an engraved invitation card: the ship's captain had cordially invited the occupants of suite six to his "Farewell Party, Monday, August 19, 1985, at 6:45 p.m. in the Bergen Lounge." That, by sinister coincidence, turned out to be the very time of Mrs. Barnett's death.

And now the blood.

Blood was on the ceiling, on the floor, on the walls, on mirrors. Spots of blood were found a dozen feet away from the bloodied bed.

The head of one of the twin beds was soaked in it. On the headboard was an ugly decoration of red spatter. On the wall of the closet beside that bed were spatters. Blood had streamed down its face and dried there.

In the bathroom, on the floor beside the toilet, was a bloodied towel. In the sink, near the drain, were spots of blood.

It was all evidence of an unbelievably savage bludgeon murder.

Between the beds was a nightstand. On it were two framed snaps of Philip Barnett, his still eyes gazing out at this awful scene.

I wondered, as I looked at the photographs: could our passive-dependent client really have wreaked this carnage? The thought intruded: Had there been someone else, a psychopathic robber who had startled Mrs. Barnett into wakefulness, then silenced her outcries? Had some dim memory of such an event percolated into Frisbee's recall? Among the final lines of his manuscript, I'd read these lines:

"I barely opened my eyes and saw him ... an indeterminate shadow of a man, my height, coming closer ... He picked up her jewelry and put it in his pocket."

A jewel thief? But her jewels were all still in the dresser drawers – and Suyehiro had pictures to prove it.

Or, as the manuscript ominously suggested, was the killer one Robert Dion Frisbee, out of his body, out of his mind?

"I feel myself levitating, my spirit spiraling me up to his mobile body, and I look down to see my body as if in a dream ... was he now me?"

Was he indeed? Could there have been a killer inside the skin of Robert Frisbee?

The thought that a third party might have committed this murder refused to leave me. That mild-mannered Robert could have done this terrible thing seemed incredible. But if he did commit this act, so explosively, in so unmeasured and reckless a fashion, could he have been in any control of his senses?

We were shown other photographs. These the jury would never see. The Crown knew our objections would be upheld.

Some were taken by the ship's photographer while the body of Muriel Barnett was still on the bed. Others show her on a morgue slab. The expression on Muriel's battered face is one of utter pain and horror. I shall spare the reader further description.

Frisbee had told us that on the evening of the murder he had taken a couple of capsules of the tranquilizer Librium, a fact that would aid greatly in making out the defenses of intoxication and automatism. But an affidavit on file from RCMP Sergeant Rehman had already warned us, "During the search of the penthouse suite there was no sign of Librium." Inspector Suyehiro confirmed this, concluding his examination by telling us that although he seized a bottle of Antabuse from a drawer beneath the bar, no other pills or drugs were discovered.

No Librium. That made me anxious. Without proof that Frisbee's mind was mangled by the additive combination of alcohol and Librium, our medical defenses would seem dangerously speculative.

Suyehiro knew what I was after in cross-examination:

"Do you have a list of everything you observed there?"

"No."

"And unless you made an itemized list, you are not going to remember what in fact was there, are you?"

"I would remember drugs."

"Did you go into Mr. Frisbee's shaving kit?"

"I don't recall I even saw a shaving kit . . . one thing I do recall is most of his items were taken out prior to my being there."

"Well, let's hear about that. Who did that?"

"I presume the people on board ship."

"So we are now finding out that certain items were removed from there before you got there."

"I believe it was just his immediate possessions."

"Well, how do you know?"

"Because – well, vaguely, this is all I can recall."

"Do you remember who the person was who may have vaguely said that to you?"

"No, I can't recall."

I made a mental note to try to locate those possessions. Hopefully we would find some proof Frisbee had a bottle of Librium capsules among them.

Oddly, Suyehiro found not a single usable fingerprint in the entire cabin.

"I take it you dusted all around the place, did you?"

"Correct."

"Various bottles and glasses and the telephone, perhaps?"

"Correct."

"Light switches?"

"Yes."

"Did you find any prints?"

"None that were usable."

It would obviously be the Crown's argument that Frisbee beat Mrs. Barnett to death while wearing his now blood-smudged robe. It was possible, though, that the robe had become bloodied while not on his person, but merely lying, perhaps on a chair or bed, near the scene of the attack. Suyehiro's theory that the wearer of the robe had hurriedly taken it off after the murder, turning its arms inside out, was also open to question. The robe had been handled by S.F.P.D. officers at the scene.

"You don't know if someone removed the robe from where it was wedged under the door?"

"No, I don't know."

"As far as you know, someone might have picked it up, examined it, and dropped it down?"

"It's possible."

"Picked it up, tried to put it on, and dropped it, for all you know?"

"For all I know, yes."

I pursued the possibility that Frisbee's gown had become blood-smudged only after the murder.

"In addition to the apparent blood spatter on the gown are some smudges, correct?"

"Yes."

"And those smudges are where on the gown?"

"On the sleeve."

"And are consistent with someone wearing that gown, perhaps bumping into some blood surface?" ·

"It's possible."

Curiously, the detectives had not seized for evidence either the half-full bottle of champagne on the bar shelf or the empty piccolo bottle in the waste-basket. Our drunkenness defense depended upon Frisbee having consumed copious quantities of alcohol, and I sought to establish there may have been other bottles in the suite Suyehiro had overlooked:

"In the fridge below the traveling liquor case, what was contained in that?"

"Gee, I can't recall what was in there."

"Did you examine it?"

"Yes."

"Can you recall whether there were bottles of alcohol in there?"

"Gee, I can't recall. I just can't even picture what was inside."

"Are you going to tell me that you doubt there were bottles in the refrigerator?"

"No, there could have been."

I thought: Not the most thorough study of a murder scene had taken place here. The San Francisco police had not gone out of their way to seek evidence helpful to Frisbee. But, on the other hand, the gaps in their case could perhaps be widened: escape holes for our client.

Chapter 16

THE END FOR PHILIP BARNETT CAME JUST AFTER NEW YEAR'S OF 1984, in his eighty-fifth year. Robert and the Barnetts had driven down to Carmel for the holidays – they abhorred being in the city during the festive time – and they'd returned home early on January 4.

Robert busied himself taking down all the Christmas decorations, and at 3:30 that afternoon asked Philip if he could go home. He remembers Philip sitting on the sofa; he remembers his last words: "All right, Robert, go. Kiss me goodbye."

Mrs. Barnett called him about forty-five minutes later.

He went over immediately. Mrs. Barnett was in the living room with Philip. He was lying on the sofa. He'd been taking a nap, and fell asleep and expired.

TYHURST INTERVIEWS

I had to clean him up a little bit and take off his jewelry and things like that, empty the pockets. And then we sat there, the two of us, just looking at him, and she wasn't crying, no emotion. She did not go into mourning, no outward grief. And she said – she tried to be very casual about it – "Of course I would like you to stay on with me as my secretary at the same salary, if you will. Do you want to?" And I said, "Yes." Very formal. And she said, "Okay." That was the only question in her mind. She thought I was going to run away and desert her.

Did she?

I think so, that is why she wanted to put that out of her mind first. Then she stood up and said, "Oh, we should look at the will."

Had you ever seen the will prior to that?

No, it was a will that he'd written himself and sealed. And she opened it, and I didn't see it at all, she just opened it to see the first page and she said, "Everything goes to me," and she put it back in the drawer.

And what did you do?

Well, I made a drink.

Do you mean a drink or more than a drink?

Well, when I say I made a drink that means I've started drinking. I'd been drinking all day, anyhow. And I sat there for two hours and talked to him more or less, because I had a question in my mind. I couldn't understand why after all those years he left me a pair of cuff-links which I had given him.

That's all he left?

Yes, I didn't know this at the time, and I talked for two hours, and I think I started to have – I don't want to be dramatic, but I think I started to have a kind of a . . . could be shock, I don't know . . . anyway, he was lying on the sofa. It took the undertakers two hours to get there. So I just sat opposite to him on the sofa . . . I was talking to him.

FRISBEE'S TESTIMONY AT TRIAL

What did you say?

Oh, I guess I was shocked and disappointed, surprised I wasn't included in his will.

Yeah.

After all the promises he'd made me, the things we'd talked about, and I just couldn't understand it.

Were you feeling loss?

Oh, yes, I still feel it.

How did you display that sense of loss?

I . . . I cried. I was crying there, sitting, talking to him.

Did Mrs. Barnett show any grieving?

I hate to say, but she showed no outward grieving to me or anyone else.

As Robert sat there nursing his sorrow, Muriel went to Philip's bedroom and kept herself busy by emptying out all of Mr.

Barnett's closets, dumping his clothes on the floor, replacing them with her own – she'd often complained about her lack of closet space. But that was her therapy, Robert assumed, removing all the physical evidence of him. Two hours later his body was gone, too, and by nightfall there wasn't much of Philip left in the apartment.

Dr. Barnett was cremated a few days later and his ashes scattered upon the waters of San Francisco Bay. Robert remembers little of this ceremony: he remained in his own private San Francisco fog. He vaguely remembers the boat, the ashes floating on the water . . . but not much became cemented in his mind. And immediately after, with no more time to mourn, he went to work for Muriel.

TYHURST INTERVIEWS

I guess we saw an awful lot of each other because I didn't want her to be alone, and I would ask her if she wanted me to . . .

Did you have any crying yourself?

Yes, I did.

What do you mean?

I sobbed while I was talking to him.

How about in the months after?

I cried at night, yes.

Did you?

I missed him, yes. I loved him. I know I sound weird because I say I loved him and I love her and I love Daniel also.

Eventually Robert was shown Philip's will, which appointed him and Philip's accountant co-executors. While it gave everything to Muriel, it did provide, in the event she predeceased him, for a cash gift of $250,000 to Robert, along with lesser sums to various friends, the Barnetts' godsons, and several charities, the remainder to establish a Philip and Muriel Barnett foundation, to benefit the University of San Francisco and its law school.

It looked as if Philip intended Muriel to inherit not just his entire estate, but Robert as well. The Frisbee insurance policy had become effective.

Robert would obey Philip even in death and continue to look after poor Muriel. He loved her, after all, like a son.

But he was a long time working through the pain of the great man's death.

Patient's name: Robert Dion Frisbee.

The patient is a cooperative, oriented, chronically ill-appearing 57-year-old man who states that his boss just died. He is quite upset over this. The patient admits he is an alcoholic and for quite some years he has been drinking on the average of one drink with orange juice in the morning, two to three martinis at lunch time, a "couple" martinis at supper time, and then two glasses of wine. He had been cutting down on his drinking until his boss died on 4 January, and then he resumed. I advised total abstention.

April 18

The patient has not had a drink since he was last in the office on 12 April. Recommended strongly that he start going to A.A. meetings with his lover, who is also an alcoholic. He is to abstain from alcohol.

May 1

Has not gone to A.A. yet because his lover has refused but he plans to go this Saturday even if his lover will not go. The patient is feeling much better. He is actually working.

May 6

Dear Dr. Raszl:

Enclosed please find my check in the amount of $45.00. I have been trying to stick to a modified low cholesterol diet. My idea of non-fat milk is non-fat nothing – except of course at cocktail hour when one slips in a dash of bitters, ounce of gin, bourbon, scotch, vodka, and a floater of champagne – then it is drinkable. (Kidding of course – been dry.)

Sincerely,

Robert Frisbee

DR. RASZL, June 15

He and his lover have gone to four A.A. meetings but they don't care for the group very much and they are planning trying another group.

Dear Dr. Raszl:

The enclosed is just about all I am able to send you – and if I don't get it in the mail soon it will start sprouting long green ugly hairs. Thank you for everything – living with a clean body, good thoughts.

Fondly,

Robert Frisbee

DR. RASZL, August 23

The patient went on a binge three weeks ago that lasted about a week. He is not going to A.A. He is planning on going to Europe within the next two weeks with his boss. He would like some Librium for the trip.

Things didn't quite stick in Robert's mind for almost a year after Philip's death; his routines, the lunches, the parties, were all clouded in a fog of alcohol and sadness. That trip to Europe, for instance, in September. Muriel and he flew there and back by Concorde – you'd think he'd remember that, but Robert simply did not. Not a single detail of the holiday came back to him when he tried to recall it. Even when Dan and some other friends showed him postcards they'd received from him.

A bill for $1,400 later came from The Lombardy Hotel in New York, so they must have stopped off there. It was where the Barnetts always stayed in New York, in the Phyllis Diller Room, the comedienne's apartment which the Lombardy managed for her when she wasn't in New York. And a bill came from the Connaught Hotel in London, and one from the Hotel Ritz in Paris. For $2,785, so he must have enjoyed himself.

Robert became a little frantic. How could he not remember this trip? He'd also begun making mistakes in the books, and even in his chauffeuring duties. He'd lose Muriel, forget which party or which restaurant he was supposed to pick her up from; he'd drive up and down the perilous hills of San Francisco from Jack's to Trader Vic's to the World Trade Club in a frenzied search for his boss.

He began making notes to himself, reminders for the day. He

entered into a daily journal all his little tasks, Muriel's many appointments, her ever-more-frequent outings. In her eighties, she was not slowing down, she was accelerating. Her husband's death was only a little blip in her social calendar.

How was her health latterly?

I think she was coming down a little bit around this time because she was a little terrified that the cancer might be coming back. And she was accident-prone, I guess. She was always breaking a leg or tripping over high heels and breaking a collar or shoulder.

How much did she have to drink?

I would say that Mrs. Barnett drank rather heavily.

Did it affect her memory in any way that you knew?

It did eventually. She started to forget her dates.

I don't want to put this too boldly, but do you think she was failing somewhat in that respect in the last year or so?

Yes, she wasn't as sharp as she had been. And she kept saying, all I want is a good few years more and that is all. She knew there was a horizon coming up.

Maybe it was as a result of an astigmatic glimpse of that thin edge between earth and heaven that she had her own will drawn up. Ted Kolb drafted it. Mr. Kolb was the family lawyer. A former golf-club mate of Philip's.

She proudly showed the will to Robert. He gratefully observed that he was named in it: $250,000, the same amount Philip had promised him if predeceased by Muriel.

Her will in fact essentially echoed Philip's – cash gifts of $100,000 to each of three godchildren, $50,000 to another favorite friend, and $5,000 to each of twenty-six charitable groups. The residue, about $3 million, was, as Philip had desired, to go to a fund to support the Philip and Muriel Barnett Professorship of Trial Advocacy at the University of San Francisco, Philip's alma mater.

Muriel just couldn't be bothered with all the fussy paperwork involved in the keeping of her accounts, so she had Ted Kolb draw up a general power of attorney for her in Robert's name. She also insisted Robert have signing power over her checking account at the Wells Fargo Bank. This was known as the Trustee account, and Muriel kept enough money in it to pay her regular bills.

Muriel rarely looked at her bank statements. She knew in a kind of hazy way that she was rich, but she wasn't one to count her dollars.

One day she glanced at an E.F. Hutton investment statement that listed her liquid worth at around $3.25 million, and said in a little delighted voice, "Robert, I'm a very rich lady." She decided she was going to start making cash gifts to friends. "So they can enjoy it while I'm still here."

She began to spend at breakneck speed. Gifts of $1,000 or $5,000 to help friends celebrate their birthdays. Regular small donations to such worthy recipients as Pets Unlimited, the Apostleship of the Sea, Guide Dogs for the Blind, the Perpetual Help Center, the Holy Ghost Fathers, and the Republican Party.

That Christmas she personally wrote out a check to Robert for $15,000. For his birthday, another $30,000. To help him move to another apartment, $5,000.

Otherwise Robert wrote out most of the checks. A lot of them were returned because he failed to include the dates or the amounts, or simply forgot to sign them. He felt lost without Philip's steadying hand, and his mourning lasted through the year of 1984.

The event that shocked Robert back at least temporarily into a semi-conscious state was Muriel's accident in October of that year.

They'd returned at night from a dinner party at which much liquid fare was served, and Mrs. Barnett was her usual jovial, tottering self. Robert offered to escort her into her apartment to help with all her zippers and fasteners, but she declined his services, kissed him good night, and bade him farewell.

She later called him at home to say she had fallen and might have to go to the hospital.

Robert hurried to her side. She had indeed taken a drunken spill, hitting her head against something – probably the marble-top dresser, although she didn't remember – and her neck was in pain. But somehow she had managed to make up her face, put on a wool cloak over a night dress, and gather her purse, and there she was sitting at the card table waiting for him, all ready for the hospital.

There, they diagnosed a minor fracture of her upper spinal cord (called a hangman's break – not as serious as it sounds). The doctors did their repairs and placed a brace on her neck, and a bandage on her left arm, which she had also injured.

Robert remembers that she was *so* uncomfortable, and he was with her from morning to night at the hospital until poor Muriel went off to sleep.

FRISBEE'S TESTIMONY AT TRIAL

I would visit her every day, um, she wasn't too happy with the hospital food. I'd bring her food I'd make up for her, soups or things easy to digest, salads, she loved fresh fish.

Why wouldn't she have the hospital food?

We'd been there so many times with Dr. Barnett that she knew what the food was like.

Did you have any conversations with her in the hospital about what her plans were?

Well, for some reason the uppermost thought in her mind was to make a codicil for her will.

Yes.

We discussed that and how it could be accomplished.

Describe the circumstances of that conversation, if you will.

Well, I don't know her inner thoughts but she was not happy with the will she had because she told me that Dr. Barnett had already established the chair at the university, and she ... her exact words were: "I don't think it's necessary to give all that money to the university any more, I'd rather give it to people."

What people?

Her loving friends and what she called "my little family."

All right.

Godchildren.

And did she make any reference in particular to the bequest to yourself?

Yes. She wanted to change the last part of her will to leave me two-thirds of her estate and one-third to the university.

All right, and what was your reaction to that?

Shock but also ecstatic reaction. I was very happy; I thought, oh, it would be fantastic, wonderful.

What kind of condition was she in when she was giving you this advice as to her intentions?

She was in her normal condition. She was taking a painkiller, um, she was able to move around and use the toilet. She had a sitting-room area in her hospital room and we'd sit up in the afternoon and talk and look at television . . . she was out of bed.

Why should I give all that money to the University of San Francisco? she asked. It wasn't *her* alma mater after all; she'd gone to Berkeley. And Philip had already established his chair, he'd given blocks of stock to the U.S.F. law school to set it up. Give to the ones you love, that was her idea. And Robert was one she loved. Like a son. He felt like her son now, truly, not her servant.

Robert remembers going home to Dan that night in a state of delirious joy. Dan could hardly believe it. Robert had never seen him so buoyed up. Get the new will signed before she changes her mind, he said. Dan could be so mercenary at times.

Robert worried that she would indeed change her mind: she tended at her age to flit from one idea to another, sometimes not alighting on one long enough to recall it. He tried to convince himself that Muriel hadn't been in a state of senility.

But when he returned to the hospital the next day with a typed rough draft of the will, she discussed it with an obvious clarity of mind, and Robert recorded some notes in his journal about minor changes she wanted. Then she told him to make up the formal document.

Robert felt overwhelmed; he would be Muriel's slave however long she might live. She was in the hospital only a few days, and when she came out her left arm was still bandaged and she was wearing a padded neck brace, so she couldn't move her neck. She wouldn't have a private nurse, so grateful Robert was with her constantly. The maid, Millie, cleaned up and helped her bathe and dress, but Robert did everything else.

Muriel's spirits were all right, but she was mad at herself for having been so stupid and now having to cancel all her engagements. She didn't want to be seen in public wearing that ridiculous collar, it would just get people talking.

Robert wrote up the codicil to her will by himself. He knew how to do it. He'd been secretary to one of the most famous probate lawyers in the state.

Why did she not go to an attorney to write this up?

Well, you see that goes back to another thing about the Barnetts. They were very secretive about their personal life with people.

But she had an attorney draw up her will in '84?

Original will, yes.

Why wouldn't she go back to that attorney then for the change?

That's why I'm trying to bring in the personality a little bit. They were secretive to anyone except Robert about their personal affairs. Their wills, their state of health. Even her broken neck, she wouldn't let people know. Nobody ever knew that Philip had heart attacks.

FRISBEE'S TESTIMONY AT TRIAL

When did you draw up the final draft of the codicil which is an exhibit here?

That would have probably been the day she came home. It happened within a series of two or three days.

And what arrangements were made with respect to having it executed?

She did not want any of her friends to witness it, and she suggested Dan, and she'd already known Mrs. DeLuca who is our next-door neighbor and we set up arrangements to have lunch at my home with Dan and Mrs. DeLuca and they would witness her signature for her.

Why those persons?

Mainly because she knew them and also they didn't know any of her close associates. She didn't want gossip about any of her own business to circulate.

So this arrangement was made for lunch at your place?

My apartment.

And how did you get her to your apartment?

I drove her over. She still had the neck brace on, and she wore what would be termed a . . . um, leisure-type of easy garment.

Chapter 17

THE CENTERPIECE OF THE TABLE THE PROSECUTION WOULD spread for the jury was a two-page typewritten document titled "Codicil," dated October 16, 1984. If valid, the document would give Frisbee almost two-thirds of Mrs. Barnett's estate of nearly four million dollars. This was not an insubstantial motive for murder, and the Crown's argument that the codicil was executed as a result of foul play proceeded on three theories:

One: Frisbee had got her so drunk she didn't know what she was doing. Two: he had drugged her to similar effect. Three: she was never permitted to read the codicil before signing it.

The latter theory was based on the apparent fact that when Mrs. Barnett put pen to it, she was wearing that stiff neck brace, unable to bend her head to see what she was signing.

There was no suggestion that the signature at the end of the document wasn't hers, although the the words "Muriel Collins Barnett" had been inscribed by an obviously shaky hand and very much lacked the firmness of her normal signature. However, it wasn't scrawled aimlessly onto the page, but written carefully above the signature line Frisbee had typed, above her name in capital letters, so I found it impossible to believe she signed it blindly. Her sight was failing, but only for distant objects. (She often told Frisbee she could read the Lord's Prayer on the head of a pin.) Assuming she were in a coherent state of mind she could not have failed to see, on the same page as her signature, the following paragraph:

"To Mr. Robert Frisbee I leave all of my personal furniture, furs, dinnerware, jewelry, crystal, and paintings. I also wish to leave Mr. Robert Frisbee, for his complete devoted attention to me, during my recent accident, and having been an employee who is knowledgeable of the affairs of the company, all of my stock, shares, and interest in Northern Machine and Marine Railways Inc. of Ketchikan, Alaska. I also wish to leave Mr. Robert Frisbee 2/3% of the residue of my estate, and 1/3% to the university as stipulated in Section B of my last will and testament."

I don't know what was made in California Probate Court of that "2/3%" figure which, strictly speaking, would give him only two-thirds of 1 per cent of the residue, but I assume it was generally agreed it was intended to be read as "66 and 2/3%."

The codicil was typed onto one of Philip Barnett's old legal letterheads. The first paragraph read:

"I, Muriel Collins Barnett, make this document a codicil to my last will and testament dated March 12, 1984. I wish to leave the following bequests."

Named in it were three persons who had not been mentioned in her previous will: her accountant Lloyd Wilkins, his wife, Vivian, and their daughter, Janet. To the former, the codicil left Muriel's Cadillac, Zenith TV, a pair of Philip's cuff-links, "pearls with tack tie and studs," and the sum of $5,000. To Vivian, "my antique lace diamond necklace with matching earrings, my Marquisite ring, a selection of one piece of furs, and a choice of my collection of handbags." To Janet, "my gold and diamond necklace with matching earrings and ring, a selection of one of my furs, also a choice of one of my handbags."

The specificity of the items and painstaking description of some of them suggested, at least to me, the voice of Muriel Barnett detailing her wishes to Frisbee, although it could be argued that he was no stranger to her extensive collection of diamonds, gold, and pearls and could describe them without her help.

Her godchildren and their families were still remembered, and in addition to the cash gifts of $100,000 each the codicil bequeathed them specific items of jewelry.

"Being of sound mind," stated the document, "and not acting under any duress, I sign this codicil."

Mrs. Barnett kept a small metal lock-box in her apartment – not a regular safe; it could be opened with a key. In it she kept her jewels and important papers. It would be Robert Frisbee's evidence that immediately after Mrs. Barnett signed the codicil, he returned to her apartment with it and placed it in this security box, and hadn't touched it since.

After Mrs. Barnett's death, the paper was indeed found by her executor in the locked security box. That helped Frisbee's cause, if one infers that Mrs. Barnett could not have helped notice it there during the ten months before her death. (Unless, say, someone with access to the apartment – someone such as Dan Kazakes – sneaked it into the box while Mrs. Barnett was on her Alaska cruise.)

What didn't help Frisbee's cause was the fact that one of the two witnesses to the codicil was that same Mr. Daniel J. Kazakes. Not your average unbiased bystander. The second witness was Concerta Ann DeLuca – Connie to her friends. DeLuca's evidence as to how the document came to be signed would be critical; presumably she wouldn't share Dan Kazakes's pecuniary bias.

The prosecution's attempt to build an air of clandestine dealing around the signing of this codicil was dampened by DeLuca when she was called by the Crown to give videotaped evidence in San Francisco.

She was a buoyant, chipper woman entering her middle years, unhesitant and frank on the witness stand. She'd been landlady to Frisbee and Dan Kazakes ten years earlier when they lived on Washington Street. She'd since moved, and so had her tenants – they were now living in an apartment on Van Ness. But she knew Mrs. Barnett, and had lunched with her and Frisbee and Kazakes several times.

Dennis Murray asked her how she came to witness the codicil:

"Well, we had lunch and I was in the kitchen area with Mr. Kazakes and we were clearing away the dishes and putting them away. Mr. Frisbee and Mrs. Barnett were talking at the table and chatting, as they always did. Muriel called us in there and asked us if we would witness that she was signing this paper, and Dan and I came in, and I looked at it and I saw my name was misspelled."

Below her signature line, Frisbee had typed "Connie DeLucca," with an extra "c".

" . . . and she said, 'Just sign it. All you are witnessing is that I am signing this paper,' and I was going to read it, and she said, 'You don't have to read it, if I wanted you to read it I would have asked you to read it,' so we both signed it, and shortly after we all said our goodbyes and Mr. Frisbee drove her home."

Dennis showed her the document. "In looking at your signature, it looks like it is signed with two c's?"

"Yes."

"And how did that come about?"

"Well, I mentioned that my name was not spelled correctly, and she said it doesn't matter, just to sign it the way it was."

The account of Mrs. Barnett's snappish instructions seemed credible, and in keeping with her briskness of character. Connie DeLuca did not suggest Mrs. Barnett didn't or couldn't see the document she was signing. In fact, the witness's memory was that Mrs. Barnett had earlier taken her collar off, that her vanity enjoined her from wearing it in public, even in front of this small ensemble.

Nor was DeLuca much help to the Crown's theory that Mrs. Barnett was in her cups. Dennis asked about the deceased's demeanor at lunch.

"Well, she was pretty good for being, you know, in the shape she was in, but she had a few cocktails and she might have been a little shaky, but I have seen her like that before. I thought nothing strange about it."

"It wasn't strange to see her have a few cocktails?"

"No, she always had. She drank every time I was in her presence."

Dennis dropped her like a hot potato and turned her over to me.

One isn't allowed to ask a witness his or her personal opinion about the good character of an accused but one may ask about his reputation in the community. (One's reputation is an issue of fact. You are entitled to ask for facts but not opinions. You invariably get opinions anyway.)

"Do you know Robert Frisbee's reputation among the community for honesty and integrity?"

"Well, he was very well liked and I always felt that he was very, very . . . nice to be around, he was very pleasant, he was a very good cook, a great hostess . . . I mean host."

"And what about his reputation generally among other people, did he have a reputation for being an honest person?"

"Yes, I believe so."

"Were you aware of any episodes of violence on the part of Robert Frisbee?"

"None whatsoever."

"What would you say about the man in that context?"

"He is a very loving, very caring human being."

One can get good inadmissible evidence if one asks the right questions.

She was equally positive about the caring relationship between Frisbee and Mrs. Barnett.

"They were very affectionate towards each other; they kissed on greeting and when departing . . . there was much touching. I felt it was mother-son, I really did. In all ways that I could see. Very loving. She depended on him totally."

I established that it was Mrs. Barnett who asked DeLuca to be present for the signing of the codicil. The witness had no inkling up to that time a document would be put in front of her.

"Mrs. Barnett in fact never discussed her private business affairs with you?"

"None."

"She was rather private in that regard?"

"Yes, she was."

DeLuca said she herself had had nothing to drink that day. As for Mrs. Barnett, her cocktails hadn't affected her mental processes; they were intact.

"No question in your mind that she knew what she was signing?"

"None whatsoever. She always asserted herself very firmly. She was very, very pronounced in her words."

DeLuca gave evidence of Frisbee's drinking problems, and Dennis seized on that in re-examination, drawing from her the fact she'd never seen him out of control, staggering or falling:

"The essence of it, that he took his drink well, didn't he; he was able to cope with it?"

"I think he could, yes."

That could complicate our intoxication defense.

"Now, the only other thing I wanted to ask you," said Dennis, "you mentioned that she depended on him. Was it also obvious to you that she trusted him absolutely?"

"Yes, with everything."

The implication being, of course, that the defendant had seriously betrayed that trust.

The fact that Dan Kazakes was scheduled to testify at the pretrial hearings the next day was the cause of a restless night in my room in the Four Seasons Clift Hotel. His cockamaimie threats to, as he put it, blow the case wide open inspired visions of his blowing up Frisbee instead. I feared he would be defensive and querulous, easily demolished on the stand.

Thankfully he was being called as a Crown witness, so Dennis Murray would not be entitled to ask leading questions of him or attack his credibility. I, on the other hand, could cross-examine him – even spoon-feed some useful answers. One has to avoid overkill, though, when coddling a witness over-eager to assist the cause – it looks bad to the jury.

Jeff and I faced a technical hitch, however, in any effort we might make to rein in Dennis if he did try to go after Kazakes. Commissioner Singh had no authority to uphold our objections. They could only be noted for the record, and were to be ruled upon later, when the trial judge reviewed the video tapes.

When Dan Kazakes showed up the next afternoon he minced past me to the witness chair exuding the pungent aroma of a few noontime nips. He was dressed casually (fortunately he'd left his collar and robes at home) and didn't exactly look the part of the evil mastermind – I think the prosecutors were hoping for something more Svengalian. In fact he seemed unusually fragile, and older than his years. As he took the oath, the microphone caught every resonating decibel of his racking cough and the skritchy scraping of his ill-fitting false teeth.

Dennis must have decided to take the gamble that our objections would later be denied at trial because he went after Kazakes from the opening bell, body punches to soften him up and bring his guard down. He insisted on addressing the witness as "sir," employing a courtroom mannerism I've always found a little too saccharine for my taste, suggesting the manner of an ingratiating prep-school pupil.

"Now Mr. Kazakes, first of all, sir, you know a person by the name of Robert Frisbee, do you not?"

"Yes, for thirty-two years."

"And in fact over that period of time you and he have been homosexual partners?"

Jeff Green was quicker off the mark than I. "I object to a leading question like that, Mr. Commissioner – outrageously leading, in my respectful submission."

All Tim Singh could say was, "Objection noted."

Dennis nodded, and calmly continued. "And over that period of time, Mr. Kazakes, you and Mr. Frisbee have been homosexual partners, have you?"

"I wouldn't say that."

"Pardon me?"

"I wouldn't say that. We're just very, very close."

Frisbee had told me Kazakes would be defensive about his sexual inclinations. There was a strong macho element to his double-sided sexuality; he was used to the aggressor role.

"Are you, sir, homosexual?"

Jeff Green: "I object to that on the footing of irrelevance."

Dennis patiently waited for the objection to be noted, and tried again. "Are you, sir, homosexual?"

Kazakes mumbled something that sounded like "no." I don't know whether he intended to amplify that by saying he was bisexual, but I wished he'd just be up-front about such unimportant matters. This would look bad to the jury.

I must have been sitting on my hands through the early part of this – maybe a little stunned at the unexpected bear-baiting – but Jeff was getting angry. "My friend cannot cross-examine this witness. I object to him cross-examining the witness."

Mr. Commissioner: "Objection noted."

Dennis was like a dog with a bone. A polite dog. "Are you, sir, homosexual?"

I complained: "He answered it already, he said, 'No.'"

"I didn't hear the answer, I'm sorry."

"The answer is no," said Kazakes.

"And to your knowledge is Mr. Frisbee homosexual?" Dennis continued.

"Yes, he is."

I thought Dennis was about to probe further, to seek out some of the more salacious details of their mating habits, but he backed off and took another road.

"Now, you, sir, are you affiliated with some church of some kind?"

Kazakes clearly didn't like this tack. His answer bristled with hostility. "My religious work is between God and myself. That's my answer to that."

"Okay, are you affiliated with any church in any way?"

"I'm not."

I decided to cover all bases; making all these futile objections was tiring. "My friend should be put on warning that all these questions in cross-examination may ultimately be ruled inadmissible, and I am maintaining a continuing objection to them."

Dennis generously asked the commissioner to note the objections, and vigorously soldiered on. "Now, sir, I'm told that people describe you as describing yourself as a clerical man, that is, a preacher or a religious man of some kind, is that correct?"

"Well, my background is Greek Orthodox, but my ministry was to counsel people, which I did for some time, and I helped a lot of people, but at this time I'm not able to."

"And for example, sir, did you from time to time wear robes of some description?"

"No."

"You never wore what could be described as robes?"

"No."

This wasn't good. I was sure Dennis could later contradict him.

"And I gather then you don't lay any claim to being a clerical man?"

"I'm retired, or disabled, whatever you want to call it."

"Did you retire from the ministry?"

"Yes. I'm not able to do that work any more."

"And what ministry was it, sir?"

"It was a non-denominational."

"Did you have a parish?"

"No."

"And when you say you counseled people, sir, what sort of counseling did you engage in?"

The cross-examination as to Kazakes's spiritual good works was taking its toll, and Kazakes's voice rose shrilly in answer:

"Spiritual counseling, and how would you like to go to a hospital and try to comfort the AIDS patients like I did? And look at them die? I went to them to comfort them, and so you are saying something's wrong?"

Dennis's tone continued to be one of exaggerated politeness. "Now when you say spiritual counseling, sir, what sort of spiritual counseling were you giving?"

Kazakes seemed to fume a little bit, then went off like a string of firecrackers. "I have had enough of this abomination..."

After Tim Singh told him he had no recourse but to answer the question, Kazakes simmered for a while, then responded:

"Well, my grandfather was a medium, and all in our family, there is about four of us, we all have that gift."

As proof of this gift, he volunteered that he'd had premonitions about Mrs. Barnett's fatal voyage.

"I told Mrs. Barnett not to go on that trip, I said, 'I don't feel right about it.' 'Well,' she said, 'it's been booked for months, can't back out of it now.' Before they left I became very ill and I told Bob, I said, 'Something's wrong.'"

Her departure on the Alaska cruise apparently made our medium sick. He was ill in bed the whole time they were away.

It surprised me that Dennis didn't grab and run with this. Here's a fellow the Crown suspected of conspiring at murder, of being an accessory before the fact, who admittedly expected a tragedy to occur.

But Dennis didn't accuse him of knowing about, or planning, the evil event that was to happen; he suddenly eased up – maybe the witness's coughing fits were getting to him – and took the witness through Frisbee's history with the Barnetts.

His answers became windy and long, but at least lacked the earlier defensive posturing. He was asked to describe the events surrounding the signing of the codicil:

"Well, the area was very small, about eight feet wide and twenty feet long. There was a little kitchen here, a little dining-room table here and then Bob had his office desk across the end here with a typewriter and all that. Mr. Barnett used to give him tapes to bring home and he would put these earphones on and type, and I was managing that building, it's seven storeys, and there was cooking going on, and Mrs. Barnett never stopped talking, Mrs. DeLuca about the same way, and I had telephone calls coming in from tenants, others coming to the front door. I was glad that day was over."

"Now, during that lunch do you remember Mrs. Barnett signing a codicil to her will?"

"Yeah, because I was a witness. My name is on there."

"Now, what was Mrs. Barnett's health like at that point in time?"

"Uh, gee . . . I don't know. The newspapers said she was eighty years old and she was eighty-five. She was getting up in years, and she couldn't see over about five feet, Bob had to take her by the arm."

But, beyond the neck injury, no serious problems did he observe. She'd had one or two cocktails at lunch.

Connie DeLuca had remembered Mrs. Barnett was not wearing her neck brace at lunch. Kazakes's version was different. "It seems to me that it was on her."

"And did she have any difficulty signing it, sir?"

"It seemed like she was, yeah. Not due to alcohol or anything like that, probably due to her neck condition."

During a break in Dennis's examination, Kazakes called me out into the corridor to confer. There's nothing particularly wrong with that, although it gives rise to suspicions of witness-coaching. That's obviously what Dennis thought.

"Now, Mr. Kazakes, I couldn't help but notice when we adjourned this morning you called Mr. Deverell outside into the hall. Do you recall that?"

"Yeah. I just wanted to remind him of something."

"What did you say to him?"

"I would think that would be between he and I."

This waffling I didn't like at all, and said, "You can answer it."

"Well, when Mr. Frisbee went on this cruise to Alaska, he bought some stuffed animals, a big carton of them, and sent them to me at home. He also bought a gold necklace that he had made up, and he had that order sent home. So he had intentions of coming home, believe me."

"Did you also ask Mr. Deverell, 'How am I doing?'"

"Maybe I said something to that effect, I don't know."

"Were you concerned, sir, about how you were doing?"

"Well, listen, I have problems on account of my health, if I sit too long . . . I want to leave tomorrow. I'm supposed to go home tonight."

For the most part I laid off this whining hothead, merely confirming Muriel Barnett's obsessiveness about keeping her affairs secret and the circumstances surrounding her gift of $100,000 to him and $20,000 to his son Jerry: those two suspicious checks signed by Frisbee on Mrs. Barnett's account just before she died.

The latter sum was a gift from Muriel, Kazakes said, to further Jerry's religious work in Australia (an "Indian type of religion," he called it). The $100,000 check was intended by her to help Kazakes start up a Greek import shop in San Francisco. He said he received it on the day the *Viking Star* departed for Alaska.

"Mrs. Barnett handed it personally to you?"

"That's right. She said 'Good luck,' and, 'If you have a few pennies left over, if you go to the hospital to visit the AIDS patients, take some goodies with you.' She walked away. That's the way she was."

He confirmed he had previously run three import stores in the San Francisco area – one in San Rafael, another in Sausalito, the third in a little town called Corte Madera.

"And you were thinking of opening up a fourth such business?"

"Yes, but it would have been a discount imports; do you know what I mean?"

"Right."

"It wouldn't be an elegant store."

"Had Mrs. Barnett been in one of these import stores of yours?"

"She had been in the one in Sausalito which my wife ran, yeah."

The $100,000 gift was, he said, Muriel's way of thanking him for filling in for Frisbee as chauffeur during a time her regular go-fer had been indisposed. The prosecution, of course, believed the whole business was simply a convenient lie to cover up an attempted draining of Mrs. Barnett's account prior to her murder. And, in truth, Kazakes's explanation seemed weak. Could there have been another explanation for Muriel's sudden generosity? A motive more compelling, more consistent with her intricate mind-set, her pattern of planning the lives of others?

I would have to spend some more time with my client.

Chapter 18

The patient states that his boss apparently fell down and fractured some bones in her neck. Because of worry over his boss he started drinking heavily again. He would start by having one drink in the morning with his lover and then he would have about half a bottle of champagne with his boss around noon time and then during the evening he would have at least three more martinis. This went on through all of November and December until this past Tuesday, New Year's Day, when he was driving a party of six home including his boss and states he only had to go six blocks but he got lost.

This shocked him into the realization he was drinking too much, and he stopped completely that day. Since then he has had problems with the shakes. He states yesterday, "My hands were shaking so much I couldn't hold a book."

He states he had a lot of trouble sleeping yesterday so he took a couple of Librium and this helped him. He states after one of his naps his lover told him that during the nap he woke up and "my eyes were staring at the ceiling and my face was blue and I was levitating." The patient doesn't remember this at all.

I suspect he had an alcohol-withdrawal seizure yesterday.

January 21

He has not had a drink since he last saw me. Says he's successfully dried out. To retry A.A. Also I advised him to go on Antabuse, 250 mg. a day; the possible complications including death were explained to him. He is to return in a month.

Has not had a drink since he last saw me. He looks much better. He is not shaky. He has gone to several A.A. meetings but his roommate is somewhat recalcitrant about going, and the patient doesn't like to go alone. He did not start the Antabuse because they advised against it in A.A. and he feels he can do it on his own.

May 6

The patient admits to drinking very heavily before he left on a trip to Europe with his employer. He started about six weeks ago and was drinking about a pint a day of vodka.

Robert doesn't remember much about those visits to Dr. Raszl. In fact his memory cells for those early months of 1985 seem to have gone into total malfunction. Dementia, wasn't that what Dr. Tyhurst called it? Robert resided, for much of 1985, in the Land of Dementia. Severe memory impairment is a symptom of this dementia. Aggravated by alcohol, Librium, and recent bereavement.

He had kept a daily journal, which the police seized somewhere along the way, and his lawyers later showed it to him. The Metropolitan Museum of Art Engagement Book for 1985, with its lovely Van Gogh illustrations. Dutifully, Robert had filled it up with all his dates, chores, and appointments. So it looked as if he was carrying on normally. Normal for Robert.

For instance, on January 8, he'd apparently taken "M.C.B." to Trader Vic's for lunch. Muriel Collins Barnett: M.C.B., it's how he always referred to her in his journal. January 14: "In office and did work." The 18th, a trip to the hairdresser, dinner that evening. On the 20th he apparently spent three hours in the kitchen preparing crab "volture" and fruit zabione. Dr. Raszl at 1:15 p.m. on the 21st.

On the 24th: another trip to the hairdresser to prepare M.C.B. for Vienna Night at the World Trade Club. Black tie, says his journal.

February 19, Dan's birthday: "Cancel, Dan not well." On some days Robert was not well either. "Bob ill," say the entries.

These mundane routines continued through the spring, says the daily journal. Jack's for lunch, Vic's for dinner, cocktails at the

Mark. Take the Caddie to the mechanic, shop for gifts, write checks, mail mail. Dr. Raszl, Dr. Raszl. Hairdresser ad infinitum. M.C.B. ad infinitum.

If Robert had been the work slave of Philip Barnett, he was now the social slave of Muriel. After a day of toil for Philip, Robert was given the night's freedom. But under Muriel's frantic reign, he was at her bidding day and night. "You're on perpetual probation," she'd said. But how could he complain? – she'd made him heir to her fortune.

Yet he began to feel suffocated.

Alcohol gave release but no escape.

His journal informed Robert he must have been busy, busy, busy arranging The Great Spring European Excursion: tickets (only $13,516), visas, outfits to be bought, and gifts for the English godson. Chauffeuring Muriel to the Oriental Express "Explorama" lecture. They'd planned to fly first-class from San Francisco to New York, then by Concorde to London. Then Venice, Lake Como, Milan, Rome, Monte Carlo, Cannes, Paris. The Orient Express. Russia.

Russia – last time he was there he just couldn't find an open liquor store. Robert didn't know if he could take Russia.

Maybe it was the prospect of being drinkless in Russia that set him off on that six-week binge before they took off. He guessed he must have been swilling a quart a day.

Of course the trip couldn't have got off to a worse start. They were in a limousine on their way to San Francisco International – in plenty of time for their morning flight to New York – when Robert discovered he forgot the tickets. They missed the plane and went back to Chestnut Street, where Robert searched in vain for the tickets to the beat of Muriel's impatient foot-tapping. Their travel agent issued new ones, met them at the airport, and they made the noon flight. Pan-Am served them a very good lunch of caviar, Caesar salad, and veal.

And how does Robert remember that? Because in addition to his daily journal, he kept another book, an imitation-leather bound travel diary into which he'd pasted his favorite snapshots of Dan and of Philip. The police seized it for evidence, but Robert was given a copy of it to read before the trial.

So he knew he'd spent two nights with M.C.B. in New York in the Phyllis Diller suite. (Caviar and champagne at Petrossian's, tour of the Trump Tower, the Laurent for dinner, where he apparently enjoyed some very delicious osso bucco.)

TYHURST INTERVIEWS

So we went to New York and London ... she's very, very involved with a Mr. and Mrs. John Cope in London, the father of her godchild, and she was going to take Mr. and Mrs. Cope to Russia as her guests. And we were in London, and as I told you I was very much into drinking.

Yes.

And I decided I was drinking too much and I knew that I should go on the wagon mainly because, number one, in these places we were going to visit, like Russia, booze is not available. So I stupidly decided to go, what we call cold turkey.

Yes. In London?

Yes. So in the morning she had tomato juice and vodka, and I didn't, and I skipped the cocktail for lunch ... I had been taking tranquilizers, too.

During that time?

Mm-hmm, because I knew there would be a terrible transition from–

What tranquilizers?

Let's see ... is Librium a tranquilizer, doctor?

Yes.

Librium.

Were you taking it during the period that you had come off the alcohol?

I doubled [my dose] at that time, yes. And so we went to an Italian restaurant ... of course this is all written down so it can't be eliminated from my memory ... and she asked me about lunch and I said I wasn't very hungry, I was rather nauseous. So I went to the men's room and I came back and luncheon was there and the last thing I recall was she said, "Are you going to eat your spaghetti?" I said, "No." She said, "Well, give it to me, I'll finish it," and I gave it to her and that was the last thing I knew.

Muriel didn't finish his spaghetti. He fell face-first into it.

"Wow, end of trip," says the travel diary.

They were at their suite in Claridge's when he woke up. He remembers the vomiting but not his stumbling, falling, and blacking out again. Then a doctor came, Alan Sinclair, and he admitted him to St. Stephen's Hospital in Chelsea, where he stayed for a few days.

The European jaunt was aborted. John Cope escorted Mrs. Barnett and wobbly Robert on a flight back to San Francisco.

Muriel crossly refused to talk about the incident – except to say it was horrible of Robert to spoil her trip. But she did visit Dr. Raszl for him, and handed him a letter from Dr. Sinclair. ("We must put your doctor on our dinner list," Muriel later told Robert "He dances and would be a great asset at one of my parties.")

DR. RASZL, May 6, 1985

I just received a communication from Dr. Alan Sinclair in London. The patient was noted to have two "eliptiform seizures" there. A systolic heart murmur was noted. Stigmata of chronic liver disease were noted. I felt the patient's seizures were probably alcohol-withdrawal seizures. I told Mrs. Barnett the patient should not drive.

May 17

The patient is getting along quite nicely. He has had no more seizures. He is on Antabuse, has gone to a couple of A.A. meetings, but he doesn't like to socialize with the people there and it makes him "depressed" to hear their stories.

The patient questioned me about driving. I advised him not to drive.

What would he have done without Dan? Dan took over the duties of chauffeuring Muriel, sometimes in her Caddie, sometimes in the Olds, getting her to the hairdresser's on time, to her lunches and her soirees.

That summer, Robert wrote to his sister:

Dearest Elly,

It is 11:30 p.m. Sitting up with a distasteful glass of soda water in lime – godawful. Today is my third birthday – of A.A. that is –

not a drop and don't really care about it any more. Philip at 86 was still drinking three martinis at lunch, several before dinner, and wine of course, and died of natural causes . . .

The three months of not driving were a trying time for Dan as he had volunteered to drive M.C.B. around town. After a long time of this he came home and said, "Robert, now I realize why you come home as exhausted from your 'easy' job." M.C.B. is demanding. Her first comment on hearing I could not drive was, "Robert, I hope you realize you are ruining my social life."

That's about it for now. Another busy day tomorrow as we are planning a cruise to Alaska August 10 and back on the same merry-go-round. She could wear out three healthy men. But she loves me and I did promise Philip I would take care of her.

Love, Bob

Robert went to several of those preposterous A.A. meetings. (Everyone was so *happy*. They were not what Robert would consider sober. On some kind of dope, most of them.)

He took Antabuse, and got sick from the fumes of the drinks he made for Muriel.

He stayed off the bottle. For weeks. Until the doctor told him he could drive again.

                              FRISBEE'S TESTIMONY AT TRIAL

Tell us how you started to drink again.

When I went back to work I started to drink again, yes.

Openly?

No, I didn't drink openly, I drank surreptitiously.

Amplify that.

Sneaking. I carried a small half-pint of vodka in my pocket, or the little bottles from the airlines.

Who were you keeping this secret from?

Everyone.

Muriel Barnett?

Everybody I knew.

Dan Kazakes?

He didn't know I was drinking. I drank a lot of orange juice and I put vodka in it.

                              148

Were you also taking Librium during this time?
No, I would have stopped that.
When did you stop taking Librium?
When I started drinking again.
Antabuse?
I stopped that completely, also.

His daily journal's entry for July 21 reads: "If you want to, you can go to the doctor's on another day. Today I am out of it, so to say." Robert is a drunken poet and doesn't know it.

Muriel's accountant, Lloyd Wilkins, passed away that summer. He and his daughter, Janet, also an accountant, had been looking after Muriel's books, and Lloyd Wilkins had been named as executor of Muriel's estate. Robert met with Ted Kolb, her lawyer, then wrote Muriel a letter:

Dearest Muriel,
As you know it is sometimes easier for me to express my thoughts on paper rather than vocally . . .
Without discussing any of your affairs, I did have a personal chat with Mr. Kolb informing him of the death of Lloyd . . . I know it is difficult for you to discuss such matters to anyone, but we must confront the facts, my dear, you will soon have to appoint another executor. Mr. Kolb thought it should be me, and Janet Wilkins as co-executrix. This has nothing to do with changing your present will, just a simple codicil in your own handwriting if you like or you could if you prefer let Mr. Kolb draw it up for you . . .
Please feel free to discuss this letter and its contents with anyone. I promised Philip, and now you, I will always have your best interests at heart.
With all my devotion and love,
Robert

FRISBEE'S TESTIMONY AT TRIAL
Why was it you wrote to Mrs. Barnett as opposed to speaking to her about it?
It's difficult for me to explain my thoughts in vocal ways. I just couldn't carry the thought into a vocal language.

Did Mr. Kolb then prepare a codicil to Mrs. Barnett's will?

Yes, Mr. Deverell, he did.

That, for the record, is Exhibit Five in these proceedings. You and Janet were named co-executors?

Yes, sir.

How did this codicil then come to be executed?

Mr. Kolb himself dropped the envelope off at the apartment on his way home and left it for Mrs. Barnett to execute. She asked Dan to come over and witness her signature and she called the neighbor next door to also be a witness to the codicil.

Why would she have asked Dan and that neighbor?

The Barnetts were almost paranoid about their private affairs.

When you met with Mr. Kolb did you discuss with him the codicil that you drew in October '84?

No.

To your knowledge did Mrs. Barnett?

To my knowledge she didn't tell anyone.

Why didn't you discuss the earlier codicil with the lawyer?

Because of her wishes. She said anything that goes on in this house is between you and I.

Robert felt distinctly uncomfortable about this business of changing the will again. Should he have told Mr. Kolb about the October codicil making him the chief heir? She would have been furious, his discussing her business like that. It was as if that codicil he had typed was their own little secret . . . Or had Muriel, her mind declining with her years, forgotten she had changed her will in his favor? Not once did she mention it. It remained in that locked security box in the Barnett apartment.

His worst fears were confirmed when he read the document Mr. Kolb had prepared for her to sign, naming Robert and Janet Wilkins as co-executors.

It concluded with these unwelcome words:

"Other than herein specifically provided for, I hereby republish my said Last Will and Testament dated March 12, 1984."

Robert was dismayed. By reconfirming her original will – by which Robert would inherit only $250,000 – would not Muriel be voiding the codicil she'd signed last October? And disinheriting him of millions of dollars . . .

Should he speak to her about it?

He couldn't.

"I hereby republish my said last will and testament dated March 12, 1984." What did you understand that to mean?

That document would eliminate any codicil that Mrs. Barnett had made out other than her last will that had been executed in March of '84.

What was your reaction?

At this time I was more or less numb. I just say, *c'est la guerre*.

At this time what did you think your inheritance was going to be in the event of Mrs. Barnett's death?

Two hundred and fifty thousand dollars.

You use the expression, *c'est la guerre*, what do you mean by that?

Well, I was disappointed, of course. Some dreams went out the window, but I just couldn't fight city hall. What would be would be. I don't think I got emotional about it. I was just stunned.

Chapter 19

THE FIRST OF SEVERAL DOCTORS WHO TROOPED TO THE STAND during the five days of commission hearings in San Francisco was Mrs. Barnett's personal physician, who identified himself as one Don Carlos Musser, a robust man in his sixties who exuded a sense of long-time service as a specialist to the wealthy. He, like lawyer Ted Kolb, had been a fellow golf-club member with Philip Barnett.

He recounted treating Mrs. Barnett for a broken arm in 1980, a carcinoma of the bowel in 1982 (a mild cancerous condition remedied by a proctologist's excisions), and the neck fracture of October 10, 1984. Mrs. Barnett had suffered an earlier fracture to her hip before Musser became her personal physician.

He described his patient as a robust person, "a tough character," far more active than was common for her years.

As to her personality:

"Well, she was a delightful person. She was pleasant, vivacious, and just really sociable."

"Do you have anything to tell us about her drinking habits?" Dennis Murray asked.

"She was a pretty good drinker. The night that she fell down and broke her neck she told me that she had had too many vodkas."

"Would it be fair in sum to describe her as a heavy drinker?"

"I would say so."

Dennis prompted the witness to remark that when drinking heavily, Mrs. Barnett never became aggressive or hostile, and "just seemed to become more pleasant all the time."

I guess Dennis called that evidence to rebut any argument that Frisbee killed her as a result of some drunken provocation on her part, but he must have known he'd get no argument from us that Muriel Barnett was not the most gentle soul in the world – Frisbee shared that view.

Over objection, Dennis asked the doctor about the "rumor," as he put it, that Philip Barnett had maintained a homosexual relationship with Frisbee. Perhaps Dr. Musser had earlier persuaded Dennis that this gay partnering was a vicious gossip spread by the accused to defame Barnett. Perhaps Dr. Musser had insisted to Dennis he be allowed to put the record straight.

"What can you tell us about this rumor?" Dennis asked.

"I know nothing about it," the witness responded with particular vigor. "In fact, I think it is pure fantasy."

Loyal golfing compatriot of Philip Barnett that he was, and sometime sharer of locker-room facilities, Dr. Musser couldn't bring himself to believe that his golfing buddy had also dabbled in a less acceptable form of sport.

In cross-examination, Musser agreed that Mrs. Barnett was a private person about her business affairs and personal concerns. This kind of evidence would bolster our argument that it would be typical of Mrs. Barnett not to have disclosed to anyone the contents of the October 1984 codicil in favor of Frisbee. The Crown's theory was that the victim's failure to tell anyone – even her lawyer – about this codicil was proof she knew nothing about it, that she had been hoodwinked by Frisbee and Kazakes.

It was also important to us that we establish that Mrs. Barnett was alert and aware, not under the influence of some mind-debilitating drug, when she signed that pivotal piece of paper at the Frisbee-Kazakes apartment only a week after her neck accident.

Jeff Green asked:

"On release from hospital in 1984, she was a completely aware and competent individual?"

"Yes."

"Capable of managing her own affairs?"

"Yes."

"Capable of making her own life decisions?"

"Yes."

"There is no suggestion whatsoever that she was in some kind of bewildered state as a result of medication that she was on?"

"None at all."

The medication, it turned out, was Tylenol 3.

Dennis Murray, in re-examination, urged on the doctor that the codeine contained in Tylenol 3, when mixed with generous parts of alcohol, could somehow become a major mind-altering substance.

Musser was careful to back away from any suggestion he might over-prescribe drugs. "An ordinary dose of half a grain of codeine wouldn't make any difference, but if she took a lot it might."

"And what would that difference be?"

"Well, it could make her unconscious."

"And on the way to unconscious what would it make her?"

Probably Dennis held a secret hope that the witness would come up with something like, "It would make her act abnormally." Cause her to sign documents she hadn't read.

Instead: "Well, I really couldn't say."

"Would it have any effects on her mind?"

The doctor wasn't biting. "Well, yes, it would. I can't tell you exactly what it would be, though."

Dr. Musser had referred Mrs. Barnett to an orthopedist after she broke her vertebra. Dr. Victor Prieto testified he had fitted her with a "four-poster" brace, so called because it's assembled with two posts in front, two in back, to hold the neck steady.

Dennis was still anxious to show that Mrs. Barnett was under the influence of something a little more useful to the Crown than Tylenol, and obtained from Dr. Prieto a hesitant recollection he had also "probably" prescribed "some Halcion for sleep." This he described as a Valium-type medication.

Jeff Green had earlier examined Dr. Prieto's report and found no mention of this common tranquilizer.

"When you say you probably prescribed Halcion, that is because you can't remember?"

"I can't recall, I have no record."

And Tylenol 3, he agreed, would not slow her mental processes. Clearly the Crown's argument that Mrs. Barnett had been drugged into a state of mindless submissiveness when she signed the October codicil was weakly supported.

Conversely, it was critical to the defense to prove that Frisbee, when and if he murdered her, was under heavy drug and alcohol intoxication, sufficient to render him incapable of any murderous intent.

Dr. Raszl, the earnest young practitioner who had so painstakingly tried to steer Frisbee away from the perils of drink in the months following Philip's death, was called as a defense witness. The Librium he had prescribed for him, he said, was the standard drug used to treat alcohol-withdrawal syndrome, moving the dependency from alcohol to the drug itself. "The drug is gradually tapered down and in this way we are able to detoxify patients."

Jeff Green asked: "I suppose the purpose of prescribing Librium would be pretty well defeated if the alcoholic patient continued to drink?"

"The effect can be additive."

"Do you mean the effects of Librium could be additive to the effects of alcohol?"

"Yes."

Additive – that is a word we liked. If the alcohol alone had not been sufficient to deprive Frisbee of an intent to kill, the additional effects of Librium could have made the difference.

Dr. Raszl also testified that Frisbee suffered from an alcoholic cirrhosis of the liver. Untreated, such a cirrhosis could result in death. (*The Concise Oxford* on cirrhosis: "A chronic disease, especially of alcoholics, in which the liver hardens into many small projectiles.") Ironically, if Frisbee's arrest had not curtailed his drinking, it was even odds he would have met his Maker before having met his jury.

His cirrhotic condition would be focal to our drunkenness defense. We would ultimately be building a case that a liver so diseased metabolizes alcohol poorly, enhancing the effects of alcohol.

Raszl gave evidence that Frisbee was pleasant to deal with but a passive dependent personality, or, as he put it: "I did not see him as a very aggressive, driving type individual."

Jeff Green knew he'd be getting into heavy weather with his next series of questions. He asked Dr. Raszl his reaction on learning Frisbee had been charged with Mrs. Barnett's murder.

"I was shocked."

Ernie Quantz's objection was noted.

"Why?"

Ernie's further objection was noted.

"I just did not see Robert Frisbee as a person who could or would commit a crime like this. He had always seemed to be quite fond of Mrs. Barnett, and he had never really, as I recall, spoken of her in any derogatory terms. He was always quite laudatory."

Jeff took Raszl through Frisbee's history of alcohol-withdrawal seizures. Frankly, we were unsure where this was taking us, but the possibility existed that our client had felled the victim during some kind of violent, mindless psycho-motor attack. Dennis Murray, anticipating such a defense, worked hard to pin our witness down.

"Just so that I understand this history of seizures, with the exception of when Mr. Frisbee drinks heavily for a continual period of time, then stops totally in drinking, he has never had a seizure?"

"That's correct."

"So as long as Mr. Frisbee was drinking on a continuous basis he encountered no problem?"

"Right."

In other words, his seizures came only after sudden withdrawal from alcohol. On August 19, 1985, the day of Mrs. Barnett's death, Frisbee had hardly been on a withdrawal program.

Dr. Raszl had referred Frisbee to Dr. Jerome Goldstein, a professor of neurology who examined him after the aborted European holiday. Goldstein went further than Raszl. He said seizures such as suffered by the accused could occur either in the withdrawal phase or "in the acute alcoholic phase."

Alcohol abuse, he said, can trigger such seizures as a result of biochemical changes in the brain.

Dennis again saw looming the defense of an involuntary act by Frisbee as a result of alcohol intake.

"Is there a distinction in what happens between an alcohol-withdrawal seizure and an acute alcoholic phase seizure?"

"No . . . they are basically the same."

"The first stage is a feeling that something is not right?"

"Generally."

"And the next stage is accompanied by falling to the ground?"

"Lapse of consciousness."

"And then a revival and some confusion about what's been going on in those minutes when you were having the seizure?"

"That is correct."

Dennis probed away until he finally managed to elicit from the witness that "in all medical probability" it was unlikely Frisbee had a psycho-motor attack on the day of Mrs. Barnett's death.

Chapter 20

THROUGH THE SUMMER OF 1985, ROBERT, WITH HIS SNEAKY LITTLE alcoholic ways, airline bottles clinking in his pockets, continued to lie to Muriel about his drinking, lied to Dan, lied to himself.

He continued not to take Antabuse. He continued not to go to A.A. meetings. He continued not to be honest with Dr. Raszl.

Dan, however, continued to drink. When he was in his cups, he would bitch about Muriel. She was possessive of Robert, wanted too much of him; Robert was allowing himself to be a slave. When did Bob ever get an evening off? What kind of normal home life could the two of them have?

And sometimes: awful, biting, subtle threats from Dan that he might have to look elsewhere, find someone else. Robert was accused of not holding his own in this relationship, this marriage of middle-aged men, the psychic and the secretary.

If Robert was able to spend less time at home, then Dan would just spend more time at 1000 Chestnut Street. Over recent weeks, he'd become a regular habitué there, a kind of semi-resident brother-in-law with bar privileges. Although Muriel didn't complain about his presence, there was this ever-so-brittle tension in the air when Dan was around, in the bar, in the kitchen, in the pantry, prowling about like the family cat.

Muriel was grateful to Dan, of course, that he had served her so uncomplainingly after Robert's grand mal attack in London, doing the driving, running the innumerable errands that Robert would normally perform. And she was grateful to him, too, for attending her parties, serving as an extra man, helping out with the widow surplus.

But still ... there was this little buzz of negative polarized energy whenever Dan came to visit. Muriel was polite, but, well, not exactly torrid in her expressions of feeling toward Dan. Was she a little jealous? Of all the time Dan demanded from Robert, time that Muriel didn't own? Or maybe some of that catty enmity that the great Dr. Philip Barnett felt toward Dan had rubbed off on her.

Robert felt torn between the two of them, felt them pulling at opposite sleeves, dividing him into non-functional halves.

In Muriel's presence, Dan talked continually about starting up another import-export business. Yes, it was true that the last time he tried to run a few little Greek gift shops he went broke, but he'd learned from his mistakes. And he dropped hints to Muriel that her financial help in opening up another such business would be received not ungratefully. Robert doubted Dan had any real intention of opening another shop. He was just trying to cadge money from Muriel, and Robert felt uncomfortable about this, about Dan's constant wheedling.

One day Dan announced to her that his son, Jerry, had just written him from Australia: he wanted to start up a little religious center there. But (Dan informed Muriel) poor Jerry lacked the resources to do so. The financial resources.

Maybe he should go to Australia to visit his son, Muriel suggested in her sweetest way.

Well, that will cost, too, said Dan.

August loomed – the fateful, terrible month of August. Cruise to Alaska.

Muriel intended to combine business with pleasure, to stop off in Ketchikan to preside over a banquet and board meeting of the directors of Northern Machine and Marine Railways Inc., the company whose shares Muriel had inherited from Philip and which she was winding up. Secretary Bob would of course be in attendance.

As Robert made the travel preparations – buy tickets, buy clothes, get shirts from laundry, Muriel to the hairdresser's – Muriel was considering yet another change to her will.

She had intended to give $100,000 to her English godson Jason Cope upon her death. But the Copes were about to be evicted from their Belgravia flat, and needed money now to buy a piece of property. Could the will be changed, they asked, so $50,000 of the inheritance could be advanced immediately?

No problem, said lawyer Ted Kolb. He would simply draw up a new will for Muriel, and have it ready for her to sign on her return from Alaska.

Muriel instructed Robert to make an appointment for her with Kolb at his office on the afternoon of Monday, August 5, to discuss the new will.

Muriel had still not mentioned to anyone her generous gift to Robert, in her codicil of October 1984, which left him two-thirds of her estate. No hint issued from her that she intended to tell the lawyer that this new version of the will should name Robert as the chief beneficiary. Had she signed that codicil as a cruel joke? Or had she simply changed her mind?

C'est la guerre. The bride giveth; the bride taketh away.

August 5 was a heavy day. Before the visit to the lawyer Muriel and Robert had a very busy lunch at Trader Vic's.

The conversation began innocuously. Chit-chat about the Alaska trip. Have you paid the travel agent, Robert? Are the monthly checks all made up? Should I store my furs at your place? What jewels should I take?

TYHURST INTERVIEWS

She also told me she would prefer I start drinking again in a social way. She wanted to make sure that if we went on this expensive trip that I was just not going to sit. She didn't want to be seen drinking in the bar of the ship without a drinking companion. So I think that day at Trader Vic's I openly came out and went off the wagon.

Yes.

When I'm sober I'm a different person of course than when I drink. When I'm drinking I become a little more charming, voluble, talkable.

But you're quite voluble with me now and you haven't been drinking.

Well, with strangers I would have been . . . I can't talk to strangers.

Well, I'm a stranger; you're talking with me quite a bit.

I feel comfortable with you. I don't know why. You are not asking me about a baseball game or football game or who is going to be the next president, as one psychiatrist did, and I didn't know who Mr. Reagan was. I do now.

Now that Muriel had freed Robert from the bondage of temperance, the Trader Vic's lunch became rather wet. Robert became more charming and talkable.

Muriel started in about her health. She was having "symptoms," she said. Similar to those when she had that cancer of the bowel. She wasn't, of course, very explicit when discussing that very private and personal illness, or her present symptoms.

She seemed oddly subdued. Robert felt there was much, much more she wanted to tell him. He remembers wondering: Was she . . . well, seeing that horizon, the end of her time? She had visited her doctor only a few days earlier. Had he discovered some new form of decay eating away at her vital parts?

"I am going to give Dan $100,000," she said.

Robert was startled. The gift, she said, was to help him open up that import shop.

She would also finance a trip for Dan to visit his son in Australia. In addition, Muriel said she wanted to donate $20,000 to Jerry, for his good works.

Robert was on his third martini by now. He was not sure if he was hearing her correctly. What was all this business about giving money to Dan? Was there a hook? A hundred thousand dollars to start an import shop: surely she knew Dan would just spend the money on booze.

A ticket to Australia . . .

It began to dawn on Robert. She hoped Dan would never come back.

Her intentions became clearer still when she offered Robert $300,000.

Strings were attached to this gift. He must use it to buy an apartment for himself. Close by, a block away on Chestnut Street. Mrs. Lucille TeRoller, one of Muriel's tea-and-bridge cronies, was planning to sell her apartment at 1080 Chestnut Street. Three hundred thousand dollars would buy it and furnish it.

Guilt-ridden was Muriel. That is how Robert saw it. Filled with an unspoken remorse over reducing his inheritance.

She'd heard that Mrs. TeRoller was going to sell her apartment and stay in the country, and she wanted to buy it for $250,000, and have it furnished for the balance of the check.

What did you think about that?

Well, I was amazed at that, also. I was wondering if she was trying to make up for the fact that she knew the codicil had been more or less thrown out, and this was a gift to make up for what she thought I might have lost.

Did she indicate why she wanted you to be closer to her?

Yes. I was the only one she could call when she needed someone.

Robert would be her nearby neighbor, would always be within a two-minute walk of Muriel's home. Available. On immediate call if her "symptoms" got worse.

She didn't say anything about whether Dan might be expected to live with him there. But he drew a kind of inference that she didn't wish that. Clearly, Dan was being paid to disappear from his life. Bought off with a ticket to Australia and a hundred thousand bucks.

And then she dropped the final bombshell. She was intending, she said, to take an apartment in London for several months to be near the Copes. Robert would be expected to remain with her there. Dan, of course, should not expect to accompany him.

Bells sounded for Robert. Muriel was clearly intent on prying her toy poodle from Dan Kazakes's steely grip. She wanted Robert all to herself.

Woozily, Robert let Muriel lead him to the lawyer's office. Ted Kolb went briskly about making notes for a new will. Yes, $50,000 could be advanced to the Copes, and the will altered to accommodate that. The new document would be ready for Muriel's signature on her return from Alaska. No problem. And no mention from Muriel of that codicil of the previous fall.

Just before the Alaska trip, Robert drove up to Guerneville, to visit Muriel Frisbee, Dwight's widow and Robert's cherished wicked stepmother. Well into her years by now, she'd had a recent bout of illness that had Robert worried.

Meanwhile, the pace of preparations for the Alaska cruise grew hectic.

Muriel gave Dan a key to the Chestnut Street apartment and instructed him in certain duties until their return: check the mail every three days, park the Caddie in the garage, turn over its engine once in a while so the battery won't go dead, bag up the furs and store them at your place (Muriel didn't really trust Millie, her saucy Salvadoran maid).

On August 9, Robert and Muriel visited the ship, and were shown their quarters. On the morning of the 10th, embarkation day, Muriel selected the jewels she would take with her on the *Viking Star*, and gave the remainder to Robert who put them in his safety deposit box at the bank. Then he visited Mrs. Barnett's liquor locker.

For Saturday, August 10, Frisbee's journal read: "Jewelry to safe deposit box. Bar – 1 C.C., 1 Stolie, 2 Scotch, 2 B.E. Gin. Ship to Alaska, Go Man Go."

FRISBEE'S TESTIMONY AT TRIAL

We were all excited about getting to the ship, and Mrs. Barnett's watch was thirty minutes faster than mine. I thought we had all the time in the world, but she was all dressed and anxious to get started. She said to make out the check for Daniel, and I did, and she said, "Do the others later on," and I gave her this check and she handed it to Mr. Kazakes, who was in the other room.

A check for $100,000?

Yes, sir.

Did you observe what Mr. Kazakes's reaction was?

Yes, he was surprised, he didn't realize it was coming. He thanked her and I know he kissed her, and they just talked for a while. I closed the checkbook, put it away.

Had there been any drinking going on the morning of that departure?

Yes, Mr. Kazakes and I had a little going-away brunch, we had some champagne and cocktails.

Tell us about the bon voyage party.

She had quite a few people, I think probably about twenty. They all came on board to have a cocktail and see the ship. They were in and out of the rooms.

How many of them brought bottles?

I'd say a good three-quarters probably brought bottles.

How long did that party last?

Almost two hours.

Then what happened?

Then they all said goodbye and left the ship, and we started out.

Chapter 21

IN ORDER TO CUSHION THEMSELVES FROM THE DEBILITATING effects of after-hours boredom, Commissioner Singh and his merry band of cops and lawyers were required, during their evenings off, to sample of the many seductions of San Francisco, the most popular being the Redwood Room of the hotel where we were barracked, the Clift, a grand and venerable establishment a block from Union Square.

Our other favorite hangout was the Curtain Call, a sing-along bar on Geary Street opposite the hotel (sadly, the place has since made its curtain call and no longer exists).

The bartender of the Curtain Call trailed the long cord of a microphone behind her as she mixed Manhattans and Margueritas and led the patrons in choruses of Irving Berlin and Cole Porter standards. "I've Got You Under My Skin" served (euphoniously) with the drinks. Some of the establishment's regulars took turns at the mike, old music-hall troupers many of them. None in our retinue could carry much of a tune, except for Tim Singh, whose energetic bellows won him exceptionally good service from the staff.

Dennis Murray, committed to a trial in Vancouver, left before the San Francisco inquiry concluded, leaving Ernie Quantz in charge. On the penultimate day of the hearing, with only one minor witness remaining to be heard from, Ernie applied to break early: "Mr. Commissioner, I have an appointment to interview a woman and it was at a quarter to five and I would very much like to go to that interview. It's at an unusual location which I will never have the opportunity of going to again."

I was gracious in my concurrence: "I am sure I do not want to put any roadblocks in the way of my friend going to this unusual location with this female witness."

For the record, Ernie's late-afternoon engagement was at the Fairmont Hotel with a senior citizen who happened to be one of Mrs. Barnett's closest friends, Mrs. Isabelle Waters. We already knew what she would have to say:

"I just don't think it's possible for Bob to do it, unless he just lost his mind," she'd told Kathy Holub, the *Mercury News* reporter. "He never *ever* had a mean word to say about anybody. In fact, I always thought he was more or less of a weak sister, you know what I mean?"

Although Ernie Quantz didn't get much help from Mrs. Waters, he often made us nervous, daily wandering off somewhere to ferret out reluctant witnesses, often coming up with annoyingly useful tidbits of evidence. He had an irritating habit of continually dropping tantalizing hints to Jeff and me that he was on the verge of unmasking the whole sordid story behind the Frisbee-Kazakes grand conspiracy.

In the meantime, Jeff and I did our own investigating, taxi-cabbing to the various theaters of action: the Frisbee-Kazakes apartment where Mrs. Barnett signed the codicil (an attractive older building on Van Ness), Jack's Restaurant and Trader Vic's and the World Trade Club, and the ugly condo monster that is 1000 Chestnut Street.

This fourteen-storey building is about as tastefully designed as the local county jail, a massive rectangular slab so out of keeping with the attractive homes across the street that their owners must have wept to see it rise. It and a couple of other concrete extrusions on the north side of 1000 Chestnut Street don't much enhance the neighbors' property values, let alone their views to the north.

Philip Barnett built it in 1954, then sold it for $2.5 million, retaining a two-apartment complex for himself and Muriel. The property must be worth many more millions now. Near the summit of classy Russian Hill, at the corner of Chestnut and Hyde, it commands enormous views of mountain, ocean, and waterfront. Just below are Fishermen's Wharf and Ghirardelli Square.

Beyond, San Francisco Bay is speckled with boats moving aimlessly, amoeba-like.

The locked garage entry to the building, which Frisbee commonly used while at the wheel of his employers' Cadillac or Oldsmobile, is on the Hyde Street side, where the Powell Hyde cable car regularly clangs past the building, its holds overflowing with grinning tourists as it plummets north down the hill toward Fishermen's Wharf.

It's a well-guarded complex. No stranger passes through the small lobby to the elevators without permission from the steely-eyed doormen on duty. Two of them were on the job when Jeff and I visited. Yes, they had heard about Mrs. Barnett's murder. No, they had not been working on the day she and Frisbee left for the ship. The doorman on that day would have been Mr. Clarence Johnson. They declined our request to see the Barnett apartment. The present owners might not be keen on a visit from a couple of lawyers investigating a murder.

We wondered if we should seek to interview this Mr. Johnson. Apparently no one else had. Probably a waste of time, we decided.

We strolled a block to the west, to the corner of Larkin, where stands another tall condominium building, almost as architecturally bland. This is 1080 Chestnut Street, where Muriel's friend, Lucille TeRoller, lived. Hers was the apartment, Frisbee told us, that Mrs. Barnett intended him to buy with the $300,000 she'd given him.

Jeff and I had been concerned the jury might not give much weight to evidence we proposed to call from Frisbee about this proposed real-estate transaction. So far we had not corroborated it. A lot depended on this evidence being believed. Otherwise, that $300,000 check found on his person could give rise only to dark speculation on the part of the jurors.

We asked the doorman at 1080 Chestnut if Mrs. TeRoller still lived there. No, she had indeed sold her apartment, had moved out several months ago, out of the city – exactly where, he didn't know. We obtained the name of the rental agent. Mrs. TeRoller must be interviewed. If she denied that she had ever discussed the sale of her dwelling with Muriel Barnett, our client could be accused of making up a convenient lie to explain his possession of Muriel's check to himself, which Frisbee himself had signed.

On the second-last night of our stay at the Clift, I made the mistake of giving Ernie Quantz the key to the little drink-now-pay-later bar in my room. I guess Ernie knew I couldn't charge a bar bill to my client (many lawyers' expenses come out of their own pockets) and on the assumption the defense was being overpaid anyway, he was generously offering the contents of my bar to those who had joined us there after a long day of evidence: Tim Singh; Anne Dyke, the official court reporter; Jeff Green and me; and Jeffry Glenn, my local criminal lawyer friend.

As Ernie handed around the champagnes, Courvoisiers, and Johnnie blacks, he cheerfully dropped several sinister hints that he had uncovered the ultimate key to the case. A major Crown witness. A gentleman who would establish Kazakes's full complicity in the murder plot. Someone the defense might carelessly have overlooked. If they hadn't done their homework.

Under our edgy cross-examination he remained coy. Seems this gentleman was at 1000 Chestnut with Mrs. Barnett and Frisbee and Kazakes before they departed for the *Viking Star*. This witness later observed some curious comings and goings on the part of Kazakes. In and out of Muriel's apartment.

Reminded of the Crown's promise to make full disclosure to the defense, and in the face of unspecified threats to his physical well-being, Ernie gave us a name: one Clarence Johnson, doorman at 1000 Chestnut Street.

And what will he say? I pressed.

Mr. Johnson would say that shortly after Muriel, Frisbee, and Kazakes left for the ship, Kazakes returned to 1000 Chestnut with a key to the apartment. He removed an object from the premises and then drove off.

The object?

The lock-box, apparently. The little security box in which Mrs. Barnett kept her important papers. Where Mrs. Barnett's executor found that codicil after the murder . . .

Ernie scooped some more bottles from the bar and shared them around. "What'll you have next, Bill?" he asked. "Hey, can somebody get some more ice?"

I needed a drink. I took a few.

V. Roy Lefcourt (I kept telling myself: *don't* call him Leroy) had invited Jeff Green and me to cocktails at his home that night, then to dinner in an Italian restaurant.

We arrived about two hours late at the Lefcourts, by which time I was feeling, to coin a phrase, totally frisbeed from the effects of Ernie's hospitality, and consumed with worry about having left him and the others in my room pillaging the bar.

I called the hotel room from the restaurant. Ernie had a complaint – my bar was nearing empty. (My bill, I calculated, was nearing half a grand.) They were hungry, Quantz advised. Where were we having dinner? Is Lefcourt paying for it? Ernie knew Kazakes had retained Lefcourt with that $100,000 check, Muriel's departing gift to him, and I guess Ernie figured there must be enough left over to set a few more places at Lefcourt's table.

The several celebrants, having commandeered the Clift's bar-and-TV-equipped limousine, soon arrived at the Italian restaurant.

Under the influence of an extravagant amount of spirits we made a regrettable and typically Canadian spectacle of ourselves in front of our more sedate American hosts. I made a gallant show of arguing for the check as we closed the place up, but we managed to stick V. Roy with it.

Throughout the evening, Ernie Quantz continued to predict the imminent collapse of the case for the defense. Kazakes had borrowed Muriel's security box, had slipped the fraudulent codicil in it, had returned it later to Mrs. Barnett's apartment so her executor could find it there.

The next day, with pounding heart and throbbing head, I returned to 1000 Chestnut and found Clarence Johnson was on shift. A black man, sixty-six, graying and handsome, he had retired after thirty years with the U.S. Post Office and had been a doorman at 1000 Chestnut for the last two years.

He recalled Mrs. Barnett fondly, a true lady, always pleasant. But Robert Frisbee, I gathered, was not on his most-admired list.

"He hardly ever said much to the doormen unless it was come and get something, or pick up something, or do something." I assumed he and Frisbee had had encounters during which our client, harried with Muriel's demands, was a little too brisk with him.

Yes, he confirmed, Mr. Dan Kazakes had driven back to the Chestnut Street apartment on the day Frisbee and Mrs. Barnett had departed for the Alaska cruise ship, and, yes, he had carried out of the apartment some kind of box.

Chapter 22

"HELLO WORLD," WROTE ROBERT AS THE *ROYAL VIKING STAR* plied the North Pacific. This was the first entry in his travel diary since he'd penned the immortal words, "Wow, end of trip," after the epileptiform psycho-motor attack, or whatever they wanted to call it, that blackout in Old London Town over his plate of spaghetti.

It was night, and Robert was at the writing desk and Muriel was dreaming Elizabeth Taylor dreams in Elizabeth Taylor's bed. Close quarters, the mistress and the slave in the same bedroom – that was the only rub to this cruise, so lovely otherwise, so diverting from the upsetting roller-coaster ride of fortunes won and lost. "Instead of separate staterooms, for a few dollars more we can have a penthouse suite." That's what she'd announced. What would people think, their sleeping in the same room? Muriel didn't care.

Robert sipped from his first-prize bottle of Mumm's as he scribbled away, recording the events of the day, about he and Dan flag-bedecking their beautiful stateroom, about the bon voyage party, how Dan, so distinguished in his clerical suit, gave a blessing for the ship and wished them a safe voyage.

"Unpacked," Robert wrote. "Have a very good table, number 90. M.C.B. poor veal, me good lamb." He poured another little glass. Just one more. But he was going to cut down. Muriel wanted him to control his drinking. Not stop. Just slow down.

"Bergen Lounge for drinks, and watched the dancers. Rather rough, bouncy weather but clear. Took a chance on the casino. This 'A.A.' won first prize, a large bottle of Champ! It will be a very liquid voyage!"

What else should he add?

"Michael is the Greek butler. Eva is the stewardess."

What did you do, the first thing, aboard that vessel?

Well, I always went immediately down to the dining room to secure our table and to leave a tip for the maître-d'.

What was your mood during this voyage?

Pardon the expression, very gay.

Did Mrs. Barnett say anything about being thrilled about having this particular suite?

The butler had told her Elizabeth Taylor had just vacated this suite and she was happy thinking she'd be sleeping in Elizabeth Taylor's bed.

You have given evidence about how you were sneaking drinks before the trip. Were you doing this on the trip as well?

Yes, I was.

What did you think Mrs. Barnett would say if she caught you drinking without her?

I don't think she would have liked it.

Mrs. Barnett wanted you to control your drinking. How well were you doing in that regard?

Not very well.

What was your daily drinking routine?

We'd have morning tomato juice with vodka, and while Mrs. Barnett was in the bath I usually went up to the bar by the pool and played the mileage game and had a drink at the bar there. I'd come back, and I'd probably comb out her hair. We'd order our own cocktails as a rule before lunch in the suite, have our cocktail around 5:00.

Now, you were sharing a bedroom with Mrs. Barnett. Have you ever done that before?

Not in this close confining area. We shared a room, a suite at the Ritz and Carlton hotels, and the Phyllis Diller suite in New York.

How did you work it out?

It wasn't that comfortable. We were always on the defensive about who had use of the facilities at what time. We worked out a little schedule; she likes to bathe around 11, and as a rule I like to bathe in the afternoon. I do snore, I don't think she was very happy about that.

Was there any tension surrounding that arrangement?

Not visible, but I think I did feel a little tense, as I had to wear pajamas and socks and slippers and ascot, no naked body exposed. One didn't kick one's shoes off and just relax.

After the ship departed, Muriel reminded him about the checks he was to fill out: the $300,000 for his apartment, the $20,000 for Dan's son in Australia. "You better make them out, Robert, before you forget." He did her ladyship's bidding.

On August 11, Robert woke up to another bouncy day at sea. His two morning Bloody Marys didn't quell the tremors in his stomach, and so he went to the reception desk, where a clerk was handing out seasickness pills, and he later washed down a couple with a martini.

Muriel simply was not going to come out of her room when the weather was like this. She was not one to sit out on the sundeck even in calm waters. She might poke her head out the balcony door once in a while, but that was it. Muriel was essentially an interior person.

Robert attended a lecture about the wonders of Vancouver, and spent the rest of the day flitting from bar to bar before escorting Muriel to the Captain's dinner. Caviar. Lobster from Maine. Very good.

At 3:00 the next morning he woke up with a start.

FRISBEE'S TRAVEL DIARY

Monday, August 12

Very rough night when at 3 a.m. there was a tremendous crash, and found out later we had hit a whale, and broke windows in the dining room. Everyone was sick but M.C.B. and Robert. Had a delicious lunch of flank steak and marshmallow with chocolate ice cream.

In the afternoon sun-baked and watched the arrival of the Bay of Vancouver. Very much like the entrance to S.F. with a bridge like the Golden Gate designed by the same man. They are getting ready for 1986 Expo and all along the pier were flags of all nations. Docked around 5. Lamb curry for dinner.

Tuesday, August 13

Up at 8 and had breakfast in the room looking out at the Vancouver harbor. At 11 met with B.C. Limousine Service, a blue Cad. Went for a drive through beautiful Stanley Park by the Sea. Then the aquarium and the zoo – not much of a zoo.

Then to an outstanding restaurant situated in a beautiful garden called, "The Tea House Restaurant," we thought a former home, it was so lovely. We had some drinks and for main course delicious roast pork, for M.C.B. very good frog's legs. Had a King's Delight for dessert, which was a pretty swan filled with ice cream and whipped cream sitting on a black cake of hot fudge.

Then to the Expo 86 Movierama, and a trip on a flight ship as if you were right in the machine. Back to the ship and sunbathed and drinks. To the Captain's cabin for private cocktail party. Met Mr. and Mrs. Max Biegert from Phoenix, chatted. Went to dinner and had some lobster bisque (fair) and then some very good lamb curry. Went to listen to the orchestra, and danced. The Biegerts came and sat with us. An outstanding show, just about the best so far. To bed about 12:45.

Wednesday, August 14

En route to Juneau. Went through inland passage, and on each side of the ship you can almost touch the land and fine greenery around you. Did M.C.B.'s hair at 11 and went to lunch.

French Night. Had escargots and rack of lamb, very good. Watched the show, and then a drink at the casino. M.C.B. won $15.

Robert was having too merry a time; he didn't want to leave the ship in Juneau. But there was that annual meeting of Northern Machine and Marine Railways to deal with, which was the excuse for this cruise, after all. Their plans were to fly to Ketchikan, spend two nights there, and rejoin the *Viking Star* in Sitka for the voyage home.

He *should* have stayed on the ship. From the word go, everything went wrong. First that mix-up with customs. The purser was all in a dither, claiming he didn't know Robert and Muriel were disembarking in Juneau, and he had to hurry them up to get them off the ship and through customs. And *they* wanted to look at everything, of course. All these tedious formalities just because they'd been in Canada.

Then, wouldn't you know, problems with their flight reservations – everything was supposed to have been *arranged*, and obviously nothing was. Robert the Taurus (persistence, ardor, boundless patience) was being rather tested this day. But they finally got on board a plane and made the forty-five-minute flight to Ketchikan.

In the meantime, one of Robert's molars had started acting up. Maybe rotted away by too much King's Delight with ice cream and whipped cream and black cake with hot fudge. For three days Robert had been nursing this tooth, and the patient was not responding.

Bumping into a whale: was that a bad omen?

First thing in the morning he went to a dentist in Ketchikan.

FBI REPORT
Dr. J. Terry Thomson, dentist, on August 16 treated Frisbee for a toothache. Found two absessed teeth in lower jaw, needed to be extracted but Frisbee asked they be given temporary repair until he got to his regular dentist in San Francisco. Dr. Thomson described Frisbee as "strange." He elaborated by stating Frisbee manifested mannerisms of a homosexual and appeared to be in very poor health, so he was relieved that Frisbee did not desire to have his affected teeth extracted. He would have been treated as a high risk patient, meaning that he would have to be alert for other complications. Paid $50 cash.

Fifty dollars a minute. Robert was not going to have this toothdrawer poke around in his mouth with those rubber gloves, or pull *any* of his precious teeth. Better to live with the pain.

Cumulatively, the stresses of these last days sapped Robert. On his return from the dentist's office, he suffered a disaster in his hotel bar. A good old-fashioned drunkarama. Somewhere along the way he must have gone out and bought some silly stuffed animals, a big carton of them, and had them packaged and sent home to Dan. That's what he found out later. How he made it through dinner that night with the directors of Northern Machine, he does not know. He can't remember much of it.

In the Hotel Ingersoll he finally had a room to himself. Despite aching teeth and hangover, there was at least peace and privacy. And freedom, for the night, from Muriel.

FRISBEE'S TRAVEL DIARY

Saturday, August 17

Up early at 6:15 to take a plane back to the ship. Had a disastrous trip, 3 1/2 hours to go a distance of about 300 miles. Stopped in Wrangell, Petersburg, Juneau, Sitka (one flight took ninety minutes). They had to call the plane back as they had left without me.

Yes, in curing his hangover, Robert had secluded himself in the airport bar at one of the stops (he can't remember which one – it involved some tiresome change in planes), and missed the boarding call. Robert assured Muriel they had lots of time, but the plane was already taxiing down the runway when Muriel emerged from the ladies' room and, after a frantic search for Robert, found him in the bar. They called the plane back, but Muriel just absolutely refused to speak to him after that.

Robert had to control his drinking.

He finally hauled himself back aboard the ship in Sitka, bedraggled and sore. He drank apple juice with his caviar that afternoon. (Not bad.)

The *Viking Star* had turned her bow south. Last stop, Victoria. In two days.

"August 18, at sea," he wrote in his travel diary. "Went to see a show on whaling. Had to see a picture about India. Then bar and rest. Had an outstanding holiday buffet, truly beautiful salmon and lobster for lunch. For drinks, more Norwegian vodka. And then on to the show of Norwegian folk dancers."

That was the last complete entry Robert wrote in his diary. In anticipation of the following day, he scribbled, "Aug. 20, Victoria." He had somehow gained an extra day. It was only the 19th.

Chapter 23

THE SAN FRANCISCO HEARINGS CONCLUDED ON FRIDAY, November 21, 1986. The trial in Victoria was to open ten days later, on Monday, December 1.

I used that time to prepare my cross-examinations from transcripts of police and private investigator interviews. Since no preliminary hearing had been held in Provincial Court, most of the witnesses the Crown would produce were still faceless strangers. It would be a game of blind chess for the most part.

In the meantime, our efforts to track down the history of the sale of Lucille TeRoller's apartment at 1080 Chestnut Street, which Mrs. Barnett had wanted Frisbee to buy, had been met with a comforting success. Russell Stetler, the San Francisco P.I., learned her co-op had been sold several months ago for $225,000 – slightly less than the $250,000 Frisbee told us it was being offered for. But close enough. Even more significant, we learned, the apartment went on the market on August 6, 1985, the very day after Frisbee's wet lunch with Muriel Barnett in which she told him she heard Mrs. TeRoller was planning to sell it. That was the day Mrs. Barnett proposed giving Frisbee $300,000 to buy and furnish it.

Frisbee's explanation for that mysterious $300,000 check now seemed on more solid footing. We knew his evidence could not now be contradicted.

I spent several days preparing written submissions upon several issues of law and jurisdiction that were to be argued at the opening of the trial. The U.S. trial system requires that all such issues be resolved well before the jury is empaneled. The Canadian system is less efficient – jurors are often forced to sit on their hands in a starkly furnished jury room while lawyers and judge slug it out in the nearby courtroom, debating the issues of admissibility that arise from time to time.

One of our points of law had to do with what is commonly known as the rule against double jeopardy: a person may not be tried twice for the same offense. The argument was inspired by the fact that a U.S. federal judge had dismissed the government's case against Frisbee before his extradition to Canada.

Another was based on a section of the Criminal Code that says that no foreign citizen may be tried in a Canadian court without the consent of the federal Attorney-General. We would contend that the consent filed with the indictment was both inaccurate and inadequate. Bob Higinbotham, one of our firm's partners, had argued a similar issue before the B.C. Court of Appeal and volunteered to make the argument for Frisbee.

I had ordered photostats of the various and voluminous paper exhibits, and they arrived a few days before the trial. I scanned Frisbee's Daily Journal for clues as to his state of mind during the several days before the cruise to Alaska.

August 5, after the meeting with lawyer Ted Kolb to discuss Muriel's new will: "At 5:35 left office, stopped at Home Drug, busy traffic, had to park by hydrant 3 or 4 minutes to pick up film, and there was an officer across the street on a red light and I pulled out and the car stalled. He may have seen my license – and a ticket?"

Here is Robert Frisbee, just after the lawyer told him he was preparing a new will for Mrs. Barnett . . . and he's worried about a parking ticket? This was a man contemplating murder?

August 6: "Dinner with Dan and M.C.B. at the World Trade Club." August 7: "Out of it." August 8: "Call M.C.B. about jewels, pick up." August 9: "To hairdresser, pick up shrimp." August 10: "Ship to Alaska, Go Man Go."

Where was the murdering mind in all of this?

Also copied for me were the diaries that Muriel Barnett had faithfully kept each year, little advance reminders for her social calendar, scribbled memories of happy times. They composed a curious picture of a woman whose passions never seemed to surface as more than a bubbly froth.

"Reward for return," she'd written in her diary for 1985. The finder could call either her or Bob Frisbee.

I opened it to the first week, to January 4, the day her husband died.

"Philip died in my arms at 4:00 p.m."

Romantic in a way, but in her arms? It sounded like a fib – she'd told Frisbee Philip expired while napping on the couch.

Eight days later: "Philip buried at sea. Beautiful day, beautiful ceremony."

She seemed to pick up the pieces rather rapidly: January 17: "Scott's for lunch – invited by Lloyd!" January 23: "Lunch at Osetria Romana. Very good." February 14: "Beautiful Valentine Party."

Bob Frisbee's name appeared on almost every page. Lots of "Bob ill." April 14: "Jack's with Lloyd (Bob ill)." April 16: "Home all day. Bob came over (very weak, shaky)."

October 10: "Broke my neck!" Following that, nothing, just large X's across each date until November 18.

At the end of the book, she had scribed a "Recipe for Friendship":

"Take two heaping cups of patience, one heartful of love, two handfuls of generosity, a dash of laughter, one headful of understanding, sprinkle generously with kindness and plenty of faith and mix well. Spread over a period of a lifetime and serve everybody you meet."

It was hard not to read this treacle without a pinch of cynicism. I suspected there were large, empty, and unexplored spaces buried within the psyche of this alcoholic fluttering butterfly. Perhaps at some level she knew that. Spoiled and over-sheltered, had she truly been capable of love?

The entry for January 4 in her 1985 diary hinted that she and Frisbee had honored the first anniversary of Philip's death in different ways. "Philip left me one year ago," she wrote, almost implying a betrayal. "Bob is ill."

May 2: "Bob had epileptic fit! Doctor Sinclair took him to

hospital! Cancel trip." May 3: "Beautiful Hurlingham Country Club for dinner with Diana and John (Bob in hospital)."

What had she to tell us about the Alaska cruise? The penthouse was "beautiful." Vancouver was "gorgeous." The banquet at Ketchikan was "very good." Norwegian Day was a "marvelous show!"

The last days of the life of Muriel Collins Barnett seemed to have been filled with unalloyed rapture.

On the fateful 19th, she'd penned this: "Victoria, B.C. Car and driver 11 a.m. (Max and Thelma Biegert with us)."

And for the 20th, to remind her of where she would be, two lonely words: "At sea."

Poor Muriel, I thought. However empty and imperfect a person, she could scarcely have deserved so brutal a passing.

◇   ◇   ◇

As I waded through the books and papers that littered my desk, Jeff Green continued to work with Dr. James Tyhurst, who had been conducting a series of jailhouse interviews with our client, causing Frisbee not a little distress. At their first meeting Frisbee took a dislike to the psychiatrist, who insisted on digging relentlessly into his fragile ego, reminding him of much of his past that he'd tried to forget.

He had been examined by half a dozen psychiatrists by now, and none of them – even those retained to assist in his prosecution – had managed to strip off so many layers of Frisbee's emotional skin. He begged us to protect him from this cruel, probing doctor of the mind. We begged him to cooperate. Eventually Frisbee became more comfortable with the doctor.

When Jim Tyhurst visited our office, we'd ask how it was going with Frisbee. He would stoke his pipe and say, "It's coming, it's coming."

The Victoria courthouse and its grounds occupy a city block on Burdett Street just east of the main commercial zone. A couple of blocks to the west, toward what is known as the Inner Harbour, are to be found the vine-clad, many-gabled Empress Hotel, offering afternoon tea for the tourists; the resplendent Parliament Buildings, which are lit up at night like a sideshow tent at a carnival, and the Provincial Museum, worth a long and thoughtful visit, a showcase of natural and human history.

Clustered nearby are all the geegaw and doodad shops, parasite businesses that live off the crumbs dropped by tourists on pilgrimages to such curiosities as the Undersea Gardens ("enjoy a fun-filled performance narrated by Aqua Maids, featuring the star of the show, Armstrong the giant Pacific octopus; shake hands with a sea cucumber in our touch-and-feel tank,") the Royal London Wax Museum ("Kings, queens, and presidents are no longer just names in a history book ... here they live!"), and Miniature World ("Over 40 great little attractions combine to thrill and delight the young and the young at heart.")

I myself have never summoned the strength to visit any of those establishments.

The courthouse is remarkable only for its stolidity and functionalism. A ground floor, and six storeys above it, a dozen courtrooms. Just within the main entrance on Burdett Street is a concession stand where lawyers can buy their essential drugs: nicotine, caffeine, and acetylsalicylic acid. During mid-morning and mid-afternoon breaks you will find several barristers gathered there, making loud complaint about the varied injustices that have just been perpetrated by their respective judges.

Jeff and I generally used one of the Courtney Street side entrances to the courthouse because our law office (and trial headquarters) was just across the street, on the third floor of a new office building.

The trial was to be held in one of the large jury rooms on the second floor. It was set for three weeks.

That was perfect, we thought: the trial would conclude a few days before Christmas. The jury would be imbued with the spirit of the season, their hearts bursting with love, mercy, and forgiveness. There is no better time to conclude a jury trial, as most criminal lawyers will tell you, than a few shopping days before Christmas. Good will to all men. Deck the halls with boughs of charity. No one wants to see the poor accused person trundled off to jail to the strains of bells jingling and carolers singing.

On the other hand, January, the hangover month, the month when the bills come in, is the worst time to defend before a jury. It is a time of stern, hard-headed decision-making. The mind quickly dismisses all reasonable doubt; transgressors must pay the price.

Our object was to get the evidence in quickly, to avoid being bumped over into the mean season. We had calculated carefully: two days of preliminary argument, two weeks of evidence, wrap up in a couple of days with addresses of counsel and the judge's instructions to the jury.

A carefully prepared trial, with admissions of indisputable fact, with cross-examinations prepared and contained and concise, without time-wasting objections over picayune points, could be kept within those time limits. Unless the unforeseen occurred. We had not factored into our time estimates the probability of the unforeseen. One must always do that.

How quickly and efficiently we could complete the trial would depend somewhat on our judge. Some are quick, some are slow. Some are bright, some dull. Some are pleasant, some a pain in the ass.

The case had been assigned to Mr. Justice Lloyd McKenzie, a veteran judge, formerly one of Victoria's best respected trial counsel. He is an imposing, square-framed man of florid complexion (we learned to assess his temperature by observing the intensity of blush on his face). He's erudite, and given to an often delicate turn of phrase.

I'd had only one criminal trial in front of him, a thrill-kill murder that I prosecuted. Like this one, it was a case involving a gay accused, but a being as unlike Frisbee as is possible while still of the human species. That fellow was a body-building psychopath who killed a man for the sheer orgiastic pleasure of it. It was an appalling form of plagiarism, from fiction to fact: he had read a best-selling thriller by Lawrence Sanders, *The First Deadly Sin*, and was inspired to mimic the actions of the villain, a psychotic serial killer. Cruising Granville Street, he'd picked up a lonely immigrant Portuguese man and stabbed him dozens of times with a pair of scissors, then boasted about it to his roommate.

I had been thrown into the case with only a weekend's preparation. My partner, Josiah Wood, was involved in one of those drug conspiracy trials-without-end, and couldn't adjourn it, and passed the file to me. In our busy office this kind of occurrence was commonly known as the last-minute lateral handoff. (For this and other sins, Josiah has since been appointed to the B.C. Court of Appeal.)

I recalled Lloyd McKenzie, from that trial, as incisive and quick and careful. I won all my major arguments in front of him, and the accused was put away for life. (He later escaped. A container with his name on it was later anonymously sent from Florida to his parents' address in Ontario. It contained human ashes. The police, no fools, have not closed their file.)

Justice McKenzie, who had seemed so stalwart a dispenser of justice in that case, seemed a fair choice for our trial. On the other hand, my role then was as prosecutor. To prosecutors, Crown-minded judges always seem fair. Maybe he wouldn't appear so admirable from the other side of the courtroom.

On the weekend before the trial, I reclaimed my gown, vest, and wing-collared shirts from the dry cleaners (in Canada, the accoutrement of barristers does not, as in England, include wigs) and readied myself for the courtroom wars.

By now, of course, we had interviewed Frisbee exhaustively. I was, if anything, over-prepared. I felt uncommonly tense, distracted, unable to focus on even the mundane aspects of getting through the weekend. On the Sunday before the trial opening I stared bleakly at the tube for a few hours, watching the annual Grey Cup game, held in Vancouver that year, for the championship of the Canadian Football League. Tiger-Cats 39; Eskimos 15.

I went to the law library that evening to polish my arguments on the law. Conciseness and clarity; judges don't like long-winded arguments while a jury is waiting.

That night I didn't sleep well.

Peter Jensen, a criminal lawyer friend, told me once, "A little piece of you dies whenever you do a major trial."

The unforeseen occurred on opening day, before even the first play from scrimmage. Justice McKenzie missed the ferry from

Vancouver, where he'd been sitting the previous week. He'd arrived at the mainland ferry dock in good time for the 7:00 a.m. sailing, but it was booked, full of football fans returning to Vancouver Island from the Grey Cup.

He made it before noon, but we'd lost half a day. He apologized to the jury panel, saying he'd not anticipated there'd be so much traffic returning from the "Gay Cup."

I drifted an anxious look at Jeff Green, beside me. Was this Freudian slip a grim portent?

The jury panel comprised fifty-three respectable-looking men and women from greater Victoria.

The U.S. jury selection process is time-consuming, and involves both prosecution and defense attorneys questioning jurors as to views and biases, before accepting or rejecting them. In Canada, only in unusual circumstances may a jury panelist be questioned. Essentially, you get what you see.

The panel is summonsed from a voters' list and is intended to represent a cross-section of the community. All one really knows about the panel members (barring receipt of any inside information) is name, address, and occupation.

The names were available in advance of the trial, and had it been permissible to send someone to interview them, we might have done so. But a Vancouver lawyer once got knee-deep in trouble for doing this; it's simply not allowed. We did check the names against the city directory, which lists occupations. (One wants to know if a jury panelist is married to a police officer. Indeed, we discovered that one woman panelist was married to a Coast Guard officer.) We would give extra consideration to choosing male jurors shown as single (there was just that extra chance they might be gay), and challenge those likely to side with the forces of law and order (watchmen, meat inspectors, bankers). And those with sour, throw-away-the-keys expression on their faces.

A fair mix of the sexes was advised. Although the murder victim was a woman, we felt no fear of the female juror. Obviously a woman was far more likely to feel sympathy toward Robert Frisbee than would some homophobic macho lumberjack.

But the defense is armed with only twenty challenges – that is, we had the right to summarily dismiss twenty jurors – and after we'd exhausted those, we were without a say in who would occupy the remaining seats in the jury box.

We placed asterisks against the names of a few prospects we liked: the single music instructor, the single male nurse and part-time taxi driver, the single seamstress. We wrote "No" against the names of the Canada Post supervisor, a woman whose husband was a ferry captain, another whose husband worked for Federal Fisheries. And we wrote a question mark beside the name of a woman against whose name Nancy, our secretary, noted: "Her son I think was a client (sexual assault)."

When we got to court, the names of the music instructor and the nurse-taxi driver had disappeared from the jury list, apparently because the sheriff had – for no accountable reason – released them from their obligation to attend.

What we ended up with was a telephone worker, a retail clerk, a bookstore manager, a clothing store manager, a draftsman, a museum technician, a seamstress, a forestry worker, and four homemakers. Seven men, only five women – fewer than we wanted.

A very WASPish crowd, they were, not unusual in Englishy Victoria. But all of pleasant demeanor, no vindictive countenances, and most of them had had the confidence to look me in the eye, an important test.

They also all had a good look at Frisbee, in the prisoner's box behind counsel table. I openly consulted with him during the jury selection process (my psychologist wife, who once served on a murder jury, told me jurors look for signals as to whether a lawyer seems to believe in his client. If he evidences little caring for him, the more likely the lawyer feels he's defending a guilty client).

Frisbee, with his white shirt and tie, with his bifocals, looked bookish and tolerably innocent. He had wanted to knit, but I preferred that he occupied himself taking notes. He did so throughout the trial, determinedly, copiously. It kept him from being nervous, he told me.

The rest of the opening Monday and the whole of the following day were set aside for our legal arguments, and the jurors were excused until Wednesday.

We argued all through the Monday afternoon. We argued all through Tuesday. On Wednesday morning the judge – reprovingly, I thought – announced he had still been unable to resolve "the complicated matters which you left me last evening about 5:00." He called for more argument. It wasn't until shortly after noon that he rendered judgment (all our arguments were rejected, so the public was not treated to the inglorious spectacle of an accused person walking out of a courtroom, free on a so-called legal technicality).

The judge did, however, agree that despite his earlier finding that the ship was in Canadian waters at the time of the murder the jury would be entitled to come to a different conclusion, and acquit if in doubt.

We finally brought the jury in at 12:30 that afternoon. We were already half a day late out of the starting gate.

The clerk read the indictment to the accused:

"Robert William Dion Frisbee, you stand charged that on or about the 19th day of August, 1985, while aboard a vessel, to wit, the *Royal Viking Star*, in the Strait of Juan de Fuca, within Canadian Territorial Waters near County of Victoria in the Province of British Columbia, you did commit first-degree murder on the person Muriel Collins Barnett, contrary to Section 218 of the Criminal Code of Canada and against the peace of our Lady the Queen, her Crown and dignity."

The ancient language embossing the final words of the indictment provided a nice solemnity to the occasion, and Frisbee, doubtless hurt that he could ever be accused of affronting the dignity of our Lady the Queen (he was a great fan of hers), seemed to muster what fragile strength he possessed as he stood not so intrepidly facing his peers.

"How do you plead, guilty or not guilty?"

Two timid words fluttered from between his lips into a great vacuum of silence in the courtroom.

"Not guilty."

I patted him on the shoulder and sat him down. He returned a nervous smile.

He wrote us a letter that day:

"I feel very at ease with you and Mr. Green– it's your ball game, and you have displayed your expertise in pitching a no hit, no run, no error game. (Is that right? – I don't know baseball at all.)"

Chapter 24

CROWN COUNSEL TRADITIONALLY "OPENS" TO THE JURY
before the first witness is called – outlining the evidence he or she
proposes to call, essentially getting a first kick at the cat. One is
not really expected to exhort a jury to tar and feather the accused
at this preliminary stage, but one can subtly start to move their
minds in that direction.

"In a nutshell," Dennis Murray summarized for them, "the
Crown's case of first-degree murder is not that it was well carried
out, and not that the plan was a sophisticated and well-developed
one, but that nonetheless the accused planned the murder of
Muriel Barnett." It was, he said, a very simple case.

Dennis knew better than to try to paint a picture of Frisbee as a
snarling sociopathic villain ("I don't expect we'll present a view of
some sort of fundamentally sinister person"). He bluntly stated
the Crown's theory of motive: the accused was one who after
many years of service to the Barnetts had developed a resentment
and an unfulfilled expectation of reward from Mrs. Barnett.

Some of his witnesses would appear in the flesh; others on a
video screen – "in a desperate attempt," he made a point of
informing the honest taxpayers on the jury, "to save the Canadian
taxpayer a few dollars."

He warned them not to believe all of what certain of his witnesses had to say. He had in mind one in particular – "a chap by
the name of Kazakes who you will see on the video." The good
reverend, he intimated, might not be a trustworthy source of the
truth.

Dennis sketched out the evidence pointing to motive and

murder, and promised the jury that despite "some glitches here and there along the way," they'd be out of there in three weeks.

In time, I prayed, to wish Robert Frisbee a Merry Christmas.

Crown and defense had agreed to speed things up by jointly filing all the relevant exhibits at the start of the trial. The documents included Philip Barnett's will (Exhibit 1), Muriel Barnett's will (Exhibit 2), her power of attorney to Frisbee (Exhibit 3), and the October 1984 codicil prepared by Frisbee (the troubling Exhibit 4). We filed checkbooks, canceled checks, bank documents, photos. The bottles of Famous Grouse scotch whiskey and Demestica wine were tendered. Frisbee's daily journal and his travel diary went in. So did the diaries that Muriel Barnett painstakingly kept. And Frisbee's bloodied robe.

But not his manuscript. The Crown planned not to produce it – unless Frisbee took the stand.

Because the witnesses from the *Royal Viking Star* lived or were stationed in such remote places as Cyprus, Austria, Sweden, France, Norway, and the Far East, many had to be flown halfway around the world to Victoria. The Crown permitted each of them, for some reason, to bring along one companion free, and all stayed in one of the better downtown apartment hotels.

Vigorously championing the cause of the Canadian taxpayer, the Crown hoped to pare its hotel bill by sending home each witness, and friend, immediately after he or she had taken the stand. Jeff and I felt there would be problems in agreeing to this – often witnesses have to be recalled to amplify their evidence – but we acceded. Rather too quickly, I felt, in retrospect.

Theodore Kolb, Mrs. Barnett's lawyer, was the first of the San Francisco witnesses to be called.

Jeff and I had met him prior to court, but only briefly, and had asked him some questions about his evidence, and generally sized him up. He was a burly, confident man who'd been in practice since 1945 and seemed still in his best years. He was at home on the witness stand, and lacked the usual courtroom nervousness.

He was the gentleman who drafted Mrs. Barnett's will. And whom she had consulted – just prior to the Alaska cruise – about drawing a new one. He was key to the Crown's theory that Frisbee murdered Mrs. Barnett to prevent her from signing a new will on her return from Alaska, a will which would render the October codicil completely nugatory.

We had reasons to be careful with Mr. Kolb. For many years he'd been friend, confidant, and golf-course pal of Philip Barnett – from first tee to nineteenth hole. A hearty masculine sort, he would not be expected to show much affection for a person he might see as the gay parasite who lived off Barnett for many years, then rudely accused him of being homosexual himself.

"Now your area of specialty," Dennis Murray asked him, "if you were to put it in a nutshell, sir, would be what?"

"Estates, probate and litigation."

Straightforward. To the point.

Had he known Philip Barnett?

For over forty years. One of the leading trial lawyers in San Francisco.

Did he know Barnett in a personal capacity as well?

Yes, he'd been a regular weekend golfing companion for ten years before his death.

No elaboration. No evasiveness.

He said he attended to the probate of Barnett's estate, and drew a will for his widow.

"And in a nutshell, sir, what did she leave to Mr. Frisbee in the event of her death?"

"Two hundred and fifty thousand dollars."

"Again in a nutshell," Dennis asked (he never ran out of nutshells, his favorite verbal decoration), "the overall effect of her will was to do what else?"

The bulk of the balance, said Kolb, was to go to endow a chair in trial advocacy at the University of San Francisco.

Had he drawn a power of attorney that, in a nutshell, would give Frisbee signing authority over her banking affairs?

Indeed he had. As well, in June of 1985 he drew a codicil to the will naming Frisbee as her executor (following the death of her former executor, Lloyd Wilkins). That was the document that contained the language, "I hereby republish my last will and testament," which Frisbee believed voided the October 1984 codicil, in which he would inherit two-thirds of Muriel Barnett's estate.

Kolb, however, was of the opinion that the October codicil – which he discovered only after Mrs. Barnett's death – was not rendered null and void by this language, and the jury heard some expert evidence from him that codicils involving minor amendments do not destroy a prior will unless inconsistent.

(That, of course, did not alter our position: if Frisbee believed, however erroneously, that the October codicil had been destroyed by the language of the later codicil he would be without a financial motive for murder. In this case, ignorance of the law was indeed an excuse. The problem: would the jury believe that the long-time secretary to one of California's most noted experts on wills was indeed so ignorant of the law?)

Dennis gave Kolb a copy of the October codicil to look at. By its terms, Kolb said, Frisbee would have been entitled to ten times the $250,000 he was to have inherited under the original will.

Kolb recalled that Mrs. Barnett met with him twice to discuss another change to her will, permitting an *inter vivos* gift to her godson in London, Jason Cope.

The first meeting was in June 1985, in Jack's Restaurant, with Frisbee present.

"What was he doing, sir?"

"He was taking notes."

Jurors turned to look at Frisbee. Taking notes.

The second meeting with Mrs. Barnett and Frisbee was in his office in August, just before they left for Alaska.

They again discussed the will. "I asked her, did she want any other changes, and she said, 'No, the rest stays according to my original will with the residue going to the university for the scholarship chair.'"

There seemed an almost rehearsed quality to this answer. I wondered if his memory of her words was quite so clear. He was implying, of course, that Frisbee had been clearly alerted to the fact that a new will would largely disinherit him.

"Did she mention anything during the course of that meeting about two-thirds to Mr. Frisbee?"

(FX2)SAN FRANCISCO, Aug. 22--HELD FOR *heed 198.*
INVESTIGATION--Robert Frisbee, 58, is being
held by San Francisco police for investigation of the murder of Muriel Barnett, 80-year
old widow of attorney Phillip Barnett. Police
say Frisbee was Mrs. Barnett's traveling
companion. Police say she had been killed
aboard the cruise ship Royal Viking Star.
(AP LASERPHOTO)(sjv50929chronicle/chris
stewart) 1985 SLUG: CRUISE DEATH!
(SAN FRANCISCO-OAKLAND OUT)

FILE

A younger Muriel and Philip Barnett at a society costume ball in San Francisco.
(Photo by V.M. Hanks, Jr.)

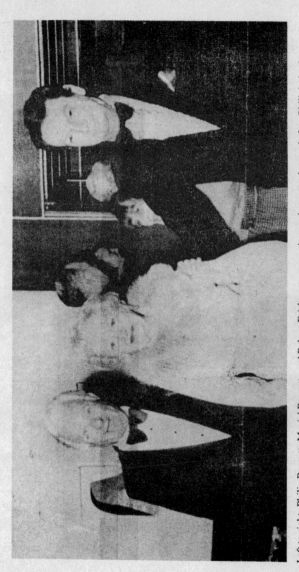

Left to right, Philip Barnett, Muriel Barnett, and Robert Frisbee on a vacation cruise several years before Philip's death. (*San Jose Mercury News*)

The *Royal Viking Star* cruise ship, which would set sail from San Francisco to Alaska on August 10, 1985. (AP/World Wide Photos)

A polaroid snapshot taken of Muriel Barnett and Robert Frisbee having cocktails aboard the *Royal Viking Star* a few days before her death.

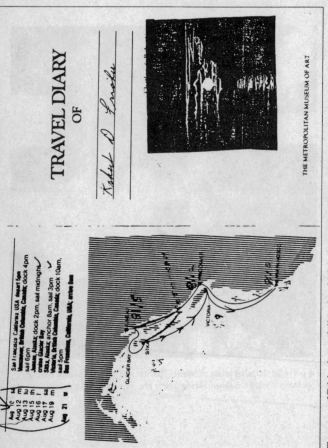

TRAVEL DIARY

OF

Robert D. Frisbee

Aug 10   th
Aug 12   m   San Francisco California USA depart 5pm
Aug 13   th   Vancouver, British Columbia, Canada; dock 4pm
Aug 15   f   sail 6pm
Aug 16   _   Juneau, Alaska; dock 2pm, sail midnight ✓
Aug 17   sa   cross Glacier Bay
Aug 19   m   Sitka, Alaska; anchor 8am, sail 3pm ✓
Aug 21   w   Vancouver, British Columbia, Canada; dock 10am,
                      sail 5pm
                      San Francisco, California, USA; arrive 8am

GLACIER BAY

SITKA

VICTORIA

The cover of Frisbee's travel diary in which he kept a daily log of activities during the Alaska cruise.
The last complete entry was August 18, the day before Muriel Barnett was murdered.

A prime suspect in the Barnett slaying, Robert Frisbee is shown here shortly after his arrest when the *Royal Viking Star* docked in San Francisco. (Chris Stewart, *San Francisco Chronicle*)

An envelope containing one of the letters Frisbee wrote to his lawyer from the San Francisco Jail (where he was held for a year), hand-decorated with a cheerful bouquet of flowers.

"Not a word."

He couldn't have been more emphatic. The Crown was starting off strong, with a firm, assured witness.

The new will would be ready for Mrs. Barnett on her return to San Francisco. The effect of it, he said, would be to revoke all previous wills and codicils.

"What would happen to Mr. Frisbee's two-thirds in the codicil Exhibit 4?"

"It would go out the window."

"At that meeting, sir, did Mr. Frisbee speak up and say anything about the October 16th codicil?"

"Not a word."

Nor had Kolb heard about any gifts to Kazakes of $100,000 or to Frisbee of $300,000.

Dennis asked him to look at Mrs. Barnett's signature on the October codicil.

"It looks very shaky. We had serious doubts about whether it was her signature when we first saw it, but experts have confirmed to us that it was. But this was shortly after she had a major fall and that might explain the shakiness of the signature."

Part of this hearsay was rather helpful. The Crown could not now be heard to say her signature was forged.

In cross-examination I drew from him that he had once advised Mrs. Barnett she should alter her will through a handwritten codicil. Quite frequently, he said, persons like to do that in privacy.

"That might have been the case, particularly with Mrs. Barnett, who was private about a lot of things?"

"That is correct."

The Crown, still intent on proving Mrs. Barnett had been hoodwinked into signing the codicil, that she really had never seen what she signed, wanted the jury to believe, of course, that she would have confided its existence to Kolb had she been aware of it. As with other witnesses, I tried to underscore her obsession with privacy.

"She didn't discuss a lot of her own business affairs with you?"

"No, she didn't."

"She was the kind of person that really didn't like others seeming to pry into her business, even lawyers?"

"When she asked my opinion, I gave it to her, but when she didn't ask it, I didn't volunteer any ideas because I think she would have resented it."

I asked whether the other provisions of the October codicil – aside from Frisbee's gift – had been admitted to probate: the various gifts of money, jewelry, and other items Mrs. Barnett had bequeathed to various of her friends.

Other than the bequest to Frisbee, to which he had abandoned his claim on the advice of his San Francisco lawyer, "the whole codicil was admitted to probate," Kolb said.

I had learned this information from Kolb during our earlier interview, and had been a little astonished. The California Probate Court had passed judgment that the codicil was valid – how could the Crown continue to argue the document was fraudulent?

"So in effect with the exception of the gift of the residue, this codicil of October 16th was admitted to probate with the intention that all of the other gifts be perfected?"

"That is correct."

"No one challenged the codicil and suggested these weren't her wishes?"

No one had done so. And the period for challenge had expired. The estate, even as Frisbee's murder trial was proceeding, was being sorted out for distribution – diamond necklaces, turquoise bracelets, gold earrings, and all: the various gifts listed in the so-called fraudulent codicil.

I had always been curious as to why, after Philip died, Mrs. Barnett was content to continue to honor her husband's wishes to endow the University of San Francisco law school.

"That university was Philip Barnett's alma mater?"

"It was, class of '27."

"It was not, however, Muriel Barnett's alma mater?"

"Not that I know of. I doubt it. It was a man's school."

The judge, perhaps thinking it odd that a law school would be gender-biased, sought clarification. "The law school was strictly a male preserve?"

"Not now, but until ten years ago it was."

I asked, "Aside from the fact that she had been married to Mr.

Barnett, she had no particular loyalty to the University of San Francisco?"

"None that I could imagine."

That seemed ample reason for Muriel Barnett to wish to change her will to reduce the university's share in favor of Frisbee. But still, I wondered, was there some specific reason for her having refused to discuss this with Kolb? I remember thinking I should probe into this further with Mr. Kolb. But only at extreme peril does one ask questions if one doesn't know the answers.

Kolb said he had seen Frisbee and Mrs. Barnett together at the World Trade Club three weeks after her neck accident.

"She didn't seem to be impaired mentally in any way?"

"No."

She was not wearing her neck brace at the time. "Mrs. Barnett was very vain and I don't think she wore it in public."

Okay. Corroborated what Frisbee would have to say.

Through Kolb, I introduced two interesting exhibits, postcards that Mrs. Barnett and Frisbee had mailed from the *Royal Viking Star* to their London friends, the Copes, and which later the Copes forwarded to Kolb. Both were dated August 11, 1985, the day after the ship departed San Francisco. The picture side showed a Royal Viking Line ship working its way across the ocean.

"Dearest family," said Frisbee's card, "another beautiful trip. Feel tip-top . . . Guess who won a prize of an enormous bottle of Mumm's champ. Robert! M.C.B. cannot drink the whole bottle, so may have to take my first champ bath!"

Very jolly was Robert Frisbee two days out of port. Not exactly consumed with murderous thoughts.

Muriel was equally full of cheer: "Isn't this a beautiful ship? We left S.F. yesterday, and will be in Vancouver, Canada, tomorrow. Then on to Alaska. Much love to you three from Robert and Auntie Muriel."

Her handwriting appeared a little shaky.

It was time to start drawing a picture for the jury of the role Frisbee played in the Barnetts' lives.

"After Philip Barnett died, I take it that Mrs. Barnett began to lean very strongly on Robert Frisbee?"

"Progressively more so."

"Essentially he was at her every beck and call?"

"Oh, I would imagine so."

"He was always there for her?"

"There is no question about that."

"As far as Mr. and Mrs. Barnett were concerned he appeared to be caring, prepared to do whatever their wishes were?"

"Certainly appeared so."

"You never saw any friction between them?"

"None that I can recall."

"Thank you," I said, and sat down.

Dennis rose to re-examine. He seemed concerned that Frisbee – quite graciously, the jury might have thought – had waived all his claims under the October codicil. On advice of his U.S. counsel, Lefcourt, he'd signed what Kolb described as a "declination to inherit."

"In other words, Mr. Frisbee filed a document saying, 'I'm not laying claim to that two-thirds?'"

"That's correct."

Frisbee of course had not waived his claim to the $250,000 bequest in her original will, and Dennis wanted to get that in front of the jury.

"What did Frisbee get out of this estate?"

I objected. "That, with respect, is not a question arising from examination, and I suspect the answer, in fact, is he hasn't got anything at this point." The estate, in fact, had not yet been disbursed.

Dennis didn't appreciate my giving evidence. "I suspect the answer is $250,000," he announced to the jury.

The judge upheld my objection, for what it was now worth. Anyway, it was all going to come out in the wash before the trial was over.

When Justice McKenzie asked if there was any reason the witness could not be excused from further attendance, I hesitated, then said, "No, I have no reason."

It was after 5:00 p.m. We adjourned to 9:00 a.m. (These, for trial lawyers, are long, strength-sapping hours. A more typical day extends from 10:00 a.m. to 12:30, then from 2:00 to 4:00, with fifteen-minute breaks each morning and afternoon – a four-hour daily grind during which the brain is constantly pumping and grunting, working close to overload. But we had to make up for lost time to beat the Christmas rush.)

As I left the courtroom I felt a vague sense there was business unfinished with Mr. Kolb, having to do with Mrs. Barnett's reluctance to discuss with him her wishes, as expressed to Frisbee, to abbreviate that major gift to the U.S.F. law school.

Frisbee had told us adamantly that Mrs. Barnett felt no fondness for that male bastion of higher education: she'd gone to Berkeley. And Philip, he told us, had already, in his lifetime, provided enough funding to establish the Philip Barnett chair of advocacy.

Answering lawyers' questions is thirsty work, and Ted Kolb seemed pleased to accept an invitation for drinks with Jeff and me in a cocktail lounge near the courthouse.

We didn't want to find ourselves on the bad side of this congenial fellow – he had yet to apply the final touches to the settling of Mrs. Barnett's estate, and Frisbee still had not received his $250,000. (And we had yet to receive our $60,000 retainer from that.) He reassured us he expected the funds to be released within days.

We'd wondered how he had so skillfully managed to persuade the law school not to contest this substantial bequest to Frisbee: after all, were our client to be convicted of murder, that $250,000 gift would lapse (one just isn't allowed to make a killing from a killing). But the law school, he told us, hadn't wanted its bequest to be tied up for months, perhaps years, of legal wrangling, losing bank interest along the way. And, Kolb intimated, he was on pretty good terms with the Board of Regents of that law school.

Turned out he graduated there. Turned out, in fact, he himself was currently a member of its Board of Regents. An important role of the Board of Regents was to help raise funds for the law school.

I realized: Ted Kolb naturally would want to ensure the law school was adequately funded.

And would not Mrs. Barnett have been more than a little reluctant to disappoint Philip's close friend by disinheriting his beloved alma mater?

And that, it struck me, was obviously why she had not disclosed to Kolb the terms of the October codicil. I was quite sure Kolb had exerted no undue pressure upon her to maintain that large gift to U.S.F. It was simply quite typical of Muriel not to want to offend Kolb in this way.

And, to avoid such awkwardness, perhaps also to avoid witnessing the horror on his face if she gave her fortune to Frisbee, she had advised him the university would continue to be her chief beneficiary.

To make up to Frisbee, she'd offered cash gifts to his lover Kazakes and to Frisbee himself. It was exactly how the mind of this carefree, stress-avoiding woman worked.

Kolb was shortly to be on a plane back to San Francisco. I imagined he would have been more than a little distressed about being re-subpoenaed and having to stay another day.

When I caught up to Dennis Murray later that evening, I made a deal. We would not inconvenience Kolb if certain matters were stated as facts before the court.

The next morning, with Dennis's generous concurrence, we put on record the fact that Kolb was a member of the university's Board of Regents and involved in raising funds for it. I now had a basis for arguing why Mrs. Barnett was reluctant to tell her lawyer about the codicil. And for disproving allegations about its illegitimacy.

Frisbee's $250,000 was wired from San Francisco that day. Good old Ted Kolb.

Chapter 25

THE CROWN, STUBBORNLY ADHERING TO ITS THEORY THAT Kazakes and Frisbee were knee-deep in trickery over that codicil, had Clarence Johnson, the doorman at 1000 Chestnut Street, waiting in the wings the next day to testify that Dan Kazakes, as the ship embarked for Alaska, scuttled back to the apartment and sneaked out with Mrs. Barnett's security box. And, presumably, placed the codicil in it before returning it.

Kazakes had testified in San Francisco that Mrs. Barnett had given him a key to her apartment and to her mailbox, instructing him to collect the mail every few days while she was on the Alaska cruise, and to run the Cadillac's engine once in a while.

Dennis had asked him: "Did you, when you brought the Cadillac back, go into her apartment?"

Kazakes couldn't remember: "I can't recall. Uh . . . what day of the week was it that she left, was it Thursday, Saturday, or what?"

Dennis insisted: "When you took the Cadillac back did you go into the apartment?"

"I don't . . . I don't think so."

"Did you at any time when they were away on this cruise take anything out of this apartment?"

"No. Nothing at all."

Armed with what he assumed to be Kazakes's blatant lies, Dennis hoped to use Clarence Johnson to prove Kazakes and Frisbee were acting in fraudulent concert. We hoped we were ready for Mr. Johnson. He could cause irreparable damage if he convinced the jury Kazakes was fooling around with the little lock-box in which Frisbee – so he told us – had placed the codicil ten months earlier.

The next day our 9:00 a.m. start, for some reason I can't remember, became a 10:10 start. Reasons for delays are multifarious: late-arriving witnesses, last-minute scrums among counsel, misplaced exhibits. Again, we would have to accelerate our pace.

Clarence Johnson looked a little ill at ease as he took the stand to be sworn.

Dennis asked him what his job was at 1000 Chestnut Street.

"I'm the doorman, port security, whatever has to be done, garbage man for the day shift."

On August 9, 1985, he'd gone up to Mrs. Barnett's apartment and brought down all her luggage, put it in her car.

"And I stand by until Mrs. Barnett came down."

"Yes."

"And she came down, I helped her around the side of the car. She sat in the front. The secretary got in the back and the car left."

"Now when you say the secretary do you mean Mr. Frisbee?"

"Yes."

"Who was driving the car, sir?"

"Uh, it was a fellow, he told us he was the priest."

"Okay, had you seen this fellow who was driving the car before that day?"

I had no doubt Dennis planned to spin for the jury an elaborate and sinister mystery about the role of the priest. I tried to alter his script.

"I might be able to save my friend some trouble. This is Mr. Kazakes. I admit that as a fact. Mr. Kazakes had a key to the suite. I admit that as a fact."

Nothing to hide, I was telling everyone.

"Thank you, my lord," said Dennis a little curtly. One doesn't like one's tempo to be interrupted, especially when working with scripted questions.

"Does that help?" I innocently asked.

Apparently not. Dennis asked when had "this chap who we described as a preacher" started coming around 1000 Chestnut?

"He might have been coming a long time, I don't know, because I only seen him after that trip they went to . . . I guess they went to

Europe. Afterwards they came back, and that's the time I seen this other fellow driving Mrs. Barnett's car, because I did question him, and he said he was doing the driving because Bob couldn't drive."

"Okay, but this chap . . . this preacher chap, you began to see him around the summer of 1985 for a couple of months?"

"That is correct."

Dennis asked what the "chap" was wearing on the day everyone left for the ship.

"With respect," I said, "my friend doesn't have to keep referring to him as a chap or the preacher. I've admitted the man is a Mr. Kazakes."

The judge nodded. "All right."

"I appreciate Mr. Deverell's comments, my lord," said Dennis, who clearly didn't. "Now, what was this chap wearing, sir?"

"He was wearing a black suit and he had on a collar like a priest, you know, how they turn around a little white patch in the middle. Every time I seen him he had that particular suit on, or either he had a chain with a cross on it."

This was intended to paint the preacher chap as a liar. The jury would soon see the Kazakes video in which he had vigorously denied wearing "robes." (However, he hadn't denied wearing clerical garb.)

"After they all left did you see this . . . this chap again?"

"I did. I'm not sure how long they were gone, but about approximately thirty minutes he was back and he pulled up, and I said, 'Why are you back this quick?'"

I objected, a little tardily, as Johnson was recalling that Kazakes said something about returning for "the papers."

"Now, just a minute. This smacks of hearsay to me."

"There's no question about it," said Justice McKenzie. As a good judge should, he did his best to explain to the jury in simple terms one of our most arcane rules of evidence: "Ladies and gentlemen, hearsay evidence is the statement of some third person who's not in the witness box. In the ordinary course of living we quote people all the time, he said this to me, she said that to me, but we can't do that, the laws of evidence won't allow it. Now, there's a degree of tolerance that's allowed, and there has been a good deal of tolerance here with no objection, but there is an objection now and I won't allow it."

Dennis pressed on, eliciting from Johnson that the chap had returned alone in the Barnett Cadillac.

"And he came into the building and he went up to the Barnett apartment?"

Johnson was being careful. "I do not know whether he went to the apartment or not because I didn't follow him."

"And when he came back out, sir, did he have anything with him that he didn't have when he arrived?"

"He had some sort of box."

"Okay, and was that the last you saw of him, sir?"

"That was the last I saw of him."

Dennis abruptly sat down. Was he expecting me, in cross-examination, to do the rest of his work? Ask the witness to describe that box? And perhaps perform a courtroom pratfall by inviting Mr. Johnson to identify the security box which, although not yet an exhibit, was sitting on a table in the courtroom? Wily counsel have been known to set such traps.

I first asked to him identify, in a photograph, the building down the street from his, 1080 Chestnut. I wanted the jury to remember that address – the building housing Lucille TeRoller's cooperative apartment, the one which Mrs. Barnett intended Frisbee to buy.

I then began a gentle tiptoe dance around the business of the security box.

"Now, you gave evidence Mr. Kazakes went into the building and brought down a box. Remember the box?"

"I told him–"

"Never mind what you told him – you saw him come down with a box, that's what I'm interested in."

"He came down with a package or a box . . . yeah, a box."

"A box with a handle on it?"

"That's right."

"Well, describe the box, the dimensions of it."

"I wouldn't know the dimensions of it. It was sort of a brownish box with a little handle on top of it."

A little handle on top of it. I breathed a little sigh of comfort.

"And do you remember seeing that earlier when you were packing up the luggage?" He seemed unsure. I helped him: "It was sitting on the piano up in the Barnett suite."

"To my knowledge," he agreed, "it was sitting on the piano when I went into the apartment."

I thanked Mr. Johnson and strolled over to the exhibit table where sat both Mrs. Barnett's squat metallic gray security box and Frisbee's portable bar. I made a show to the jury of studying the latter item: a sort of brownish box with a little handle on top of it. And asked no further questions of Mr. Johnson. (Beware that one question too many.)

I was confident now that after all its eager fishing, the Crown had managed to hook only a red herring. After Ernie Quantz had confronted us with that paralyzing information about Kazakes slipping out of the Barnett apartment with what the Crown confidently had assumed was the security box, we'd sat down with Frisbee and asked him to recall, once again, the events of the day of departure.

When it came to such critical matters as where his next drink would come from, Frisbee's otherwise-ragged memory suffered few gaps. He clearly recalled that the first thing he did when he and Mrs. Barnett got to the ship was unpack his portable bar.

"And I realized there was no bar."

After a few moments of near-panic, Frisbee exhorted his roommate to drive back to 1000 Chestnut, and return with the portable bar. Kazakes dutifully did so.

I decided to wait for a more appropriate time in the trial to nail the point home.

Ruth Berlin was the Barnetts' third-floor neighbor at 1000 Chestnut. A gentle woman in her later years, she was called to the stand by Ernie Quantz to provide some background into the relationship between the Barnetts and Frisbee.

After Philip's death, Muriel Barnett was, she said, "very dependent" on Frisbee, and they were close.

Ernie asked about Mrs. Barnett's condition after her neck accident.

"She seemed more frail, she didn't walk as steady, but her spirits hadn't changed."

"And how would you describe her spirits?"

"She was usually quite an upbeat person. She had injury before, but she accepted it."

I'm not sure what advantage the Crown intended to gain from her evidence, but Mrs. Berlin was clearly not unsympathetic to Frisbee. Indeed, as I discovered in my earlier interview with her, she would be helpful to the defense.

I asked her in cross-examination about Frisbee's condition after his return from the aborted trip to England. Frisbee, she said, looked as if he had been quite ill. In fact, she recalled Mrs. Barnett telling her that during a meeting with the doctor "Robert was told he could never drink alcohol again or it would kill him."

(This is classic hearsay, by the way, but as the judge implied to the jury, he wasn't going to do counsel's work: if no one else objected to it, he wasn't about to.)

"Your observation was that Robert was intensely faithful to Mrs. Barnett?"

"He was devoted to her."

I paused, let that one sink in.

"And would you agree she was very lucky to have him around especially after her accident?"

"Yes."

"Mrs. Barnett was a person who did not openly discuss her business affairs, is that fair to say?"

"She was very private."

Good witness.

Chapter 26

AFTER THE DEATH OF LLOYD WILKINS IN JUNE 1985, HIS DAUGHTER Janet took over his accounting practice, and was appointed, with Frisbee, as co-executor of Mrs. Barnett's $3.7-million estate. A matter-of-fact, apparently diligent woman, she evidenced little sympathy for Frisbee, and when we briefly interviewed her before she took the stand, she seemed reluctant to offer us much help. She was staunchly on the side of the prosecution.

In the courtroom, Dennis asked her to recall a visit to 1000 Chestnut Street on July 19, 1985, about a month before Mrs. Barnett's death.

She had met Muriel Barnett and Frisbee for lunch that day at Jack's before accompanying them back to the apartment. When Mrs. Barnett went to her room to change, Frisbee led Janet Wilkins on a tour of the apartment – it was her first visit there. He showed her where various documents were kept, showed her the security box and the key to open it, which was in the drawer of a secretary. She didn't recall Frisbee opening the box.

"Okay, was there any conversation around a person by the name of Kazakes?" Dennis asked.

"Yes, he said that Mr. Kazakes would be taking care of the mail, I wouldn't have to do that, while they were gone on their trip."

"Yes, and was Mrs. Barnett present when that was said?"

"No."

"Did he say anything else about Mr. Kazakes?"

"Just that he would be given the same sort of tour so he would know where things were, too."

She was among a dozen guests at the bon voyage party on board the *Royal Viking Star* on August 10, and observed Kazakes there in clerical garb: "collar and cross, a black outfit."

On August 20, she learned about Mrs. Barnett's death. Two days later, Kazakes telephoned her.

I rose to ward off any damaging hearsay response. "I don't know whether I should jump up to object, but my friend knows what the law is."

"On any issue of what the law is I defer to Mr. Deverell," Dennis said.

"Very gracious," I replied. We were getting chippy.

It was no courtroom secret that one of the matters Kazakes phoned Janet Wilkins about was to make arrangements to return Mrs. Barnett's furs to the estate. He had been keeping Mrs. Barnett's more valuable fur pieces in his apartment while she was on the Alaska cruise.

His evidence at the San Francisco hearings was this:

Dennis Murray: "Did you at any time have anything to do with Mrs. Barnett's furs?"

Kazakes: "That was prior to her leaving. I put them in a plastic bag and I had them in my house. They were turned over to the estate."

Dennis: "Would you describe how that came about?"

Kazakes: "Well, she wanted me to have them at my place because her maid, a Nicaraguan girl, she was in and out of the apartment and all her relatives and everything."

The Crown had cooked up a theory that the scoundrel Kazakes had simply walked into the Barnett apartment and stolen the furs, and probably planned to sell them after Mrs. Barnett's death. After the murder, he was forced to return them to the estate. The theory was poorly grounded, I thought: according to the terms of the Frisbee codicil, some of the furs were to go to Janet Wilkins and her mother, and if Kazakes knew about those bequests, as the Crown alleged, it was unlikely he would have dealt with her minks and sables in so brazen a fashion.

Wilkins said she was surprised to learn Kazakes had the furs: she'd been told nothing about this.

What Kazakes also told her was that she might find Frisbee's codicil in Mrs. Barnett's security box. That was the part of the conversation I didn't want the jury to hear. My objection didn't faze Dennis. One can often get around the hearsay rule by asking a question framed like this:

"As a result of that conversation what did you do?"

Which was indeed the question Dennis asked.

"I subsequently went back to the apartment and looked for a codicil in the security box."

She found it. She'd never seen it before, nor had she known of its existence. She turned it over to Mr. Kolb.

So the Crown, still gnawing away at its Kazakes-Frisbee conspiracy theory, established that Kazakes, with easy access to the apartment, apparently drew her attention to the contents of the security box. But far worse was to come. In his opening, Dennis had given us warning, telling the jury that Frisbee had drained unauthorized amounts of money from Mrs. Barnett's accounts. I had taken that to mean the big checks for $300,000 and $100,000, and was frankly caught by surprise.

Frisbee, said Wilkins, had been pilfering from her trustee account.

I knew Frisbee had made a botch of his employer's books: checks were out of order; stubs didn't match checks; dates were often not accurate. But I didn't know Frisbee had actually fiddled the books. (He had not lied to us, but he'd not offered the information.)

As Dennis led Wilkins through Mrs. Barnett's checkbook, I began to feel a queasiness in the pit of my stomach. I remember smothering an urge to turn to Frisbee, to give vent to the ire I felt. (During the testimony of various witnesses, I would often consult with my client, if only to let the jury observe he was not being forgotten, but this wasn't the time.)

The majority of checks which issued from this account had been drawn and signed by Frisbee, the remainder by Muriel Barnett (hers were mostly personal gifts to friends and godchildren). Janet Wilkins had gone to some effort in matching the numbers on the cancelled checks to those on the checkbook stubs.

"Check 184 is a September 1, 1984 check. Can you just describe what you found in check number 184?"

The amount on the stub, we observed, was $400 (Frisbee's monthly salary). Janet Wilkins: "The debit that shows up on the

207

bank statement for check number 184 is $2,400." And the cancelled check with the bank statement had disappeared.

Similarly, check 186: the stub showed payment to Frisbee of $100. The bank statement showed check 186 as having been cashed for $500. The cancelled check had disappeared.

And so it went. Check 214. "In a nutshell it's a stub that reflects $400 to Robert Frisbee, a check that reflects $2,400, and the cancelled check is missing?"

"Yes."

The nutshells piled up. One hundred dollars became $1,100; $300 became $1,300; $500 showed on the stub, $2,500 was pocketed by Frisbee. All salary checks for Frisbee, or petty cash amounts to him, or, in a couple of cases, checks to pay his Visa account.

"Are you able to express an opinion with respect to what appeared as a pattern in this bookkeeping?"

"Well, there is consistent under-reporting of check amounts, as to what actually went through the bank account."

"And that starts in September of 1984?"

"That's right."

"And continues through until the period of time immediately prior to the departure of the cruise?"

"Yes."

Not just a murderer was Mr. Frisbee. A jury can forgive murder. But killing someone to cover up one's small-time thievery: that's beyond the pale.

Finally, Dennis referred Wilkins to the checks Frisbee signed August 10, the day the ship sailed for Alaska: $300,000 to Frisbee, $20,000 to Jerry Kazakes. On each stub was recorded merely: "To Alaska." Then, after many blank pages, the $100,000 check to Dan Kazakes, given to him just before the ship departed (which Frisbee explained he had dated August 6, in error). Nothing recorded on the stub.

Dennis saved the punch for the end:

"Now, finally with respect to the tour that Mr. Frisbee took you on of the apartment where he showed you the various things, did he express to you why he wanted you to have this tour?"

"So I would know where things were in case anything happened on the trip."

"Those are my questions. Thank you, my lord."

The judge looked at me. "Mr. Deverell?"

I looked at the clock. Fifteen minutes to lunch break.

"My lord, I don't expect I'll be longer than an hour, so if we commence at 2:00 I would appreciate it."

Justice McKenzie took pity on me. "All right."

I turned to Frisbee. He couldn't look me in the eye. He had kept from me, kept from Jeff Green, from Dr. Tyhurst, and all who had interviewed him, the extent of all his petty thievery. But although the Crown had failed to honor its commitment to full disclosure, it was I who was at fault. The books and bank statements had been there for me to examine; I had been warned by Dennis's opening remarks; I had not gone after my client hard enough during the pre-trial interviews.

I skipped lunch, and went to the courthouse cells instead, where Frisbee was waiting for me in a state of abject fear.

Yes, he had, over the course of a year, skimmed about $10,000 from Mrs. Barnett's account. He had destroyed her cancelled checks when they'd come back from the bank. Not that she ever looked at them anyway.

He pleaded for understanding. He'd been living beyond his means . . . all those years of slaving for the Barnetts . . . a monkey on a string working for peanuts.

He said, with a childlike shame, "I'm sorry."

I felt like telling him he was grounded for the next week.

I spent the rest of the noon break poring over Wilkins's exhibits, then went to the concession stand for a fast coffee.

Larry Still, the courthouse reporter for *The Vancouver Sun*, drew me aside.

"Looks bad," he said. "But the sword cuts both ways, doesn't it?"

"What do you mean?"

"Why would he kill the fatted calf? He had a nice thing going there."

I took a few seconds to absorb this.

"Isn't it in his interest for her to live to a ripe old age? That way he could carry on taking a little here, a little there."

I blinked. "You're right."

Larry smiled. Larry has covered hundreds of murder cases; he's developed a clever, lawyerly mind.

"Takes away from his motive to murder her, doesn't it?" he said. "The only way he'd get caught is if she dies and the books get opened."

I carefully placed Larry's useful comments in my mental speech-to-the-jury file, hoping the Crown might cut itself a little on its own sword.

It was important, in cross-examination, to diminish the impact of Janet Wilkins's evidence that Frisbee wanted her to "know where things were in case anything happened on the trip." That answer, I felt, had been handcrafted by Dennis in an attempt to suggest Frisbee was contemplating that some dastardly event might indeed occur aboard the ship.

The thrust of Dennis's examination was to suggest that Frisbee, after Muriel Barnett had gone to her room, went to particular pains to show the accountant where the security box and its key were located. As part of the accused's cold and deliberate plan to murder Mrs. Barnett, he would want to ensure that her executor would not overlook the security box (and codicil) after he'd bumped her off.

Muriel Barnett's daily diary for 1985 was before the jury as an exhibit. I showed Wilkins the entry for July 19.

"That was the second time you met at Jack's with . . . "

"Yes, that's right."

". . . with Bob Frisbee and Mrs. Barnett. You see that is her handwriting, isn't it?"

"Yes."

"And it says, 'Lunch at Jack's with Bob and Janet Wilkins. Janet at 1000 Chestnut to oversee the situation.' Do you see that?"

"Yes."

"Essentially that was the purpose of your trip to 1000 Chestnut Street, was it not?"

"Yes."

"Because you had just been named co-executor of the estate it was important that you find out where everything was kept?"

"Yes."

"That was the purpose of Mr. Frisbee showing you around?"

"Yes."

"There was nothing surprising or remarkable about that?"

"No."

"No. You had not been in the suite before?"

"Never been there before."

"In fact it was Mrs. Barnett who wanted you to come up and look around there?"

"I don't know that but I suppose so."

"Well, she invited you up there to 'oversee the situation,' as she put it in her notebook?"

"To oversee."

"And that was your understanding?"

"Yes."

That, I hoped, let a little air out of the Crown's balloon.

I ran through a number of the checks with the witness to establish Frisbee's careless (doubtless gin-induced) bookkeeping practices: wrong dates, unsigned checks, blank stubs. I also established there was nothing unusual about his removing blank checks from the checkbook before going on long trips: he had done so prior to their flights to Europe, presumably to avoid having to take the whole checkbook.

"As of the time Mrs. Barnett and Robert Frisbee were taking this trip to Alaska, how much was in this particular account?"

"About $130,000."

That was before the Kazakes check for $100,000 hit the bank.

I referred her to Frisbee's check for $300,000.

"Quite clearly as of that time this $300,000 could not have cleared that account?"

"No."

Nor did Mrs. Barnett currently have sufficient funds in her other accounts to cover it. So here was Robert Frisbee with a useless check for $300,000 in his pocket when arrested. Obviously he must have known it couldn't clear, so (I was now in a position to argue) what devious purpose had he for making it out to himself?

Seeking to rub a little salted red herring in the wounds of the Crown, I strolled over to the table where sat the security box. The Crown, apparently no longer interested in its theory that Kazakes had lugged it out of 1000 Chestnut Street, had so far carefully neglected to tender this crucial piece of evidence as an exhibit.

With Herculean effort, I raised it from the table.

"This then is the – this is how you get hernias – the metal box you were referring to?"

"Yes, it is."

"For the record, this is a gray metal box. The drawer is brown; it says on it, 'Safe Manufacturers National Association,' and it's very heavy. May that be an exhibit, my lord?"

"It's all right with me," said the judge, "but now the Registrar will have to lug it up and down."

"I'll help," said Dennis.

"We'll let Mr. Murray do that," I said.

Clarence Johnson had described a handle. I asked the witness: "There's no handle on this, is there?"

"No."

The judge: "Exhibit 43."

We excused the witness.

Chapter 27

VICTORIA, ALTHOUGH THE PROVINCIAL CAPITAL, IS A BACK-water media town, and the fourth estate was uncharacteristically slow to realize the news potential of the Frisbee trial. The city's one daily, *The Times-Colonist*, began covering the trial with its usual pedestrian, give-the-facts style of journalese, and it was not until the big Vancouver dailies perked up their ears that the case became a front-page celebration among the media.

By Thursday, December 4, the fourth day of trial, *The Vancouver Sun* and its little sister, the morning tabloid *The Province*, were in high gear. The *Sun*'s front page offered a teaser: "A courtroom drama with all the elements of a classy fiction whodunit" had opened in Victoria, wrote Larry Still.

Wealthy widow, luxury liner, $2,000-a-day-penthouse suite, blood-soaked bed, secret will: all the ingredients were there to convince Larry's editor to keep him in Victoria as long as it would take.

"A slight figure in a dark suit and tie, Frisbee sat quietly in the glass-backed prisoner's box, peering intently over the top of gold-rimmed bifocals as the trial proceeded," he wrote. "Lawyers in the trial, unfolding in a wood-paneled courtroom carpeted in crimson, add further class to the proceedings." They included "noted author William Deverell, whose crime novels are best-sellers," wrote Larry, whose review for the *Sun* of the noted author's first effort, *Needles*, had cruelly panned it as being over-violent and pornographic (thus propelling it onto the best-seller list).

Barbara McLintock, for *The Province*, also had a headline-grabbing lead: "He killed his rich boss before she could cut his

213

share of her multi-million dollar estate," she boldly wrote, acknowledging Dennis Murray, in his opening, as the author of this cruel allegation.

"A small, bespectacled man with straggly brown hair that refuses to stay tidy, Frisbee looks like a male secretary from a Charles Dickens novel," she wrote on another occasion, describing the trial as "a torrid tale of high society intrigue . . . a story of lust, greed and death rivetting the attention of sedate Victoria . . . Spectators addicted to the plot are jamming the courtroom."

Scooped by the print media, the television networks were quickly on the scene, but, unable to bring their cameras into the courthouse, they hired sketch artists who portrayed arm-waving lawyers (must remember to run a comb through my hair once in a while), a frowning judge, a scribbling Frisbee, earnest witnesses. Outside the courthouse entrances camera crews stood like watchdogs, forcing the lawyers to run the gamut each day.

"Are you going to write a book about it, Mr. Deverell?" one of them asked me.

"No," I said.

Soon the San Francisco papers were getting a daily feed, and reporters were flown in by the big Toronto dailies, *The Toronto Star* and *The Globe and Mail*. "Stuff of soaps," proclaimed the latter. "Courtroom spectacle offering intrigue not seen in a Canadian courtroom in many years," said the former, complete with "wise-cracking judge," jurors who "alternately appear mystified and bemused" and a "bestselling author of thrillers receiving the accolades of a fan as he puffs on a cigaret in the corridor during a break."

It was tempting to ask the judge to sequester the jury, to remove them to the lonely confines of a hotel to avoid being influenced by the onslaught of publicity, but we knew the judge would not accede. It is traditional in Canada merely to warn jurors not to follow media reports, and to confine them only after the final addresses by counsel and judge, granting them their freedom when a verdict is reached or the jury hung.

The press brought out the crowds, and by the Thursday of the first week, the benches of our courtroom were filled with drama-seekers and sensation-lovers, as well as the usual courtroom groupies, mostly older men and women who prefer (quite properly) a sex-and-blood murder trial to the tumid fare on the daily soaps.

Their curiosity did not go unrewarded that Thursday: the Crown called a witness who knew the Barnetts as intimately as anyone could, their maid of many years, an attractive, spunky immigrant from El Salvador blessed with the lyrical name of Milagro Romero Dearnaley. Millie to her friends.

Frisbee had told us he and Mrs. Dearnaley had formed a kind of gentle, kidding affection over the years, and that we were not to fear her. And in her interview with Russell Stetler, Lefcourt's investigator, she had described Frisbee as "a wonderful person." Yet she proposed to offer one piece of damaging evidence about which, during our pre-trial interview with her, she was adamant.

Assistant prosecutor Ernie Quantz first drew from her that she met Frisbee when she entered the Barnetts' employ in the spring of 1980. She worked as their maid five afternoons a week until Philip died, three a week after that.

What duties had she seen Frisbee perform? Ernie Quantz asked.

"He took care of the mail, answering things that needed to be answered, making arrangement for the Barnetts' social life, fixing Mr. Barnett's hair, Mrs. Barnett's hair. Was errand boy, everything the Barnetts asked for."

"How would you describe the relationship between Mr. and Mrs. Barnett?" Ernie asked.

"I think it was wonderful. He called her the bride all the time until he died."

"Was there ever any difficulties in their relationship that you saw?"

"Normal, like any marriage will have."

"All right. Somewhat like your own?"

"Right, like that."

"Maybe like Mr. Quantz's," I offered.

Ernie ignored me. "How would you describe the relationship between Mrs. Barnett and Mr. Frisbee?"

"I think it was really nice, they get along just fine."

Ernie asked her how Barnett and Frisbee managed their working relationship.

"Well, Mr. Barnett really didn't like Mr. Frisbee as a secretary and sometime he could be really nasty with him."

"And that would be when Mr. Frisbee did what?"

"Did mistake ... like he called him a lousy secretary making mistake with the letters and making mistake with the numbers and things like that."

Despite that, they were "extremely close."

Up to this point in the trial, no witness had confirmed just how close they'd become. Kolb had denied any suggestion of physical hanky-panky between Barnett and his submissive servant, and Frisbee was in danger of seeming a liar when he ultimately took the stand to give the bare facts, as it were.

When the FBI first interviewed Millie Dearnaley, several days after the murder, she had nobly defended Barnett's name. The FBI report recited:

"She advised that any allegations about Mr. Barnett's homosexuality are preposterous. Mr. Barnett was a 'real man.' She felt that Frisbee was a homosexual. She advised that Frisbee had a roommate, a Greek Orthodox priest by the name of Kazakes. She thought that Kazakes drank and smoked too much to be a priest."

But when FBI agent Jan Smith later interviewed Cammie Adams, manager of 1000 Chestnut, the story changed:

"Adams explained that Millie Romero Dearnaley, who was employed as Muriel Barnett's maid, told Adams she misrepresented certain facts to the interviewing agent. During Dearnaley's interview, she advised she did not believe Philip Barnett and Robert Frisbee maintained a homosexual relationship, when in fact she told Adams there was no doubt in her mind Barnett and Frisbee knew each other intimately. Dearnaley went on to say she purposely said this to protect her former employer's reputation, as she thought very highly of him. Adams further said Dearnaley related stories of dinner parties she was aware of wherein Daniel Kazakes would attend and would, at each one, become extremely inebriated."

Millie Dearnaley was not very fond of Kazakes.

On the stand at the trial, Mrs. Dearnaley recalled having seen

Frisbee and Philip Barnett sitting together in the TV room of the apartment.

"Mr. Frisbee was touching him, touching his genitals and then they were kissing their lips. That was on one occasion. Then he was helping Mr. Barnett to give a bath and Mr. Frisbee was touching again, and they have the door wide open, so I was again seeing kissing and Mr. Frisbee touching Mr. Barnett's genitals."

She observed such events on two or three occasions – when Mrs. Barnett was not in the apartment.

"I would like you to describe Mr. Frisbee's reaction to the death of Mr. Barnett."

"He was very upset. Long time after his death, we used to talk family matters, and then Mr. Frisbee jump into Mr. Barnett's death, looking at his picture and crying."

Frisbee had not hid his disappointment at not being remembered in Barnett's will.

"He was very unhappy, he was complaining around the building, with the managers, with the doormen, with everybody."

After Mrs. Barnett's neck accident, she "was in a really bad shape. She was very pale and used to cry of the pain."

Now came the bad part:

"You've indicated she was taking medication during this period?"

"She was. She really needed it."

"And were you able to observe whether that medication affected her in any way?"

"She looked like she was drunk. Her head go to the side and she talked very slow, and while you were talking to her, then she fall asleep."

"And who would be administering that medication to her?"

"Mr. Frisbee help her with that."

I looked at Frisbee. He shook his head.

This unhappy version did not match Frisbee's. He'd told us he did not in fact give Mrs. Barnett her medication. Her evidence was also contradicted by Dr. Musser's in San Francisco, where Jeff Green had asked him:

"There is no suggestion whatsoever that she was in some kind of bewildered state as a result of medication that she was on?"

"None at all."

Millie Dearnaley recalled that Mrs. Barnett's first outing since the accident was the lunch at the Frisbee-Kazakes apartment: Thanksgiving, November 22. Clearly she was wrong – the lunch was October 16, and Kolb had said he'd seen Mrs. Barnett at the World Trade Club three weeks after the October 10 accident.

One of Millie's functions, while Mrs. Barnett was away on her trips, was to collect the mail from the box and leave it on a table in the apartment. When her employer left for Alaska, she noticed that the mail had been disturbed. She had received no instructions that Kazakes would also have access to the apartment, but she saw him in the building:

"He came to park the car, then I saw him once getting out of the service elevator, and he was drunk. He looks scared when he saw me and he was very unfriendly, so he say, 'Hi, goodbye.'" The incident occurred a few days before she learned of Mrs. Barnett's death.

Ernie concluded his examination-in-chief. It was six minutes to lunch break. The judge asked if I wanted to start cross-examination now or at 2:00 p.m. I picked up the hint, and we adjourned until the afternoon.

By 2:00 p.m. Ernie had thought of another question. Justice McKenzie naturally gave him permission to reopen.

"I knew I should have started my cross-examination," I complained.

"Well, that's the price you pay," said the judge.

"Mrs. Dearnaley, at one point did you decide to leave the employment of Mrs. Barnett?"

"Yes, I did."

That was shortly before the Alaska trip, and Mrs. Dearnaley discussed her decision with Frisbee.

"And what did Mr. Frisbee say to you?"

"Well, first he told me that I should stay because Mrs. Barnett was very fond of me, and she really need me, but then I told him I . . . I was not going to put up with a lot of things, so he said, 'Better stay 'cause you are in the will.'"

I wasn't sure what the intended effect of that evidence was: Mrs. Barnett's original will (not the codicil) included a $5,000 gift to

Mrs. Dearnaley "if she is still in my employ at the time of my death."

Frisbee did her a favor in telling her about it, I suggested to her in my cross-examination.

"I didn't think it was that much, anyhow," she said. Millie Dearnaley was underwhelmed by the generosity.

I asked her how she came to be hired by Philip Barnett.

"He just came and, 'Millie, come close to me where I see you. Turn around. Turn to the other side. You look pretty. You are hired.' That's all."

At the time she thought Frisbee was their son, "or something very close to the family."

She got along with him "very good."

"Just before this trip to Alaska did he leave you with any chores to do?"

"Yeah, he left me some handmade things that he said belonged to his grandmother. I was going to iron for him and give it him back when he returned."

"So they would be ready," I asked innocently, "when he and Mrs. Barnett returned?"

"Exactly."

Every little piece of evidence that suggested Frisbee didn't leave on that trip with murder on his mind would help.

"Just prior to that trip to Alaska was he acting differently or unusually, or . . ."

"Not at all, no."

"Didn't seem weird or tense or anything like that?"

"No, no, no. He was really happy to go on that trip. He even had a hat and he said he was going to be the captain of the ship. He was dancing all over the apartment."

"In his captain's hat?"

She nodded. I could picture it. So could the jury. Some of them were looking at Frisbee and smiling. Frisbee looked embarrassed.

I went through the usual questions about Muriel Barnett not wanting people nosing into her business, then asked her to confirm that after her husband's death Mrs. Barnett started spending money more freely.

"For herself, yes."

"For herself. Like what?"

"Extravagant clothing, more furs, going out more frequently, inviting a lot of friends to different clubs."

"And she would buy outfits from the very best shops in San Francisco?"

"Very much, yes."

"Her favorite color was what?"

"Light blue."

"What color was her bathroom?"

"Same color, light blue."

"What color was Mr. Barnett's bathroom?"

"Pink."

I thought I'd throw that entertaining trivia in.

In her interview with private investigator Russell Stetler, Millie Dearnaley said Mrs. Barnett liked to support charities where "her name was going to blow up," but was not truly generous "between her heart and God." I pushed her a bit about this.

"My opinion?" she asked.

"Yeah."

"She wasn't too generous."

Particularly with Frisbee: "for what he deserved."

The judge took over: "Excuse me a moment. You don't think she was very generous?"

"Not in my personal opinion, no." Feisty Millie was clearly not all that enamored of her employer. "Mr. Frisbee get some of the things but not because she really was generous. I think he deserved a lot of those things."

The judge: "He deserved a lot of those things?"

"Yes, he really did more than was necessary."

For some reason the judge seemed troubled by this. Maybe he wasn't seeing it the same way as I. He asked: "So you are saying Mr. Frisbee got things because he deserved them not because she was being generous?"

"Exactly."

I pushed it as far as I could go: "He was practically her slave?"

"In a way."

Frisbee, she agreed, had had no private life. But he never complained.

220

I asked her to recall a conversation she had with Frisbee after Mr. Barnett died.

"I asked him why he did so many thing, I couldn't understand, it's too much. Then he said, 'I promised Phil that I'll take care of his bride until she died.'"

As to Mrs. Barnett's drinking habits: "She drank a lot for her age."

"What do you mean by a lot?"

"Like two bottles for lunch sometimes."

Justice McKenzie seemed shocked. "Two bottles for lunch?" he asked.

"She could drink it easy."

"Two bottles of what?" I asked.

"Wine, whatever."

She agreed that on the night of Mrs. Barnett's accident, she was so drunk she couldn't find her own floor from the elevator. She hated being seen by the public in her neck brace, and refused visitors while recuperating. When Millie Dearnaley was impertinent enough to ask her why, she got a sharp response: "'Whatever goes on in my house, that's only between you and Robert.'"

Frisbee's drinking?

"A lot of the time he show up drunk, was shaking, he was pale, he fall asleep on the couch, he forgot things. He jump in one conversation to another."

After the London trip, he'd been told by Mrs. Barnett to recuperate, not to show up for work for a month. "But he still comes, he show up in bad shape."

Frisbee also developed serious memory problems, she said.

"He would forget what happened on the previous day?"

"Most likely, yes."

"Not to mention the previous week?"

"Never mind the previous week."

I connected these problems to Philip Barnett's death. They continued, following that, she said, over a year and a half. "He told me he was lost without Mr. Barnett."

She'd never known Frisbee to perform any act of violence or raise his voice to anyone. He was a "very soft person, very loving."

Millie Dearnaley had earlier asked me if she could talk to

221

Frisbee, to wish him well. I didn't see why not. As court recessed, I guided Millie to the prisoner's dock. She gave him a hug. The jurors watched as they filed out. They would know Frisbee was not being deserted by his real friends.

Before the sheriffs marched Frisbee away, he adjusted my bib and my robes. (He often did that; he just couldn't stand the way I sloppily presented myself.)

Larry Still's story the next morning: "Dearnaley told the jury she once saw Frisbee fondling Barnett's genitals and kissing him on the mouth as the prominent lawyer sat in a chair with his feet on a stool," and later "while bathing him in his pink bathroom."

"Gay feelies in the pink bathroom," as one newspaper chose to describe it. The next morning there was not an empty seat in the place.

One of the courtroom regulars asked me if I was going to write a book about the case. I said no, I only write fiction.

Chapter 28

SEVERAL TASKS CHALLENGED THE DEFENSE IN OUR HANDLING of the several shipboard witnesses to be called. To make out the defense of automatism it was necessary to show that Frisbee was very much in a dazed state when the crew found him in Penthouse Six. To lay the groundwork for the defense of drunkenness, we would hopefully show that Frisbee exhibited signs of having been seriously under the effects of alcohol. Some witness statements supported our case for intoxication; others clearly didn't.

The problem: Frisbee had carried on intelligible conversations with crew members after the body was discovered, had made telephone calls from the suite, and he hadn't been staggering, falling, or slurring his speech. Frisbee had, of course, trained himself over the years to appear sober when drunk, and our medical evidence would indicate that the shock of discovering Muriel Barnett's body would cause an immediate, adrenalin-stimulated sobering effect.

We would also want to canvass with the ship's witnesses the possibility that a third person may have been in the room, a thief-murderer perhaps. Although we were not betting all our chips that a defense based on that theme would succeed, it was vital to leave open to the jury a verdict based on Frisbee's total innocence – or the judge might take that verdict from the jury. We felt that many of the curious circumstances surrounding the timing of the murder weighed against the likelihood of Frisbee being the perpetrator – unless he was very drunk.

Another area we would tackle involved an accusation that he had deliberately staged an accidental fall on the part of Mrs.

Barnett. The Crown would be adducing much credible evidence to this effect.

Finally, we wanted to show that Frisbee's demeanor both before and after the murder was not that of a man consumed with a murderous passion. In this regard we expected some help from a couple of shipmates whom Frisbee and Mrs. Barnett had befriended.

A couple of days out of San Francisco they had struck up a chatting acquaintance with Max and Thelma Biegert, comfortably retired Arizonans from Paradise Valley, a suburb of Phoenix, who occupied a cabin on the promenade deck.

The Biegerts were the last persons to have seen Muriel alive. They'd spent the day with her and Frisbee, touring Victoria.

Jeff and I had read their prior interviews and talked with them: both were engaging, honest, and concerned. They'd taken a liking to their odd shipmates.

Their first conversation was struck up over a piece of jewelry that Thelma Biegert observed Mrs. Barnett to be wearing, a gold elephant brooch encrusted with diamonds and emeralds.

They shared drinks in the different bars of the ship, and Frisbee became voluble and open in their presence, describing his history with the Barnetts, even letting them know – according to the FBI's interviews with them – that he was named in Muriel's will.

Investigator Stetler's report stated: "Mrs. Biegert said she found Mrs. Barnett and Mr. Frisbee 'fun people to be with' and 'just enjoyable.' Mrs. Barnett appeared 'well-traveled,' and Mr. Frisbee 'such a sensitive person.' Mrs. Barnett was 'not well in the first place,' but she was enjoying the cruise. Mrs. Barnett and Frisbee were 'so fond of each other that it was kind of like a mother-son relationship.'

"Mrs. Biegert said that the crime in her opinion 'just doesn't make sense.' She added that it 'blows my mind' to think that Frisbee is charged in this case, since acts of violence would appear to be so remote from his temperament. She noted that quite a number of people on the ship's staff would have had keys to the Barnett-Frisbee suite, at least by inference from the number of people who had access to the Biegerts' rooms."

Mrs. Barnett had told Thelma Biegert she owned a number of

valuable pieces of jewelry, and the possibility the elderly woman had been robbed and murdered was clearly in her mind.

On the witness stand, Max Biegert described to Dennis Murray a limousine tour of Victoria that the foursome had made. Mrs. Barnett had leased the car. "She didn't like to go on tour buses. She asked us to accompany them."

They met at the dock at 11:00 a.m. and set out in the limousine to do the sights: the tidy city, Butchart Gardens' acres of floral display, Fable Cottage's gingerbread and elves, with a stop for lunch at Chauney's, one of Victoria's older and better downtown restaurants.

While the two women went to the restaurant's restroom, Frisbee ordered vodka on the rocks for himself and Mrs. Barnett. Her drink was waiting for her when she got back.

"Mrs. Barnett asked Robert Frisbee what cocktail she had, what it was. And he said, 'It's vodka on the rocks.' And then she asked him, 'Robert, what do you have?' and he said, 'I have Perrier.'"

I had no problems with drink-sneaking Frisbee's little white lie. Muriel Barnett had told him to tone down his drinking, and was probably monitoring him.

They returned to the ship at 4:30, half an hour before sailing, and arranged to meet at the captain's farewell party that evening, said Mr. Biegert.

"We had made arrangements, as I recall, to meet in the Venus Room or some lounge. I think it was 6:30 or 6:45 we were to meet there, the four of us."

Max Biegert was asked to describe Frisbee's demeanor that day.

"Well, we had a very nice day, he was very attentive to Mrs. Barnett, there was nothing that indicated any friction, any problem, any tensions or pressures between anyone."

When Frisbee and Mrs. Barnett failed to show up at the captain's farewell party, Mr. Biegert testified that they went on to dinner by themselves. A waiter handed them a note which simply read, "Call Bob," giving a cabin number.

"So I dialed him on the phone about 11:30, he answered, and I said: 'Robert, this is Max,' and he said, 'Yes, Max, it's terrible, Muriel is dead.' And I was really taken aback, and I said, 'Bob, well, what happened?' He says, 'Well, she was dead. I was taking a nap and I woke up in my cabin and she was on the bed with blood all over and she was dead.'"

The next morning, they talked on the phone again, Frisbee asking if they would come by his cabin and talk with him. This was the cabin in which the captain placed Frisbee under ship arrest.

"There was a guard there, and he let us in, and we went in his room and talked with him for about half an hour."

Frisbee gave few more details of his ordeal of the night before. He'd awakened from his nap, he told the Biegerts, and found Mrs. Barnett partly on the bed, her knees on the floor.

The three of them then went up to the Biegerts' cabin, the guard docilely following them, then remaining outside their door.

"Then while we were in the room our telephone rang." It was a call from San Francisco for Frisbee, but Biegert didn't know from whom. (Apparently this was Kazakes.) The caller delivered more bad news for Bob Frisbee: his wicked stepmother, Muriel Frisbee, Dwight's ex-wife, had just expired in Guerneville, California. On the very day that Muriel Barnett was killed.

"Well, what else can happen?" was Frisbee's dejected comment as he put the phone down.

They left the cabin for drinks in the Neptune Bar.

"And the guard – I don't know what happened, but the guard didn't follow us, and we walked out of the cabin, and there was no guard or anything around us."

There followed a Keystone Cops-like search for Frisbee aboard the vessel. The guard, one Olav Rugholm, quartermaster, was not summoned to Victoria to give evidence. As with other members of the ship's staff he had never been informed that Frisbee was suspected of murder and doubtless wasn't taking his duties with utmost seriousness. He later told a sheriff's officer in Norway, however, he had indeed caught up to the three at the Neptune Bar.

From the interview with the sheriff:

"As the witness was wearing work clothes, he was unable to follow the accused and the couple into the Neptune Bar, so he ran to the outside of the bar along a glass wall in order to, if possible, keep watch in a discreet manner. However he lost sight of the three of them and immediately reported this to the bridge over the radio. A search was instituted all over the ship."

The ship's officers stubbornly refused to make any formal shipboard announcement about Muriel's mysterious death, probably feeling it unwise to concern their passengers with the thought that a murderous psychopath might be on the loose. Although the crew were admonished not to speak to anyone about it, rumors abounded. G.L. Abrahamsen, who occupied a stateroom neighboring the Barnett suite, recalled hearing that the guard outside Frisbee's cabin had fallen asleep, and later observed ship's officers patroling in pairs in the search for Frisbee. Other rumors had Frisbee escaping or jumping over the side. But they "found him at lunch at his usual table," Abrahamsen said.

After a couple of hours, Frisbee and the Biegerts were found in the Bergen Lounge having a sandwich. Frisbee had drunk some champagne but wasn't intoxicated, according to Rugholm. "After he was found in the Bergen Lounge he was taken back to his cabin on Deck Three," said the Norwegian sheriff's report.

One might have thought the ship's officers would have turned the ship around, brought her into Victoria or some other nearby port, and summoned police to the vessel. But the captain stayed the course, and merely ordered Muriel's body delivered to a cold storage unit, radioing ahead to the San Francisco police and the Norwegian consulate there.

Dennis concluded his examination-in-chief of Max Biegert by drawing from him evidence that was not particularly helpful to our drunkenness defense. During their late-night phone conversation on August 19, Frisbee "was very, very coherent, and very direct in what his comments were."

In cross-examination, I asked Max Biegert: "In the course of your conversations with Mrs. Barnett, I understand you had learned something about her state of health?"

"Yes, I think she told Thelma that she had cancer."

This was important to us, because Frisbee would later be telling the jury that during his lunch with Muriel a few weeks before the Alaska cruise (the lunch at which she announced her plans to make large gifts of cash to him and Kazakes) she stated she was having "symptoms." Frisbee had assumed she was referring to a recurrence of cancer. (That might have been an additional reason for her sudden bout of generosity; she knew she couldn't take her fortune with her.)

This suggestion of a returning cancer was also verified by a paragraph near the end of Frisbee's manuscript: "We got along very well, but we were straining our relationship progressively. I really will go all out for a private room. She felt, and with reason, she wanted absolute control over my waking hours. She was not well, and had the same vague symptoms as she had previously when the doctor said, 'Cancer.' She just did not want to be alone any more."

During the Victoria tour, Frisbee didn't seem at all tense, Biegert said. Nothing unusual about his demeanor. The witness characterized Frisbee as having seemed a very gentle person.

I showed him a Polaroid snapshot taken – by their chauffeur – of the four of them during one of the Victoria stops. (It was found in the Barnett suite.)

"And all four of you are standing there smiling quite happily?"

"Oh, yes, we'd had a nice day."

Thelma Biegert confirmed her husband's evidence as to Frisbee's demeanor in Victoria.

"They were charming as always in your company?" I asked her.

"Yes."

"No indication of any tenseness on the part of Robert Frisbee?"

"No."

On their return from the tour, Muriel Barnett told her she was going to have a shower and a lie-down. That was the last time the Biegerts saw her.

When Frisbee and Mrs. Barnett didn't show up for the captain's party, Thelma Biegert recalled – although Mr. Biegert didn't mention this in his evidence – that she and her husband went by Mrs. Barnett's penthouse suite shortly after 6:30 p.m. They didn't knock. It was deathly quiet in there.

Chapter 29

MICHAEL GEORGIOU MICHAEL, THE BUTLER WHO DIDN'T DO IT, was one of the Crown's key shipboard witnesses, the first to see the body. Flown to the Victoria trial from Cyprus, he took advantage of the government's offer to pay for the companion of his choice. He brought along his mother.

In police interviews just after the murder he had seemed over-wrought, excitable, unable to remember clearly the scene in Pent-house Six. In my own interview with him he impressed as the kind of witness capable perhaps of error, but not prevarication.

Ernie Quantz intended to call evidence from him which would imply to the jury that Frisbee had attempted to disguise Mrs. Barnett's death as resulting from an accidental fall. He led up to that carefully.

"You basically attend to the needs of the passengers on the penthouse deck?"

"Every needs they have, plus your duties to make sure they have everything, canapés, caviar, lobster, anything they want."

Each morning he would serve Mrs. Barnett and Frisbee break-fast, each evening bring a tray of canapés to their room, he said.

"I asked Mrs. Barnett the first day: 'What would you like normally before you go downstairs for dinner at 7:30?' and she says to me she loves caviar, so every night I used to bring caviar for her the same time." At 6:45 every night. Ironically, the very time of death of Muriel Barnett on Monday, August 19.

Michael duly showed up that Monday evening with his caviar and canapés. "I knock the door and then I got an answer from inside the penthouse. 'Who is it?' And then I answer, 'Michael, sir, I bring the caviar for Mrs. Barnett.'"

"Wait a minute," came a voice. The voice of Robert Frisbee.

"And that's the gentleman seated here in the prisoner's dock?" Ernie asked.

Michael looked over to Frisbee and beamed a smile at him. "Yes. Hi."

Frisbee looked up from his notes, a little startled. He smiled back.

Ernie asked what happened next.

"Suddenly Penthouse Eight which is next door, he opened the door and we started talking, and I asked him how your day because custom to ask the passenger how's your day, did you have a nice day and all this. And then the door open and Mr. Frisbee holding his head and he told me she's dead. He was . . . looked shock. All I did, I walk in here, she was lying bed here."

He was asked what Frisbee was wearing.

"A trouser."

"Do you recall if he had anything on his upper body?"

"Um, I think a shirt but not, not closed – open shirt. White shirt."

Mrs. Barnett, he said, was lying on her back on the bed, "looking up at the ceiling." Presumably through sightless eyes.

This innocuous-seeming evidence, that Muriel Barnett's body was supine upon the bed when he first saw her, carried dangerous ramifications for Frisbee, because the stewardesses who arrived soon after would testify they observed the body in a kneeling position at the side of the bed, her head and upper torso on the pillow. The inference: Frisbee had, between Michael's hurried departure from the suite and the stewardesses' arrival, moved the body to that position in an attempt to fake her injuries as resulting from an accidental fall, perhaps against the night stand.

"I have realized could be physical death. And right away I walk out the door. I told the stewardesses. And right after, I went to our pantry and I called the nurse, the captain of the ship and the doctor."

A few minutes later the doctor came running down the corridor. "The doctor asked Mr. Frisbee what's happened. He says he thought she fall on the dressing table."

He followed the doctor into the stateroom. Frisbee was sitting on a couch.

"Myself, I left right away so I don't know what's happened afterwards."

"Did you see him walk at all?"

"Yeah, he walk."

"Did he have any difficulty in walking?"

"No."

"When you saw Mr. Frisbee the second time you came back, how would you describe his emotional condition?"

"Different because of what happened."

"How was it different?"

"Not . . . not normal."

"Are you able to explain that?"

"Shock, I say, shock."

"How long was it between the time you left Penthouse Six and when you returned?"

"Well, the stewardesses, they came first. I can say after ten seconds, ten-fifteen seconds."

That struck me as a very brief time for Frisbee to have changed the position of Mrs. Barnett's body to a kneeling one.

I could have started my cross-examination, but the day had been a long one, and evening adjournment was only minutes away. And we had made up for lost time. The judge agreed to let me commence the next morning.

◇   ◇   ◇

Although Frisbee had told everyone within earshot he didn't know what happened, he also kept insisting that Muriel had probably hit her head in a fall. The Crown planned to make a lot of hay out of the suggestion that Frisbee contrived a scenario of accidental death in those seconds that Michael left him alone in their suite. My cross-examination would be directed to showing that Michael was in such an agitated state when he first entered the suite that he had made a simple error of observation.

Legal case histories are replete with examples of careless perception on the part of witnesses to crimes, and of errors made when reconstructing one's memory of them. The steel-trap minds of the most meticulous observer become unhinged in moments of turmoil. It was unlikely that Michael Michael, so excitable and easily flustered, could be accused of maintaining the cool detachment of, say, a hardened police officer when observing a newly bloodied corpse in a blood-spattered room.

The next morning, Friday, Justice McKenzie asked that we quit early for the weekend to permit him an early ferry back to Vancouver:

"If possible let's not have a witness who comes from Siberia and wants to catch a train. Can you handle that?"

Dennis assured him he could. He was equally confident that the Crown would have all its evidence in by the following Thursday. That would allow a week for defense evidence and summations. We seemed to be on schedule to obtain a verdict while the Christmas spirit was still with us. And hopefully with the good people of the jury.

When the jurors were called in, Michael Michael bounded like an eager rabbit to the stand.

I asked him about the bon voyage party in San Francisco. He recalled thirty to thirty-five people being there.

"Everyone was coming and bringing bottles."

"And did you bring more bottles in yourself?"

"I remember some champagne."

"In addition, you provided three complimentary bottles of alcohol?"

"Bottle of Smirnoff's vodka, whiskey . . . Black Label and Jack Daniels."

"And a bottle of champagne?"

"Mumm's."

I confirmed that his invariable routine was to show up at the Barnett cabin at 6:45 each evening with his canapés. It was essential to establish that Frisbee, on August 19, had been expecting Michael to turn up at that time, and must have known it would be a very inconvenient moment to commit a murder.

On each occasion Michael would knock at the door, be answered, and walk inside with his tray.

On August 19, he came on evening duty at 6:30 and first attended to a couple of "big parties" on the penthouse deck.

"Were they noisy parties?"

"Loud parties."

Then he took his tray to Penthouse Six. "And that was about what time?"

"6:45."

"Did you check your watch?"

"Yes."

He said he found the door unlocked:

"If you are outside the door you can realize whether it's locked or not locked. There is a white color and a red color, that means . . ."

He struggled to explain. "An indicator," I said.

The white color meant the door is unlocked, he said, and the lock showed white that evening. Also, when Frisbee opened it for him, he did not hear the clicking sound that lets one know the door is fastened from the inside.

This was good evidence for us, if one assumes that a coldly calculating murderer prefers to perform his deed behind a locked door.

Frisbee opened the door "thirty seconds to a minute" after Michael announced himself.

"Now, when you came into the suite you saw Mrs. Barnett lying on the bed?"

"Yeah, that's right."

"You said she was lying on her back looking up?"

Michael seemed suddenly unsure: "If you see somebody with all blood all over the places you no stand there to figure out whether it's this side or this side. What I remember her face was facing with eyes open, so that's . . . I ran away to ask for help."

"You were pretty excited, weren't you?"

"Shocked."

"Fair enough, and you just don't remember if the body was lying on her back, side, or what position on the bed. You glanced in and you ran out?"

"Glanced and I run. But it was facing . . . I remember, I can see her face, and eyes open. But if you see somebody full of blood you don't wait to figure out how she is there, you know."

But he insisted that her entire body – however she was facing – was on top of the bed. "Her whole body, she was on the bed. That's no doubt. But if you, from two, three feet, you can see somebody about five kilos of blood and everything, you cannot figure out this side or this side, because you see blood, you know, it is something which for me I remember always."

"It was very confusing for you at the time, wasn't it?"

"Yeah, I would say that."

That was about as far as I could take him. My suspicion was that what he was really remembering was Mrs. Barnett's position after Michael had followed the doctor into the suite, by which time the stewardesses had lifted her body back onto the bed. But I would save that for later argument to the jury.

"You exited from this door and shouted as soon as you got out the door?"

"No, I left it open."

"I'm sorry, I didn't mean 'shut it,' but you *shouted*, you yelled for the stewardesses?"

"I shouted the whole ship. You know, if you see somebody dead in front of you, you shout the whole ship."

I smiled at this. "You shout the whole ship, you bet you do."

"You get them up."

Frisbee, he said, was standing motionless in the living room when he went for help. The two women came running to the suite "five to ten seconds" later, an even shorter time lapse than he had earlier estimated.

I was positioned now to argue that in the several seconds before the stewardesses arrived it was improbable if not impossible that Frisbee had time to walk into the bedroom, carefully reposition the body, then return to the living room where the stewardesses found him.

Chapter 30

EVA ANNA KERSTIN FALK, ONE OF THE STEWARDESSES MICHAEL summoned, seemed much cooler of head than the butler. She was a slim, attractive Austrian who gave careful, measured evidence.

"Me and my assistant were working in Penthouse One and cleaning up the penthouse, and then the butler, Michael, came in to us," she told Dennis Murray. "And he said, 'Miss Eva, Miss Eva, you have to come to Penthouse Six. Mr. Frisbee said that he thinks that Mrs. Barnett is dead.' So then the two of us run into Penthouse Six. We saw Mrs. Barnett lying in the bedroom with her head on the bed and kneeling, kneeling with her eyes on the floor and her head on the bed, and she looked lifeless, and Mr. Frisbee was standing up in the living room.

"We took her up and placed her on her back on one of the beds, and my assistant is a nurse, and she took the pulse, and also I phoned the doctor."

She asked Frisbee what happened. He said, "I think she fell."

The doctor came a few minutes later, and Falk left the suite.

Dennis asked her how Frisbee looked and acted.

"What I recall from Mr. Frisbee was that he was very calm."

I was unsure what she meant by "calm." It seemed an inappropriate reaction to his employer's death.

"First he was standing, looking at us, and then he was sitting on the couch looking out the window facing the balcony."

In cross-examination she told me that in addition to the bottles Michael described as having been delivered to the suite, she remembered Mrs. Barnett ordering "thirteen small piccolo Henkell Trocken champagne."

"And who brought those into the suite?"

"This was like a gift order for her that was to be put into the fridge before she arrived."

She remembered seeing Frisbee knitting one day, as she was cleaning up the suite.

"He was knitting maybe a pullover, I don't know."

"A pullover, a sweater of some kind?"

"Yeah, something like that."

"You had a conversation with him about it?"

"Yeah, because you are knitting differently in the States, I think, than we do in Europe, and I said, 'You are knitting in a strange way,' and then we had a small conversation over that."

"Did you use the words, 'Are you the one who's been knitting Mrs. Barnett's beautiful sweaters and coats?'"

"Um-hmm, that could be the one."

"And Mrs. Barnett made some comment about another coat that he had knitted?"

"Um-hmm."

"And she seemed proud of it?"

"Yes."

"They were in good spirits on that occasion?"

"Yeah."

"You never saw them quarreling with each other?"

"No."

I asked about his demeanor as he stood staring out the balcony door after Mrs. Barnett's death: "His face was expressionless?"

"Yes."

"Can you agree with me that he appeared to be in a state of shock?"

"Could be. That I can't say."

"He wasn't moving?"

"No."

"Just staring?"

"Yeah, he was . . . emotionless."

Obviously that is what she meant by calm. I hoped the jury would correctly interpret that as evidence Frisbee was in a state of shock.

The other stewardess was another story. Jeannette Helan, a

petite young Swede, had been altogether traumatized by the death scene, and I realized this when I interviewed her before she took the stand. She was extremely nervous – perhaps not so much in anticipation of a courtroom ordeal as being forced to recall the events to her mind.

She told me she had carefully written down all details of the incident she could remember, sent her notes home to Sweden and, inexplicably, never looked at them again.

Of all the shipboard witnesses, she was the only one clearly antipathetic to Frisbee, and you didn't have to be a Dan Kazakes to pick up on the vibes: she thought him guilty, a cold-blooded killer of helpless old ladies. She'd endured awful nightmares later, she told me. I wasn't sure how I would handle her in court: she seemed wired as tight as a time bomb.

Clearly, Dennis Murray intended her as his star witness.

She'd been a qualified nurse for three years, but chose to work instead in the more menial capacity of a cruise-ship stewardess, and perhaps with her delicacy of temperament she found such work less stressful.

She testified that on August 19 she started work at 6:30 p.m., intending to clean up Penthouse One, but before entering that suite, while still in the corridor, she heard a "banging noise."

How many banging noises had she heard? Dennis asked.

"Two, three."

"Were they separated by a lot of time or were they all together?"

"All together."

"And did you have any difficulty hearing them?"

"No."

"Could you tell the court exactly where they were coming from?"

"No."

She joined Eva Falk in Penthouse One, and was making up the suite when Michael came in – ten or fifteen minutes after hearing those thumps. She went to Penthouse Six, a journey she said took her "one, two minutes," a time lapse, I recall thinking, that seemed improbably lengthy, especially given Michael's estimates, varying from five to fifteen seconds.

Frisbee was standing in the living room when she arrived. Dennis asked her to identify him. She looked around, saw him in the dock, and pointed. "Right," she said, "that one." And quickly looked away.

Helan went to the bedroom, saw Mrs. Barnett on her knees, her upper body lying on the bed.

Dennis showed her a photo of the bloodied bed and asked her to draw Mrs. Barnett's position on it. She sketched a stick figure, a body kneeling, her head in the pool of blood near the headboard. The witness was clearly having some problems holding her feelings in by now, and her voice was almost inaudible.

"Which way was her face facing?" Dennis asked.

"Facing down."

The stewardesses lifted her onto the bed and Helan felt for a pulse and found none. The doctor soon arrived, and attempted a tracheotomy, sending Helan out to get some clean sheets.

Helan went first to the bathroom of Penthouse Six to wash her hands and there found a towel on the floor, smeared with blood. Then she saw another towel in the wash basin, also showing blood.

Frisbee had told us he was standing in this bathroom when he returned to a conscious state of mind. Her evidence could suggest he was trying to wash blood from his person.

She fetched clean sheets, and the doctor covered the body with them. She was then instructed to call the staff captain from the phone in the living room. At some point she sat beside him on the couch.

"What was Mr. Frisbee wearing?"

"Tuxedo pants."

"Were the pants done up?"

"The zipper was open."

Robert Frisbee, with his zipper open? Not at all like the man . . . unless he was in shock, or very drunk.

"And were you able to see if Mr. Frisbee had underwear on underneath?"

"No underwears."

His state, she said, was "normal."

Dennis asked her what words passed between them.

"I asked him if he was married to the lady."

"And what did he say?"

"'No.'"

"Yes?"

"And I asked . . . I can't remember what I asked him."

She was clearly having problems. Dennis pressed her, and she recalled Frisbee telling her he was the woman's secretary.

"Yes?"

"And I can't remember . . ."

Dennis, in difficulty, became bold.

"Okay, did you ask him what happened to the lady –"

I rose. "She has said she can't remember, now my friend is putting questions to her which are leading to answers."

Justice McKenzie let him rephrase and he finally got his answer:

"He said to me that he was taking a nap and she had fell down on the edge of the table just between the beds. And that he woke up and saw her on the bed, laying on the bed like this, and that she has been falling before for half a year ago or one year ago, really bad, and that it was not the first time it happened."

Dennis appeared relieved at this abrupt improvement of memory. He asked her to recall the condition of the other bed, Frisbee's.

"It was . . . the bed was not touched by somebody who has been taking a nap on the bed."

I suspected she was over-reaching. Photographs showed his bed was indeed creased, and a blue comforter was on top of it, considerably rumpled.

"Now, during this conversation what was his emotional state?"

"He was answering my questions well." Her voice dropped again. "And I think that he was pretend crying."

Justice McKenzie: "You thought that he was crying?"

"Pretend crying."

Dennis, milking as much impact from this as possible, walked to the far wall of the courtroom: "Would you shout over here at me. Would you mind raising your voice up a little bit? What was it that led you to think that he was pretending to cry?"

"He didn't . . . there was no tears and he was very calm after he has taken away his hands from his face."

Dennis asked her to demonstrate. She put her hands to her face, withdrew them.

"And when he took away his hands, no tears?"

"No tears."

"Was he saying anything?"

"He said, 'She was a nice lady. Nice lady, nice, fine lady.'"

"Was he making any noises like crying?"

"Yes."

I stayed firmly planted in my chair. To object to this leading question would only prolong the agony of his painting of my client as an emotional charlatan.

Dennis prompted her to describe a couple of telephone calls Frisbee made from the suite:

"He want to phone a nephew in London, and . . . I think it was a lady lawyer in San Francisco."

The nephew presumably was Muriel Barnett's godson, Jason Cope. The lady lawyer? How she had surmised that, I did not know. The fact is, according to the ship's radio officer, Frisbee completed only one call from the suite – at 7:36 p.m. – collect to Dan Kazakes, a call that lasted fifteen seconds and which Frisbee ended abruptly. Frisbee also tried to contact the Copes in London, but didn't get through.

Helan remembered Frisbee saying on the telephone: "The lady, she is dead." She couldn't remember his other words. The call lasted "a couple of minutes" and he was "a bit upset" during it.

(Dan Kazakes's version of the phone call, as given in his evidence in San Francisco, was more emphatic: "He was hysterical, absolutely hysterical. He said, 'Dan, I come out of the bathroom and she's laying there and she has some blood on her,' and then the ship-to-shore radio went out." He had no memory of Frisbee telling him that Muriel was dead, and insisted he thought she was alive but injured. Nor did he remember his call to Frisbee the next day, in the Biegerts' suite. Probably his clouded recall was due to the fact that he was "ill" at that time – for which read, presumably, in a state of severe alcoholic confusion.)

"Did he make a second call?" Dennis asked.

"Yes."

"Was there any conversation in that one, or did it not go through?"

I refused to continue biting my tongue. "My lord, my friend has been taking his questions a little too far each time. Let's hear her evidence, not my friend's evidence."

"That was leading, Mr. Murray," the judge said.

The witness said she couldn't remember if that call went through.

"Now, how long did you have this conversation with Mr. Frisbee?"

"No idea."

"Can you tell us if it was more than five minutes –"

I rose and said brusquely, "Here we go again, this is cross-examination. She said, 'No idea.'"

The judge nodded: "Yes."

"Now he is trying to pin her down," I complained.

Dennis snapped back: "Well, I accept that my learned friend is concerned about the evidence, as I would be if I were in his shoes –"

"I want to hear the evidence from this witness," I barked, "and I don't want to hear it from my friend." In a Canadian or British courtroom, the word "friend" is often a euphemism for some more appropriate descriptive noun.

Justice McKenzie tried to calm the waters. "Just a moment, there is no need to raise voices, I can hear all right. You see, the difficulty is that the witness will say that he or she has no idea and of course a witness does have an idea, but doesn't have a precise idea. I think it is proper to ask this witness, Can you, to the best of your ability, estimate the time?"

I didn't think Dennis needed all this generous help.

"Between half an hour, an hour," Helan said. During which time Frisbee seemed to have no problem understanding her questions and gave responsive answers.

And she saw him get up and walk a few feet, apparently without difficulty.

At some point, at his request, she poured him a glass of champagne. Dennis asked her how he appeared "from a drunkenness point of view."

"Not drunk. That's what you mean?"

"Yes."

"Yes, sober."

Dennis, more than pleased with this portrayal of Frisbee as a sober and cunning tragedian, a weeper of crocodile tears, sat down, and cordially tendered the witness to me for cross.

Chapter 31

I REALIZED I HAD ALLOWED MYSELF TO GET ROILED DURING those angry exchanges with Dennis, and warned myself to simmer down – Jeannette Helan was a witness to be handled with kid gloves. But she had caused much damage to the defense, and would have to be confronted, and her bias against Frisbee unmasked.

"Miss Helan, you met Mr. Frisbee earlier in the voyage, did you not?"

"Yes."

"On a few occasions?"

"Yes."

"You met Mrs. Barnett as well?"

"Yes."

"And they seemed to have a normal, friendly relationship?"

"Yes."

I guessed she'd been coached to keep her answers to me short. After about ten one-syllable answers in a row I asked her: "Did Mr. Murray ask you to simply answer yes or no to my questions?"

"No."

She agreed that all the passengers knew the stewardesses came by in the evening after 6:30 to clean the suites. (This would add to the unlikelihood that Frisbee, in a conscious state of mind, would choose that busy time to commit murder behind unlocked doors.)

She recalled that after Michael ran down the hall shouting the ship, she and Eva Falk went immediately to Penthouse Six.

"Did you run there?"

"Yes."

"It only took you a few seconds to get from one cabin to the other?"

"Yes."

So much for her earlier "one, two minutes." I asked a series of questions to test her powers of observation:

"When you arrived there, Mr. Frisbee was where?"

"In the living room."

"Looking in what direction?"

"That I don't remember. I could see his face."

"What was the expression on his face?"

"That I don't know."

"You can't say whether his face appeared to be of a person in shock, or–"

"No, I can't."

"– or concerned?"

"No, I can't."

"Upset?"

"No, I can't remember."

"You just don't remember?"

"No."

"Do you remember if his eyes were open?"

"I suppose, but I don't know."

"Can you remember if he was moving about?"

"No, I can't."

"And was Michael with you at the time?"

"I don't remember that."

In the bedroom, she saw blood on the walls.

"Blood on the ceiling?"

"I can't remember if it was."

"Blood on the other bed?"

"I can't remember that."

"Blood on the floor?"

"I can't remember that exactly either."

What she did remember was that several of the dresser drawers in which Mrs. Barnett kept her jewelry were pulled out.

"It was many drawers, three, four, drawers."

"Did that strike you as unusual?"

"Yes."

"Why?"

"Because it was not normal that so many drawers was open at the same time."

She couldn't recall the condition of those drawers.

I reminded her she told Inspectors Klotz and Guinther of the S.F.P.D. she had seen a mess in the drawers. She didn't remember saying that, but agreed it was probably true. (I was still hoping the burglar-did-it defense would come alive for me.)

Her recollection of the state of the suite was remarkably different from the version she'd given to officers in San Francisco, and armed with the transcript I contradicted her on several matters which, though trivial, might help impress upon the jury that Helan suffered from a seriously flawed memory – and one that seemed programed to damage a man she was determined to believe a murderer.

But my main concern was with the "pretend crying." In my deepest heart of hearts, knowing Frisbee as by then I did, I felt he was simply not one to have play-acted his grief. Tears there may not have been, especially if he was still in shock, but Frisbee is a person whose emotions cannot be long contained.

Unexpectedly, with a stab in the dark, I was rewarded with an interesting answer from Helan.

"Do you remember Mr. Frisbee going to the washroom and throwing up?"

She paused, looked puzzled. Then a light seemed to go on for her.

"Yes, he did."

"That is something that you just suddenly remembered?"

"Yes, I do."

"When was that?"

"It was during the conversation we had, but I'm not exactly sure about it."

"You are not exactly sure when that happened?"

"No."

"But he got up and bolted for the bathroom?"

"Yes."

"Yes?"

"Because he was, you know . . ."

"Heaving?"

"Heaving, yes, heaving."

"It looked like he was going to be sick?"

"Yes, he did."

Things were looking up.

Those bloody towels that she saw in the bathroom could, I thought, have been deposited there by someone other than Frisbee.

"Can you be sure whether anyone else went to the bathroom while you were attending to Mrs. Barnett?"

"No, I can't."

"Is it possible that someone else did?"

"Yes."

As with Michael, I felt her powers of observation were clouded by her distraught condition, but she seemed not to want to admit how traumatized she was. After returning with the sheets, she said, she wanted to leave the suite.

"You wanted to go where?"

"To go out from the cabin, leave the cabin."

"Why is that?"

"Because I thought . . . I didn't have anything to do in there . . . I don't know."

"Well, had the scene not disturbed you a little bit?"

"Yes, I suppose."

"That's why you wanted to leave, wasn't it?"

"No, it was because . . . enough people in there."

"How many people were in there by that time?"

"There was the doctor and the nurse and the staff captain."

"Now, the staff captain is Captain Olsen, is that right?"

"Yes."

"And you were stopped from leaving?"

"Yes," she admitted.

"By Captain Olsen?"

"Yes."

"What did he do?"

"He grabbed my arm and said I shouldn't leave and said that I have to sit down and talk with him, Mr. Frisbee."

"You didn't particularly want to sit down and talk to Mr. Frisbee?"

"No."

"You told Captain Olsen that you wanted to leave and he said, 'Well, you are not going to leave'?"

"Yes."

Being forced to sit and chat up a murderer was not Helan's idea of a congenial way to pass the time. She was able to recall only bits and pieces of that conversation.

I thought I had now worked enough stubbornness out of the witness to try to tackle her unqualified assertion that Frisbee was "not sober" and her opinion that Frisbee was pretending to cry.

"You can't say whether he was in a state of shock or not, can you?"

"No."

"You can't say whether he was intoxicated or not, can you?"

"I can't say it, no."

"Different people act in different ways when they are in a state of shock, don't they?"

"They do."

She said he was making a kind of choking sound when covering his eyes with his hands.

"But there were no tears that you observed?"

"No."

"You can't say whether he had been crying earlier and all his tears were gone or not, can you?"

"No."

Earlier in her evidence she had said the first of Frisbee's two telephone calls was to a "nephew" in London. Suddenly, in cross-examination, she changed that to "niece."

"One was to a niece in London?"

"Yes."

"Did he say the name?"

"I can't remember that."

"Are you sure it wasn't a nephew that he said he was going to phone?"

"No, niece."

"Are you absolutely sure of that?"

"Yes."

"Miss Helan, it may be our error, but according to Mr. Green's notes, your evidence in answering Mr. Murray's questions was that he wanted to phone a nephew in London."

"No, a niece."

I couldn't fathom why she so stubbornly insisted on maintaining this obviously incorrect assertion.

"I'm not trying to trick you or anything, but it's just that that is his note."

Dennis helped out: "We have nephew, my lord, if that's helpful."

"I have nephew, too," said the judge.

"You have nephew?" I asked him.

"That is three nephews," said Justice McKenzie.

"A good majority," I said. I turned to Frisbee, another taker of notes, and he nodded. Four nephews.

I asked the witness: "Do you agree that you said nephew when you were answering Mr. Murray's questions?"

"No, niece."

"Niece?"

"Niece."

"That's what you said in evidence here today?"

"Yes."

"Niece?"

"Yes."

"Definitely?"

"Yes, I'm sure."

All of this was clearly beginning to rattle Helan. I wondered how her unwielding stubbornness about a matter so inconsequential was being received by the jury. Surely they were now in doubt about the quality of the more telling aspects of her evidence.

Comforted by this thought, driving along easily in cruise gear, I heedlessly went off the road into a thicket of trouble. The jury must have concluded by now that Mrs. Barnett's death had caused Helan an almost pathological distress, and I hardly needed to keep pounding the point home . . . but I did.

"Miss Helan, during the whole of this episode, how were you feeling?"

"Just doing my work."

"Were you feeling anything?"

"Well, I just . . . did what they told me to do and nothing more, nothing less. I didn't feel anything special about that."

This was so obviously false that I felt sorry for her.

"Didn't you start having nightmares a few nights later?"

"Yes, for a week."

Her face took on an expression of tremendous strain. I blundered ahead.

"They continued for a while, yes?"

She burst into a great, flowing river of tears. No pretend crying this. I think I went white. The courtroom was shocked into silence.

"My lord," I said, "I think the witness is in some distress."

"How much longer do you expect to be in cross-examination of her?" the judge asked, as Helan stood on the stand shaking with grief.

"Not much longer, but if she is in a state of emotion I think it is inappropriate for me to continue."

We took ten minutes.

How awful, I thought, as the jury was led out, their faces creased with sympathy for the victim of my sadistic bullying. So much of what I had won now seemed to have been lost.

While both the witness and her inquisitor composed themselves, I could see Dennis and Ernie calmly enjoying my plight. It was a classic case of a cross-examiner going too far, stepping over the edge between close, probing interrogation and a hectoring meanness.

"That is just what I didn't want," I mumbled to Jeff. He could feel my pain. We could both feel Helan's.

I was in peril of losing permanently, if not the minds of the jury, their hearts. I tried to console myself with the thought that Helan's breakdown graphically confirmed that her recall of events had been made unreliable by the enormous stress she'd been under.

Normally, I try to seek eye contact with jurors during the giving of evidence, but when we reassembled, I couldn't bring myself to look their way. As much as I wished to release Helan from my clutches and send her on the first plane back to Stockholm, I believed there were nuggets yet to be mined from her evidence.

On resuming, I said, "Miss Helan, I hope you will understand that I do not intend by my questions to make you upset."

"No, I know," she said softly.

I drew from her that after the ship's return to San Francisco, it sailed for Hong Kong, and one of her duties was to clean the unoccupied Penthouse Six, a task that I suspect did not lessen the severity of her nightmares.

"And there was still some blood here and there in the suite?"

"Yes, it was only in the . . . on the balcony."

"On the bed cover?" the judge said.

I corrected him. "'On the balcony,' she said."

She repeated: "Balcony."

"Your voices are both going down," said the judge.

"We have both become a little subdued, I'm afraid," I said in apology.

"What did you see on the balcony?" I asked.

"Blood spots on the floor."

I took some time with the jury over this, asking her to mark the blood spots on a large diagram of the suite. Blood on the balcony: significant, because there was no evidence Frisbee had been out there. Significant, too, because the balcony door was wide open, and a thief's escape route might have taken him outside that way, over the lifeboats and to safety.

"At some point Mr. Frisbee said that he had to go and pray, did he not?"

This question troubled her. "Pray . . . . pray . . . it is something, but I can't remember, I just . . . pray, it is something in my memory but I can't take it out."

"Did he say something like, 'I must go and pray'?"

"He said something . . . something in my mind about praying, but I don't . . . Can I ask you a question?"

Oh-oh, I thought. But how could I deny her? "I guess that you can."

"Have I said that before?"

"I have an indication that you said it to the police."

"Then it's right," she said, and I thanked her.

Justice McKenzie dismissed the jury for the evening, but court remained in session to hear Dennis Murray's proposal that

Helan's entire eighteen-page interview with the police in San Francisco be filed as an exhibit – for the jury to peruse, I gathered, at their leisure. I had cross-examined her on it, he argued, and it therefore became admissible – on the basis of some dubious reasoning by a judge of what we defense lawyers used to call, before its recent intellectual reformation, the B.C. Court of Apples.

I remonstrated, expostulated, and admonished against. "If I am put in a position throughout this trial that it becomes dangerous to examine a witness as to previous statements because every word that was said to investigating authorities would go before the jury, we are faced with all sorts of possibilities of prejudice."

Justice McKenzie intimated he felt bound by the Court of Appeal, but agreed to postpone full argument on the point until later in the trial. (The possibility of Helan's long police interview going into the jury room haunted me for another week, until I placed before the court a decision of the appeal court to opposite effect. Dennis finally abandoned his try.)

We adjourned for the night.

The next morning, Frisbee slipped me a note: "To let you know I am not completely stoic I had an attack of some kind for some reason last night when I turned on the TV, uncontrolled crying and closed throat and choking and shaking. OK now . . . ?"

Chapter 32

THE KINGDOM OF DENMARK WAS REPRESENTED AT TRIAL BY the ship's nurse, Anne-nette Pedersen. For some reason court authorities had been unable to locate her until after the trial was under way, and she became the subject of an international search. They finally caught up to her aboard a cruise ship in Jamaica, and whisked her up to Canada on two days' notice.

She was frazzled by that experience, and apparently became even more alarmed upon learning of Jeannette Helan's breakdown in court the previous day. I gathered someone must have named me as the villain of the piece, a heartless abuser of innocent witnesses. Before court was called to order Dennis admonished me to please try to be a gentleman and not to act the bully again. That rankled me. I told him that as long as she didn't retreat – as many of his witnesses had – from earlier statements to interviewing authorities, she would have nothing to fear. Pedersen had been interviewed by FBI agents both in San Francisco and Seattle following the murder, and I wanted those previous answers on record.

Before calling her to the stand, Dennis found it necessary to tell the court that Pedersen "is pretty edgy about giving her evidence," and he was the soul of courtesy and compassion in leading her through the events of August 19. She had not much new to offer, aside from a recounting of her efforts to assist the ship's doctor to revive Mrs. Barnett.

When asked to describe Frisbee's emotional state that evening, she became literally speechless for several seconds.

"Are you able to answer that question?" the judge asked.

"No," she said. "I just cannot find the words."

Dennis didn't push it, and after a few more questions turned her over to me.

I had no problems with her at all. She had no difficulty recalling that Frisbee made the two telephone calls, one to San Francisco and another to Britain, which didn't go through.

She agreed she "kind of noticed" Frisbee hurrying to the bathroom at one point.

"And did you hear any sounds from the bathroom?"

"Yes."

"Sounds of vomiting?"

"Yes."

"And you told the FBI agent in Seattle that Frisbee appeared to be in a daze and had appeared to be drinking?"

"Yes."

"And to the best of your knowledge, that's true?"

"Yes."

"And when you were talking to Agent Jan Smith did you tell her that Mr. Frisbee appeared to be in a dazed state?"

"Yes."

"And that was true as well?"

"Yes."

I was content with that, and thanked her.

◇　◇　◇

Dr. Roland Bengt Hansson graduated from a Swedish medical school in 1976, qualifying as a surgeon, and maintained the kind of general practice which allowed him leave to travel as a ship's doctor aboard Royal Viking vessels. A gentle, soft-spoken man obviously possessed of an amiable bedside manner, he was in the captain's cabin, steeling himself for the farewell party that evening, when he received an urgent call by beeper to attend Penthouse Six. He and the staff captain – both in formal dress – hurried there.

His attempts to resuscitate the victim were of course futile: she wasn't breathing; he felt no heartbeat. He observed that the left side of her skull was crushed.

Frisbee "seemed to be in a little bit of shock."

Dennis asked him the standard questions intended to disprove drunkenness: he had no difficulty speaking, or understanding what Dr. Hansson was asking him, no problems walking.

I was unsettled by this. In an interview with an FBI agent, Dr. Hansson had said Frisbee was shocked and intoxicated and had difficulty walking straight, although he noted no slurred speech. His memory, sixteen months later, was markedly different.

He had overheard Frisbee concluding a telephone call (the one to Kazakes) with the words, "I can't talk to you any more now," and observed him hang up.

Dennis had prepared the witness to confute any suggestion that Frisbee had suffered a grand mal seizure. He said Frisbee showed none of the typical indicia: cramps, drowsiness, confusion, tongue-biting.

In Jeff Green's cross-examination, the picture described by Dr. Hansson altered. The doctor had observed that while Frisbee was sitting on the couch, he was shaking his head.

"Talking to himself, apparently?"

"Yeah, sometimes he was, yes."

"Crying?"

"Yes, sometimes he was crying, too."

Struggling with his emotions, he seemed unable to continue his telephone conversation, and when he hung up started to cry.

"He just couldn't get the words out any more because he was choked with emotion?"

"Yes, that's right."

As he sat on the couch, he seemed to be having a conversation with himself, repeating again and again that he didn't know what happened, that he was asleep.

Jeff tackled the issue of Frisbee's sobriety:

"You also got the impression that Mr. Frisbee was intoxicated?"

Hansson seemed to want to back away from any such sweeping description. "I think he was smelling from alcohol."

"And your general impression was that he was intoxicated from some source?"

"Yes, he ... I got the impression that he'd been drinking alcohol, yes."

Despite his best efforts, Jeff couldn't get him to budge any further than to agree that Frisbee appeared to be under the influence of alcohol "to some extent." Reminded of his prior interview with the FBI, he was unable to recall his answers to their questions.

The truth is we felt a little betrayed by Dr. Hansson, not to mention the Crown, which we felt had encouraged him to back away from his earlier opinion that Frisbee had seemed drunk. After Dr. Hansson was excused we raised a great hue and cry about calling the FBI agent whom he told, only a few days after the murder, that Frisbee "seemed to be intoxicated" and found it "hard to walk straight." Ultimately, we forced the Crown to agree to admit these prior statements to the jury. It was a poor substitute for oral evidence; admissions by counsel lack much impact.

A cruise vessel of the size of the *Royal Viking Star* employs two captains: a senior captain with overall authority, and a staff captain in charge of the crew. This latter officer was Arnuf Olsen, a confident and assured gentleman with a long naval experience, who had navigated the Strait of Juan de Fuca some forty times. Ernie Quantz led him through much technical detail about the science of navigation. Olsen, as might be expected, was positive the ship had remained on the Canadian side of the international border after departing Victoria.

When the emergency call came in, Olsen followed Dr. Hansson to Penthouse Six to oversee the crisis.

"Did you try to speak to Mr. Frisbee at all?" Ernie asked him.

"I tried to speak to him but he didn't answer."

He summoned the ship's photographer to take some pictures of the scene before the body was removed, ordered a cabin be made ready for Frisbee, called the radio operator and told him to assist Frisbee with his telephone calls, then had Frisbee escorted to cabin 468.

"Did he appear to have any difficulty in walking?"

"Not as far as I could see, no."

Before locking up Penthouse Six, he glanced around the bar and noticed that two of the bottles had blood on them.

Jeff handled the cross.

"One of the first things you did is told Jeannette Helan to go and sit with Mr. Frisbee and calm him down?"

"That's correct."

"He looked to you like he was intoxicated?"

"Looks like he was drunk."

"He looks like he was drunk to you?"

"Yes."

"And he also looks like he was in shock to you?"

"Also that, yes."

"Now, when Mr. Frisbee went to cabin 468 he was permitted to take his toilet articles with him?"

"I told him he could do that."

"And those were in a bag, a small bag with a zipper on the top?"

"That's correct."

It was in that zippered bag, we hoped to prove, that Frisbee kept his Librium. Which is why Inspector Suyehiro of the San Francisco police never saw any such capsules in the suite.

Olsen and his first officer, Thor Kjellingland, who was called to attest to the ship's bearings when the murder took place (just off a Canadian landfall known by the pointless name of Point No Point), held the stand for the better part of a day, mostly with technical evidence, and again we were in fear of running behind schedule. It was by now Thursday, December 11, and the Crown was still several witnesses shy of completing its case.

"Would it not be prudent to start at 9:00 tomorrow morning?" the judge asked at the end of their evidence. "The awful eventuality we want to navigate around of course is sitting Christmas, so I think it's wise for us to start early and sit late."

Wearily, Jeff and I dragged our briefs of law and evidence to the law library, and prepared for the blood-spatter experts.

Chapter 33

FRISBEE'S BLOOD-SPLOTCHED ROBE, FOUND LYING ON THE FLOOR near the living-room closet, caused us no end of headache. None of the crew had observed him wearing it on August 19, but it offered credible if mute testimony that its wearer was Frisbee (to suggest that an intruder would don it, then commit a murder, beggared belief) and that he wore it while wielding the death bottle. In an attempt to put Frisbee in the robe, the Crown relied on the relatively new forensic science of blood-spatter analysis, and tendered a witness whose credentials were beyond dispute.

Dr. Boyd Stephens had been Chief Medical Officer for San Francisco since 1971 and given evidence in about fifteen hundred trials as an expert in both forensic medicine and blood spatter, which involves a knowledge of physical laws about the behavior of liquid in flight. From an analysis of blood spatter, an expert can often gauge the force of a blow and the direction in which a blunt object was swung.

Dr. Stephens, a pathologist, had conducted an autopsy on the body, concluding that Mrs. Barnett was struck in the left forehead and left lower head at least four times: "blunt force injuries."

Such blows, he told Dennis Murray, cause "a very low frequency resident sound, much like a gourd being struck, or a melon." An analogy that I'm sure sent chills up the jurors' spines.

He had noted injuries on her hands that may have resulted from her attempt to ward off blows.

There was "literally no blood soaking" in the kneeling position in which the stewardesses had found her. This evidence, I feared, might give the lie to Frisbee's assertion that he first saw the body on its knees beside the bed.

Justice McKenzie intervened: "Have you offered a theory, doctor, as to how this person moved from the primary position on her back with her head on the pillows, to the secondary position with the knees on the floor?"

There were two possibilities, Dr. Stephens said, "and I have no real way of telling which is the correct one."

The first was that "she came to enough to roll over and into the position in which she was found." The second was that someone moved her: "a possibility that I think is more supported by this scene but not to the point of excluding the first."

Dennis handed him Exhibit 24, the robe, and the jury was treated to some forensic theater as Dr. Stephens wrapped himself in it to demonstrate how it could have become spattered. It was a short robe falling to a point above the knees, and had shortish sleeves. Blood spatter on it was consistent with a person having worn the robe while being close to the bed, Stephens said.

What was remarkable was that although "swiping stains" showed on the right sleeve, as if the wearer had wiped a bloody surface, no spatters were found underneath the sleeve, "one of the things we commonly look for when a person is striking a bloody surface." The left sleeve, however, showed blood droplets. Frisbee, the jury could observe (as he scribbled away on his notepad), was right-handed.

The absence of spatters on the right sleeve would, he said, argue against a right-handed killer having administered the blows, but it was possible that the spatters "just simply never reached the right arm for some reason."

I knew by then that Dennis planned to demolish one of my pet theories, relating to the red spots on the balcony floor which Jeannette Helan had observed when swabbing the balcony. Dr. Stephens had informed me, before taking the stand, that a serologist – a blood specimen expert – had examined the spots. They were not, Dr. Stephens firmly announced, tell-tale droplets of blood left by an escaping thief-murderer.

Dennis asked Stephens if the spots had been analyzed. I tried to limit the damage.

"If it please the court, I think we can save some time. It's been explained to me that those are Bloody Mary spots."

"I understand that Bloody Mary has no real blood in it," said the judge, deadpan. "At least the number I've tried doesn't have any real blood in it."

C'est la guerre.

In cross-examination Jeff obtained from the doctor that neither the right nor left sleeve of Frisbee's robe showed the kind of spatter one would associate with a wearer delivering the blows that killed Mrs. Barnett.

"Would this assailant likely have blood afterwards on his or her hands and in his or her hair and so on?"

"Very likely have blood about the hands and forearms, very likely about the legs. There may not be blood in the hair."

"Another reason why you would expect to find blood spatters on the leg of the assailant if he was wearing that dressing gown is because it's a pretty short dressing gown?"

"It is, counsel."

No one from the ship's crew had seen any blood on Frisbee, although the Crown of course would argue he had a chance to wash before Michael came to the door. But if he had moved the body off the bed in the seconds before Michael returned with the stewardesses, one would suppose the effort would leave him at least a little blood-smudged.

◇   ◇   ◇

A week and a half into the trial, the Crown produced its first Canadian witness, Corporal Herbert Leroy, the chief blood-spatter expert of the RCMP in British Columbia. The Crown tendered him at my insistence – I felt he had useful additional evidence to give. He had examined the robe earlier that year and been briefed on the circumstances of the crime.

In examination-in-chief he had little to add to Dr. Stephens's evidence, but in cross I asked him: "You can't rule out the possibility that the gown had been laid on some surface on which there were spots of blood?"

"That's correct."

Could the robe have been lying near the scene of the murder and thus become blood-spotted?

"Providing it's in close proximity to where the blood source is, it's possible."

"Whether on the opposite bed or on the floor or some position near the victim's body?"

"That's correct."

In addition, Corporal Leroy agreed he'd found no significant stains to support the theory that the victim may have been placed in the crouching position she was found in by the stewardesses.

"If a person wearing the robe had in fact moved the body from one position on the bed to a kneeling position, the body would have to be lifted or pulled, obviously?"

"Yes."

"And you would expect if the person was wearing this robe there would be a lot more blood on it?"

"I would expect that, yes."

Dennis, in re-examination, blunted the effect of that excellent answer: "Had they just grabbed the legs and pulled it over, you wouldn't expect to find any stains on the robe, would you?"

"That's a possibility I hadn't taken into account, yes."

◊   ◊   ◊

Inspector Carl Klotz of San Francisco homicide had not originally been expected to give more than brief evidence, but I think Dennis Murray was sufficiently concerned about our thief-murderer theory to qualify Klotz as a burglary expert in an attempt to put that theory finally to peace.

The inspector, in the S.F.P.D. for twenty-three years, had wide experience in the burglary unit before being transferred to homicide.

Dennis asked him: "You are responsible, I gather, for all homicides that occur in San Francisco?"

One might have thought the inspector would hesitate before answering this highly incriminating question. A yes response would make the inspector one of the most successful mass murderers in all of history.

"That's correct, sir," he said.

I recall some laughter in the courtroom, prompting Justice McKenzie to amend Dennis's question: "He is responsible for investigating them."

Klotz smiled. "Thank you, my lord."

"Sounds like a make-work project," said Dennis, nicely recovering.

Klotz said he and his partner, Inspector Ora Guinther, boarded the ship in San Francisco at 10:30 on the morning of August 21. (Guinther and Klotz: not a bad title for a TV cop show.)

The door to Penthouse Six, he said, was open when the police arrived, with a guard posted. I thought this odd, because Captain Olsen had given strict orders that the suite remain locked.

"Did you look for signs of burglary?"

"Yes, sir, we did."

"What kinds of things would you be looking for?"

"Forced entry, jimmy marks on the door, pry marks."

"And did you find, sir, any signs of forced entry anywhere?"

"No, sir, we did not."

"What other things would you be looking for?"

"The room to be in disarray."

"Any particular kind of disarray?"

"All of the drawers would be turned inside out, clothing would be thrown on the floor."

"What did you find in that connection, sir?"

"Found the stateroom to be in a normal condition for one or two people residing in it."

The drawers in the suite were open when he first visited it, he said, but nothing was turned over.

Against this, of course, I had Helan's original statement to the police that the drawers were in a messy state.

He observed several items of jewelry in those drawers, undisturbed, and produced them from a bag for the jury to see.

"Perhaps just by way of example, is there a diamond-encrusted elephanty kind of item there?" Dennis asked.

There was, he said, and he'd found it in a jewelry pouch.

The judge asked Klotz to step from the witness stand and show the jewelry to the jury, who took turns goggling at Mrs. Barnett's necklaces, brooches, and earrings.

Klotz described finding, in Frisbee's wallet, the $20,000 check to Jerry Kazakes and Frisbee's check for $300,000, those apparently incriminating bills of exchange that Frisbee, despite having every chance, never thought to destroy.

Dennis asked the inspector if, when arresting Frisbee, he observed him to have any personal effects with him. I assumed we would not be hearing about any Librium.

"He had two bags."

"And he brought those with him when he was booked in?"

"Yes, sir, he did."

"And did you find any drugs or vials in his possession?"

"No, sir, I did not."

"Did you, sir, do what is referred to as a skin search?"

"Yes, sir, I did."

No drugs on Frisbee's person, in his clothes, in his bags. The inspector was adamant that no drugs had been found in Penthouse Six (apparently he was ignorant of the fact that Inspector Suyehiro seized some Antabuse tablets). But no Librium: a fact that Dennis intended happily to underscore for the jury. The Crown knew that without proof that Frisbee had packed a bottle of Librium capsules for the trip, the entire framework for automatism would collapse beneath our feet.

So where was the Librium?

Earlier in the week, we'd done some detective work. We discovered that when Canadian RCMP officers went to San Francisco to pick up Frisbee and escort him to Victoria, the San Francisco jail officials also released to them some personal effects which had been under lock and key since Frisbee's arrest: they were contained in a paper bag and a plastic carry case.

Oddly, no one had closely examined these items, nor were they ever released to Frisbee. They remained untouched in a locker at Wilkinson Road jail.

At our request, corrections officers at Wilkinson Road retrieved for us the paper bag and carry case. Nothing remarkable was found in the bag: a yellow tie, a few seasickness pills, Frisbee's wallet with a Visa card and a couple of receipts for some purchases he'd made in Alaska, and a pair of reading glasses (which Frisbee had complained he'd been sorely missing).

In the carry case, however, in addition to various toiletry items (toothbrush, toothpaste, hairbrush, comb, nail file, nail scissors, and a small bar of Royal Viking Lines glycerine soap) were an empty bottle of Advil tablets, a pill case with five brown capsules and five white tablets, and an empty pill bottle bearing a prescription number, 778535, Dr. Raszl's name, and the inscription, "Librium 10 mg/#30, 5-1-84, take 1 capsule every 6 hours as needed, Dan Kazakes, discard after 5-86."

The label contained this warning: "May cause drowsiness, alcohol may intensify this effect, use care when operating a car or dangerous machinery."

We asked Frisbee why Kazakes's name would appear on the Librium bottle. Apparently Dr. Raszl had also prescribed Librium for Frisbee's partner, and in packing for the trip Frisbee had simply taken the wrong pill bottle. He had apparently, at some point, transferred the Librium capsules, along with some Advil tablets, into the pill case.

We were careful not to alert the Crown to our discovery. I wanted to hear what Inspector Klotz would have to say when confronted with it.

After a ten-minute rest break, the inspector was turned over to me. I asked him to describe the bags Frisbee had with him.

"I can't recall if it was a plastic bag or a paper bag, but I know there was two white bags."

"One of them in fact was a paper bag, wasn't it?"

"It may have been."

"And the plastic bag, how would you describe that?"

"Again, I can't recall." Toilet articles were in it, he said.

"Did you make a list?"

"No, sir, I did not."

"Do you recall whether there was a hairbrush in there?"

"There could have been."

"Scissors?"

"Again, could have been."

"A couple of empty pill bottles?"

Now he was certain: "I did not observe any pill bottles."

"Even empty?"

"Even empty."

"All you can say is that you looked into that bag briefly?"

"That's correct."

"Okay, did you see any soap in there?"

"Again, I can't recall."

"With a Royal Viking Line wrapper on it?"

"Again, I cannot recall."

"All right, an empty bottle of Advil?"

"Again I cannot recall."

"An empty pill bottle with the number 778535?"

"Again, I cannot recall."

Faced with specifics, probably concerned now that I had facts to contradict him with, he had gingerly stepped back from his assertion that he saw no pill bottles.

The two bags, he said, were given into the custody of the deputy sheriff of the county jail. I had noted that someone had written an identifying number on the paper bag, HQ-13100. He agreed that seemed to be an FBI identification mark.

He maintained that the bag, "if it had anything to do with the case, would have been seized by our department."

"Inspector, I'm more interested in what happened than what would have happened. If you don't remember what happened, just be blunt with me about it and tell me that."

"Well, if you are referring to the paper bag, I have no knowledge."

One would have thought that the San Francisco police, especially after Frisbee had told them he'd taken Librium the evening of the murder, would have seized any suspect pills or tablets. But perhaps that would have been too helpful to the defense.

As I had with Inspector Suyehiro, I took Klotz through a long list of articles observed in the suite but not seized, examined, or scientifically tested. The inspector's memory of the crime scene was hazy at best.

I saw an opportunity to muddy the waters, as it were, about the issue of where the crime occurred. "Where, according to your understanding, was the vessel when the alleged offense was committed?"

"My understanding was they were in international waters in the Pacific Ocean, off the coast of Washington." Merely six and a half miles off that coast, in fact.

"Now, did somebody tell you that?"

"Yes, sir."

"Someone from on board the vessel?"

"Yes, sir."

"Do you remember who it was?"

"No, sir, I could not."

"And you passed that information on to the FBI?"

"No, sir, I think maybe the FBI checked also and they were informed it was 6.5 miles."

"They advised you they were taking over the case because it was within their jurisdiction?"

"That's correct, sir."

"Because it was in U.S. territorial waters that the alleged crime took place?"

"Yes, sir, that's correct."

"And they carried on their investigation for months afterwards on that basis, is that right?"

"That's correct, sir."

"Did you check with any of the ship's officers or attempt to look at the log of the ship?"

"No, sir."

Alas, police investigators are never as methodical and unerring in real life as those steely-eyed heroes who unfailingly collar the bad guys in books and movies.

I harbored the secret hope that the jury, aware that Frisbee had been negligently imprisoned for a wasted year of his life, might seek to redress this wrong with an acquittal or a conviction on a lesser charge.

The defense had counted on casting even more doubt about the location of the vessel by calling an officer of the U.S. Coast Guard who had filed a report suggesting the *Viking Star* could conceivably have been taking a short cut across U.S. waters at the time of the murder. The officer apparently balked at coming to Victoria on short notice. Since he wasn't subject to subpoena, we were forced to file his written statement as an exhibit and abandon efforts to bring him to Canada.

As to the contents of Frisbee's paper bag and plastic carry case, we ultimately shared our discoveries with the Crown, who, after their own investigation, agreed to an admission of fact which left no room for contesting Frisbee's possession of Librium capsules on the *Royal Viking Star*.

Chapter 34

THE CROWN HAD PLANNED TO TENDER TWO CALIFORNIA psychiatrists to rebut automatism, but ultimately decided not call Dr. Chris Hatcher of Berkeley. I suspected his report was too equivocal for the prosecutors, implying a possibility Frisbee had suffered a true amnesia. Dennis Murray was anxious, of course, to persuade the jury that the amnesia was feigned. Pretend tears, pretend amnesia.

The psychiatrist he did call was Dr. George Solomon, a professor at UCLA who had interviewed Frisbee for the U.S. government.

Solomon was not just another hired gun for the state – he'd often given evidence for the defense, notably in People versus Daniel James White: the allegedly homophobic slayer of Mayor George Moscone and Harvey Milk, the gay San Francisco city supervisor. White was found guilty only of manslaughter, his mind unbalanced as a result of a radical depression. (The press seized on an item of evidence suggesting the depression resulted in part from a surfeit of junk food in his system, and it was thereafter branded as the "Twinkies" case.)

Before Solomon took the stand, Jeff Green drew him aside for a brief debriefing. I asked: "What do you think?"

"I like him."

"Are you sure?"

"I like him."

I was skeptical.

Dr. Solomon was earnest and well-intentioned but may not have been well-prepared for his testimony, which was accentuated by the witness's frequent shuffling through papers, during an ongoing search for the apposite reference or quote.

Most of the psychiatrist's evidence was neutral and innocuous until Dennis asked him about "this alleged memory loss" claimed by Frisbee about the murder.

Solomon believed three hypotheses were open. One was simple deception: "He could be not telling the truth and really remembers it." The second was he could have a genuine amnesia, due to alcohol or organic brain disease – alcohol intoxication interfering with events being encoded in the brain. Of those two possibilities the second was "far more likely in this instance." A comment that I noted and double-underlined.

The third possibility was a psychological amnesia. "That would simply be because of horror, guilt, distress about events that a person had pushed from consciousness because they were just too painful to bear."

Having traveled so far down this road, Dennis couldn't avoid the next question: "In that array of possibilities, did you form an opinion as to which is the more likely?"

Solomon seemed to find no easy way to answer without offending his client and patron, and he prefaced his response with a series of halts and staggers: "Not . . . no, no, I wouldn't say that I don't know . . . Uh, I tend . . . I don't . . . I think I tended to feel that the . . . but I . . . I'm not positive in any way. . . ." Then finally: "My own personal opinion, not held on the basis of any strong evidence, is that the amnesia was genuine."

I felt like cheering this marathon effort; he had not only made it to the finish line, he had won a medal – for the opposing team.

If genuine, he continued, the amnesia could be either a result of alcohol or an involuntary blocking of memory. But he couldn't rule out altogether the possibility that Frisbee was lying about his lack of memory. "I simply do not know."

"What did you say about lying?" the judge asked.

"I said he could be lying."

"Could be lying," Justice McKenzie repeated, making a note.

"Could be, but that wasn't my personal impression," the witness amended.

For Dennis, matters didn't improve, and when he asked Solomon about whether Frisbee had the capacity to form an intent to kill, the answer was: "I felt he would have the capacity to do so; whether he did or not is another matter."

As to Frisbee's alcohol intake on the day of the murder: "I think he had quite a bit to drink on the day. I would think his degree of intoxication possibly produced a disorder of impulse control."

If Dennis had hoped to gain an opinion from this witness that Frisbee was the thoughtful perpetrator of a designed murder plan, he was plainly disappointed.

In cross-examination, Jeff had the witness serve up a few more tasty morsels. He asked about the impact of sudden emotional shock on an intoxicated person: "It has the effect of sobering him up pretty substantially, doesn't it?"

"Yes. A drunk driver might be a good example. In spite of relatively high blood alcohol a person may, after an injurious crash, sort of be jolted into being much more alert by the high levels of epinephrine in the blood, adrenalin in the blood."

As to alcohol and Librium in combination, both were sedative drugs and both affected the same receptor cells in the brain. "Their effect is additive."

Afterwards, in the hallway, we thanked Dennis for his generous Christmas donation in the form of Dr. George Solomon. He walked away shaking his head.

◇   ◇   ◇

During these last two days of the Crown's case, Thursday, December 11, and the following day, the jury were cruelly subjected to several hours of videotapes of the commission evidence taken in San Francisco. At one point a mind-numbed juror nodded off. Nobody bothered waking him.

The judge excused them for a while to let us engage in some trench warfare with the Crown over what parts of the Kazakes tapes could be played for the jury. I objected, of course, to Dennis's bear-baiting of the good reverend about his so-called ministry and sexual preferences. My complaint that the Crown had unfairly attacked the character and credibility of its own witness was greeted by Dennis with pique:

"It seems that every time I turn around in this trial, I am being unfair and I am getting more and more unfair as time goes on."

I was beginning to share that view.

The trial and some of its heated exchanges had begun to erode the easy comradeship Jeff and I once enjoyed with Dennis. Lawyers are expected to leave their hostility behind them with the exhibits when they drag their weary bodies from the courtroom, but as the trial progressed we were finding that our relationship with Dennis was being tested with increasing severity. Each side, of course, was becoming more persuaded of the rightness of its cause – this unfailingly happens during long, demanding trials – and more suspicious of the motives and the tactics employed by the other. Such is the nature of our adversarial system of law. It takes a human toll.

It wasn't easy for Dennis. He was a competitor. Defense attorneys are entitled to a certain fervency, but by long custom of law, advocates for the state must maintain a dispassionate, equable demeanor. In the heat of combat it's easy for a prosecutor to forget that the object of the game is justice, not winning. And we felt Dennis was beginning to forget.

But his lament about our accusations of unfairness was dampened down by crocodile tears, because to this point in the trial Justice McKenzie had sided with the Crown on every major issue of law argued before him. We were beginning to despair of receiving a ruling benefiting our side. In fact his lordship seemed to have begun to list to starboard, to the Crown side, through the first two weeks of evidence (at least from our biased view), often intervening in the examination of witnesses, the effect of which was usually to help the Crown clarify a murky point of evidence. Some judges do tend to get into the fray more than others. Others play an honest broker role, decline to assist either combatant, avoid injudicious asides that might insinuate to a jury where their sentiments lie.

But this argument we won. At the end of a couple of hours of wrangling, Justice McKenzie held (reluctantly, I thought) that those portions of Kazakes's evidence to which the defense took offense could not go before the jury. Dennis Murray had assumed the role of cross-examiner of his own witness at his peril. The judge ordered the improper questions and their answers excised from the videotape.

By late Friday, the Crown had called its last witness and played its last videotape.

"I make no secret of the fact that I would like very much to be on that 5:00 boat," said the judge.

I said, "I know what it is like not to make the ferry, my lord; I live on an island."

"You believe in ferries, too," said Justice McKenzie.

I should have been sharp. I should have told him I believe in their innocence.

On Monday, Mr. Frisbee would take the stand.

Chapter 35

JEFF AND I SPENT MUCH OF THAT WEEKEND IN FRISBEE'S JAIL cell, preparing him for his Courtroom D debut. He had decorated the cell with bright Christmas touches and with scenic photos from magazines: the Eiffel Tower, Big Ben, a Polynesian beach, various distant addresses Frisbee told us he transported himself to, a form of freedom from jail. An escape into memory, into his lavish reveries. Snapshots of the Barnetts and Dan Kazakes were taped to the frame of his bunk and on the walls. A table was thickly piled with his own notes, copies of exhibits, transcripts of his several interviews with Dr. Tyhurst.

We didn't know whether Dennis intended to attack Frisbee with a broadsword or a scalpel, but he may have shared our sense of teetering between victory and loss, and probably viewed his cross-examination as the juncture at which our defense would prevail or collapse. Overhanging us like a storm cloud was the fear that Dennis held a secret weapon, some lethal bolt of lightning.

Frisbee's coaches gave him pre-game instructions:

Listen to the questions carefully, Robert.

Keep your answers brief and responsive.

Don't try to give an answer if you don't know the answer. Say I don't know.

Don't try to reconstruct memories that aren't there.

Don't ramble. Don't throw in filler. Don't, in other words, confabulate.

The judge is your lordship, not your honor.

Don't be obsequious to Dennis. Be firm in your answers, but polite.

Don't argue with him.

You're not on stage. Be yourself.

Thrice I took him through his evidence, from start to end, returning to the trouble spots, the signing of the codicil, his explanations about the checks in his wallet, about the pilfering from Mrs. Barnett's account, the amount of alcohol and tranquilizers consumed on August 19.

Then Jeff Green took him on.

"I'm Dennis Murray, okay? I'm going to cross-examine you. I'm going to be rough on you. Ready?"

Frisbee nodded nervously.

Jeff thumped away at him for a couple of hours, seeking weaknesses, scoffing at answers, demanding explanations, contradicting him with the evidence. Often we would pause, suggest an answer was badly phrased; Jeff would back up a little distance, drive forward again.

He pulled phrases from Frisbee's manuscript.

"'A calumnious act to perform. Today is the day.' What does that mean, Mr. Frisbee?"

"Just . . . fantasy. I was trying to write a best-seller."

"It means you were planning a murder, doesn't it?"

"I . . . no, not at all."

Frisbee didn't react at all well through any of this: he stumbled over answers, continually apologized, and at the end seemed weary.

Be strong, we told him. Be yourself on the stand.

That was the key. How could this jury, once they had met the real Robert Frisbee, not be won over by his gentleness, his wry humor, his winsome self-effacement? How could they not forgive him his frailties, forgive him the imperfections that an experimenting God had endowed him with?

We had perhaps grown too fond of our client by now. We desperately wanted to believe in his innocence, had eagerly persuaded ourselves that if he was not exactly Anne of Green Gables, he was clearly not a callous killer inflamed by greed. But defense counsel *must* believe or they aren't doing their job – the cynical defender is an uncaring defender and therefore a poor one despite the skills he may own.

We continued to be troubled by our ignorance of what had transpired during the several minutes before Mrs. Barnett's death, and Frisbee continued to regret that his memory was empty of any lucid moment that could help his cause.

We were also feeling squeezed for time. In addition to Frisbee, our witnesses would include Dr. Tyhurst and Dr. Rosenthal. We couldn't see completing our case until Thursday, exactly one week before Christmas. The Crown might then call witnesses in rebuttal. Following that would come addresses from counsel and instructions from the bench, and the jury would then retire to deliberate. We could be pushed very close to Christmas – and who would the jury resent most if ordered locked up on Christmas Day to debate a heinous murder on the high seas? And would they rush to judgment to escape from their hard wooden chairs into the bosoms of their families?

On Monday we started at 9:00 a.m., and before I made my opening address to the jury, I played for them the videotapes of the doctors who had treated Frisbee for his alcoholism and his London seizure, Doctors Raszl and Goldstein, and after the morning adjournment, I opened to the jury. Such opening addresses tend to be brief outlines of evidence to come, but do give counsel extra innings to pile up some points.

I began: "Mr. Foreman and ladies and gentlemen, at the beginning of this trial you will recall that Mr. Murray said this case tells a very simple story. And maybe the Crown likes simple stories, but you now know that this is a very complex and bizarre story. It's a story that deals with a world so apart from our own experience that in my view it is going to be necessary, before we understand it, to understand the participants in that story.

"It's a puzzle, I don't mind telling you that, and it's a puzzle that is incapable of any neat packaging. Please don't expect that at some point during the defense evidence I'm going to turn around and point a finger at someone in the back, and say, like Perry Mason, 'You did it, did you not, Mr. Smith?' because you already know what we are ever going to know, or not know.

"Frankly, Mr. Frisbee will tell you that he does not know whether he is responsible for the death of Mrs. Barnett. I'd be overjoyed if I could put him on the stand and have him say to you: 'I did not kill Mrs. Barnett,' but you've already heard some evidence from one of the Crown witnesses, Dr. Solomon, that in his best estimate Robert Frisbee was suffering from a true amnesia."

I suppose all of that lowered the jury's expectations, but I felt it wrong to leave them with false ones, and in the end be disappointed.

The defense, I told them, had no secrets. "Robert Frisbee has nothing he can hide from you, and nothing he wishes to hide from you. He will be subject to a full and searching cross-examination by my learned and able friend, counsel for Her Majesty the Queen."

I would be asking Frisbee to recount his long and difficult history, this man from a humble background who became "mesmerized by the world of caviar and champagne." He would tell his story not to elicit sympathy from the jury, but their understanding.

After outlining our witnesses' evidence, I concluded:

"It's not up to the defense to prove that someone else did this act. It's not up to the defense to prove that Robert Frisbee did so in a conscious state. The burden is on the Crown to prove beyond a reasonable doubt not only that Robert Frisbee did the act but he did it in a normal conscious state."

I thought it important to pound this point home. A jury of lay persons, fed a diet of TV lawyer Pablum, might easily believe the defense had some obligation to actually *prove* something.

"So what you will have placed before you, ladies and gentlemen, is not a whodunit. That question, who done it, may never be answered. The other question to be put before you is how *could* he have done it, and it's not the very simple story that Mr. Murray spoke of, but a complex drama of the mind."

I turned to Frisbee, gave him my most reassuring smile.

"Perhaps the witness can be sworn."

Robert Dion Frisbee stepped cautiously toward the witness box. Every seat in the courtroom was occupied. Reporters waited like keen-eyed hawks at the press table.

"Take the Bible in your right hand," said the clerk.

Chapter 36

As I MANEUVERED FRISBEE ACROSS HARMLESS FIELDS – HIS family, his hometown, his growing up – he quickly conquered his tremors and after several minutes seemed miraculously to have discovered his métier. He was a born witness. No stiffness, no reticence, no obliqueness of response. Once in a while, never inappropriately, a quip, a hint of humor.

I watched the jury: they had the appearance of careful shoppers, checking out the goods, cautiously deciding whether to buy. Some smiled, even chuckled at the occasional *bon mot* from Frisbee. ("What was your mood during this voyage?" "Pardon the expression, very gay." That brought laughter. From all except the foreman, from whom Frisbee didn't draw a smile even when describing his army field-training experience, which ended abruptly when he threw a hand grenade softball-pitcher style.)

The only problem I encountered during my examination-in-chief of my witness: I couldn't stem the flow of his words; I constantly had to rein him in. But at the same time he impressed as being consumed with an impassioned eagerness to tell his story.

"Pause here," I would say.

"Oh, sorry," he would say.

Or:

"Mr. Frisbee, you are having a little tendency sometimes to talk over my questions before I –"

"Oh, I beg your pardon."

"– finish the question and it's hard for the court reporter –"

"Oh, I beg your pardon."

"– to take it down when we are both talking."

Or:

"As I say, he called her the bride and they were just a perfect couple."

"Over how many years –"

"He doted on her constantly."

"– just a minute. See, this has happened again, Mr. Frisbee."

"Did I interrupt you?"

And again:

"What background did Philip have in terms of –"

"Well, he was a local –"

"Mr. Frisbee, do try to let me finish the question. I know you are anxious, but . . ." I sighed. "Okay, carry on."

Robert Frisbee had finally breached the dam of his enforced silence over the last two weeks, and despite all the coaching ("listen carefully, then answer") he was like a high-spirited racehorse, chafing at the bit. Eventually, he slowed down for me and maintained a gentler, steadier trot. I wanted to train him to keep to that more relaxed speed during Dennis's cross.

I led him through the Dwight Frisbee years, his relationship with Kazakes, with the Barnetts, his descent into alcoholism, Philip's death, his depression after that, and those long blank months of faded memory.

Early in his examination, mainly to get it out of the way, I guided him across the rocky terrain of his thefts from Mrs. Barnett's account.

"I was getting to the point I'd been living beyond my means," Frisbee explained, "and I just needed some money to pay off some of my monthly bills. I had become a compulsive buyer buying things that I didn't really need. I bought Mrs. Barnett a diamond bracelet and a diamond necklace and a diamond ring and I redid the new apartment I moved into; I took all the kitchen appliances out and refurnished the apartment."

"What was your condition as to alcohol during this period?"

"I was drinking heavily then."

"Why didn't you take this problem up with Mrs. Barnett?"

"Difficult for me to face issues. If I face an issue I've usually written a letter. I didn't tell her I was in need of funds, no."

And I let it go at that. Frisbee was prepared to face Dennis on the issue.

By 5:00 that afternoon, when we stood down for the evening, Frisbee had given a history of all the events leading up to and including the signing of the codicil – and there was much still on our plate. It had been a long day but Frisbee had borne the strain well. I told him so, hoping to keep his spirits buoyed.

The Vancouver Sun gave Frisbee's opening-day performance a good review:

"Dressed in a smart tweed suit, a silk handkerchief in his breast pocket, Frisbee appeared relaxed and confident on the witness stand, answering Deverell's questions in a clipped, precise tone."

But when we began the next morning at 9:00, he seemed weary, and I hoped he'd kept something in reserve for what was no doubt going to be an even more trying day.

I took him through the events surrounding his seizure in London, his recovery, his secret return to alcohol, and his preparations for Alaska.

He recalled packing Librium, Antabuse, and headache pills for the trip.

I asked him whether he had ever used Librium in combination with alcohol. (This was of more than academic interest: any prior knowledge he had of the combined effects could negate our automatism defense. He could then be said to have willfully blinded himself to the dangers of mixing drink and drugs.)

"No, I never had."

"Did you know anything about whether or not you should or should not take Librium with alcohol?"

"No, I don't think I did know particularly about the effects of those two ingredients."

Then on to Vancouver. Then Alaska. The hectic return to the ship. Then, on August 19, on to that far outpost of former Empire, that little bit of Olde England, the City of Victoria.

It was now time to start adding up the day's drinks.

The Bloody Mary was a shipboard morning ritual. Mrs. Barnett usually had one, Frisbee usually two.

"How many ounces of vodka would you put in one of those?"

"Mine I made with three ounces and Mrs. Barnett's I made with two."

I reminded him that at the lunch at Chauney's he had fibbed to Mrs. Barnett: he ordered vodka, told her it was Perrier. Why had he done so?

"She was a little piqued at me that morning because she saw me taking an extra Bloody Mary, so I told her I was drinking water."

I asked about their return to the *Viking Star*.

"Well, there was a little upsetting incident with that," he said. The vessel was to depart at 5:00 p.m., and the limousine chauffeur had dawdled on his return, "and Mrs. Barnett, all of us, were getting anxious and tired, and we got back exactly at 4:30, which didn't please her too much because she didn't like to be rushed, so she told me to take it out of his tip. She was upset with him."

"You said you were anxious?"

"We didn't talk much on the way back because we were driving too fast also, and just anxious to get back to the ship to start getting ready for the party the captain was giving."

After arranging to meet the Biegerts for the captain's party, he and Muriel returned to Penthouse Six. He was still feeling the stress of their hurried return to the ship.

"I took a Librium first, and then I started to make a cocktail for Mrs. Barnett and myself."

"What kind of cocktail?"

"We called it a French 75. It's a combination of gin and champagne or vodka and champagne. Again in Mrs. Barnett's drink I would have put two ounces; in my own I would have put three ounces of vodka."

"How much champagne goes into those?"

"That's hard to tell, depends on the size of the glass. I was using a large tumbler and Mrs. Barnett had a cocktail glass from the ship. I usually put in the alcohol and then two or three ice cubes and then fill it with champagne."

I showed him one of the police photographs; he identified the tumbler he drank from and the stem glass used by Mrs. Barnett. He also looked at photographs of the empty piccolo champagne bottle and the half-full bottle of Moët, and he agreed he used the contents of those bottles to make his drinks.

"Can you give me your best estimate as to how many ounces of champagne you added to the three ounces of vodka or gin?"

"It would have been at least five, depending on the volume of the glass. Mine probably was more because it had more space in it."

He recalled that in many of the San Francisco restaurants he frequented, a limit was imposed: no more than two of these heady drinks per customer.

He and Muriel sat and chatted, brought out their fancy clothes.

"What were you feeling about this big evening?"

"I was looking forward to it. It was a fun evening. I felt a little shaky and I didn't feel the effects of the first pill I had taken."

"The Librium?"

"Yes."

"So what did you do?"

"I took another. I hadn't been drinking since that one small drink at lunch and I just felt shaky and queasy and I just took another Librium."

And finished his French 75. Then Frisbee took a shower, and put his robe on, and Mrs. Barnett went to the bathroom and ran the tub. He finished his drink and made another French 75. After downing it, he laid on the bed, pulled the comforter over him.

The next thing he remembered: he was standing at the toilet urinating. Michael was rapping at the door.

He recalled saying something like, "Wait a minute," then walking down a short hallway to the living room, bypassing the bedroom. Although memory was not clear, he must have gone to the closet, found his pants, and put them on. He didn't remember discarding the robe, couldn't recall if he was wearing it in the bathroom.

"I remembered I better arouse Mrs. Barnett as it must be getting time to get dressed, and I went into the bedroom and I saw Mrs. Barnett. She was more or less in a kneeling position and I ran over to her and touched her and there was blood all over her and I panicked and the first thought was to try to get some help, and I went back into the stateroom, and I opened the door and I don't know what I said. I just wanted help."

He never returned to the bedroom.

The rest was confusion: people running in and out of the suite, people shouting. He was in a daze.

"Do you recall making any telephone calls?"

"I made some telephone calls. It's not clear in my mind. I found out that I called San Francisco and I tried to place a call through to London."

"Do you recall anything you said on the call to San Francisco?"

"No, I don't recall a thing." But he believed he would have called Dan Kazakes. "He would be the only one that would be able to contact anybody in San Francisco, call them."

"Do you remember how you were dressed later on during these events in the room?"

"Actually I don't recall how I was dressed. I have to surmise I was dressed in some way from what I've heard here."

Later, when he was removed to a lower cabin, he brought along his toilet articles and his pills. After calling the Biegerts, he took another tranquilizer to help him sleep.

He recalled the long-distance call with Kazakes the next morning, and being told that his stepmother, Muriel Frisbee, had died. "I was totally discombobulated."

The last thing Frisbee did before being taken off the ship was to honor Mrs. Barnett's instructions to bestow tips on the ship's staff. "That was uppermost in my mind," he said.

"She wanted the butler to be tipped and the stewardesses and the dining-room steward, two of them. But she didn't tip the wine steward because she said, 'He really didn't do that much for us.'"

"And how did you hand out these tips?"

"I had the cash and I wrote envelopes out the next day to all the people involved."

He was faithful to his mistress's wishes until the end.

How was he now feeling about her death?

"Great loss. I miss her terribly. She was a very lovely woman."

And with that, I rendered my client unto the mercies of Dennis Murray.

Chapter 37

THROUGHOUT MY EXAMINATION-IN-CHIEF, NOT A WORD OF complaint had issued from the mouth of learned counsel for the Crown, neither hint of objection nor whisper of disbelief. He sat there impassively, making his notes, stockpiling his ammunition.

It became quickly apparent that he intended Frisbee's manuscript to be his chief weapon:

"Now, sir, first of all, while you were in prison in San Francisco you began to compose what I will loosely describe as your autobiography, correct?" Dennis asked.

"I started to make notes for a fictional novel, some of it based on my life, yes."

And into the courtroom came RCMP officers wheeling a cart filled with photostat copies of the manuscript. The original copy became Exhibit 58.

"Now I, sir, don't want to go into great detail with respect to your sexual exploits or your history, but to a limited extent I would like to do that," said Dennis. And I knew then what he had planned for Frisbee: a full frontal assault upon the man's homosexual lifestyle. Perhaps more accurately, an attack from the rear.

He started with Frisbee's brother, Francis. "How old were you when the first of these sexual acts between yourself and your brother took place?"

"I was five and my brother seven."

"And was it that your brother demanded that you suck on his penis or something like that?"

Frisbee didn't remember how it came about. He'd been too young.

Dennis went on to the "chap in the movie house." That relationship "involved you performing oral sex on him, is that correct?"

"Yes, sir."

"And during the course of that relationship, sir, he actually paid you for what you did, is that not correct?"

"In a minor way. I did have entry into the theater."

"Was he letting free entry to boys who didn't suck on his penis?"

"I don't know."

I began to realize why Dennis had held his peace during my examination of Frisbee: he intended to make it difficult for me in turn to object during cross-examination. Were I to complain about these questions, I would seem to the jury to be over-protective of my witness. Dennis would probably continue to turn up the heat, but I thought Frisbee could handle it. And perhaps win sympathy.

After eliciting some details about Frisbee's sexual roles with his various older partners, Dennis asked whether as a young person Frisbee engaged "in sex for money."

"No. I was never promiscuous. I didn't do things like that."

Dennis was eager to paint a different picture. Possibly he shared the stereotypical view of homosexuals as being intensely promiscuous and wanton. And maybe he felt the jury would share that view.

"You wouldn't characterize yourself as promiscuous?"

"Never."

"And you wouldn't characterize your relationship with men as though they were 'Johns' and you were basically a hooker?"

"Never."

Dennis quoted from the manuscript: "'There ensued amorous trips to Holyoke College, Hartford, and the thrills of weekends in New York.' Is that, sir, a description of your weekends away with Mr. Fitzsimmons?"

"Yes, in separate hotels."

"How old were you then, sir, I'm sorry?"

"Fourteen, fifteen, sixteen. Something in that area."

"And how was it, sir, that you were earning the money to pay your weekends in New York?"

"I worked part time in a candy store as a soda jerk."

Again Dennis tried to force him to agree that he had led a life of homosexual lechery, and again Frisbee denied it. The manuscript's recounting of his army years contained some silliness about "General Taylor," fantasies of sexual submission. Frisbee said it was pure fiction.

Dennis pointed to some passages in the manuscript about Frisbee's failed marriage and the death of his baby son.

"I gather you were not particularly pleased with the advent of responsibility involving a child?"

"I think I was pleased to have a child, yes. My wife wanted one very badly, and I did."

Frisbee's reaction to the death of his baby?

"Horrible. Frustrating."

Dennis confronted him with a passage from his writings:

"'Baby Bob died under mysterious circumstances and we the parents were free to copulate ourselves in a series of abortions in Washington, D.C.' Do you see that, sir?"

"Yes, sir."

"That, I gather, sir, is also a fictional account of your response to your child's death?" Dennis's question was richly accented with sarcasm, and Frisbee bristled:

"Does that sound careless to you?" he said, with uncharacteristic defiance.

"I'm sorry –" Dennis began.

"Does that sound unfeeling to you in some way?" Frisbee demanded.

"Did you feel –"

Frisbee forcefully said his piece: "He died and we moved to Washington and we did have a series of abortions – not abortions but miscarriages."

"No pregnancy resulted in a child that you would ultimately have to be responsible for?"

"No, we never had another child." Frisbee spoke those words with some sadness.

Dennis accused him of participating in Tom Leary's plan to falsify documents for sailors. Frisbee denied it.

His relationship with Dwight Frisbee, Dennis suggested, was

284

characterized by an anxiety to become his heir. Again Frisbee demurred.

"You didn't perceive of him as what I would loosely refer to as a 'wealthy John'?"

"I didn't think that unkindly of him, no."

Among the many unfortunate descriptive passages in the manuscript was one which profiled Philip Barnett as "short of cock, his lion's mane flying captivatingly in the breeze." Dennis seized on that.

"This is not the only place which I have had the pleasure to read where you refer to Mr. Barnett as 'short of cock.' Is that because in your opinion he was not particularly well-endowed?"

"Ah, yes."

Dennis for some reason seemed to take great umbrage at the passage: "And you find that, sir, worthy of ridicule?"

"Oh, I hadn't thought of it as being ridicule. Factual."

Dennis may have decided that this manner of discrediting the accused was not paying dividends. He spent some time trying to establish that Frisbee was resentful of Mrs. Barnett and her constant demands.

"You were on twenty-four-hour call, weren't you?"

"Oh, yes, I was."

"And you resented that, didn't you?"

"Not at all."

"Not at all?"

"No, I did not resent –"

"You loved every minute of it?"

"– being available for Mrs. Barnett twenty-four hours a day, no."

Dennis pointed to a passage in which Frisbee described himself as "more and more a slave to the Barnetts." He obviously read into it and similar phrases a suggestion that Frisbee chafed at this role. (Our psychiatrists would testify that Frisbee, given his curiously submissive makeup, actually reveled in it.)

"That, in my mind as an ordinary person," said Dennis, "is a feeling of resentment?"

"No, I loved Mr. Barnett very much."

"Did you love him less after he left you nothing?"

"Not one iota."

"And you didn't end up with a feeling that what he had done by his will was committing you to a further life of slavery with 'the bride'?"

"No, I committed myself seventeen years before."

"If you perceived yourself to be a slave, why didn't you quit?"

"It was just not a thought I would think of."

"What you thought of, sir, was to begin stealing money from Mrs. Barnett, isn't that correct?"

"I took funds from her account, yes."

"And that was your way of beginning to get for yourself what you thought you were justly entitled to, and that was a heck of a lot more money than you had got."

"Is that a question?"

"Yes."

"I don't know if I had those thoughts. I just knew that I was doing something unkind by paying my accounts through that checkbook."

"Well, it was more than something unkind, you were stealing from her."

"I have already admitted that, sir."

Dennis asked if Frisbee had discussed these thefts with Kazakes.

"Mr. Kazakes had nothing to do with that at all."

"Is your evidence that Mr. Kazakes was not even aware you were stealing money from the fall of '84?"

"He was not aware of it, sir."

Dennis resurrected the theory that Frisbee had drugged Mrs. Barnett before she signed the codicil.

"She didn't know what was going on in detail during that period of time?"

"She was perfectly conscious of everything about her."

"She was not, for example, falling asleep while one would be talking to her?"

"At times she would. She always did that all her life."

"And that was normal behavior for her?"

"Yes, it was. Mrs. Barnett took short, small naps constantly all her life."

Frisbee, Dennis insisted, was administering medication to Mrs. Barnett after her neck accident.

"I certainly was not."

"When Millie Dearnaley testified that you were in fact administering the medication, Millie is not telling the truth?"

"Millie is mistaken somewhere. She was only there two days a week."

"Would Millie Dearnaley have any reason whatsoever ... let me put it this way, sir: after she finished giving her evidence I watched her walk by this box and embrace you?"

"Yes."

"You are friends?"

"We are very fond of each other, yes."

"She wishes you nothing but the best?"

"True."

"She has no reason to lie about an issue like that?"

"Of course not."

Again Dennis pressed Frisbee on whether he felt a grudge against the Barnetts, quoting him this passage from the manuscript: "'They were making a fucking chambermaid out of me, and awarded me a Good Housekeeping award. I have been kept, but this is too much.'"

"Is that an accurate description, sir, of how you felt about your role in their lives, as a chambermaid?"

"No, not really."

"You had no notions in your mind of just being tired of being a slave and a chambermaid?"

"On reflection, perhaps."

"You had got to the point where you were just absolutely tired of being stuck in the role that you were stuck in?"

"It's hard to say if I was really conscious of that. That's what scared me all this time – is there that kind of resentment?"

This interesting response, I felt, demonstrated some glimmering of a new understanding, one that perhaps Dr. Tyhurst had helped him awaken to.

Dennis turned to Kazakes, establishing that Frisbee was constantly in fear of losing him to other lovers with whom Kazakes enjoyed occasional dalliances.

"It was important to you that your relationship stayed together, yes?"

"I had no power over Mr. Kazakes."

"No, but he had power over you, didn't he?"

"No, I was rather independent at times."

"Well, either you are submissive or you're independent; it's very difficult to be both, Mr. Frisbee."

"Well, I did have spasms of independency, yes."

Dennis led the witness through the events of August 19, seeking holes and contradictions, and Frisbee seemed to be taking it all well. Dennis seemed to get impatient:

"No matter how many questions I ask, you are not going to have any memory between going in and lying down in that bed and the time that you are in the bathroom?"

"Not except what I might have read in the papers," said Frisbee calmly.

Dennis may have been getting tired. He addressed the witness at one point as "Mr. Freezie."

But when he began to cross-examine him about the phantasmagorical ending to his manuscript the roof fell in on the defense.

Chapter 38

THIS WAS THE FIRST PASSAGE DENNIS QUOTED FROM PAGE 220 OF Frisbee's self-styled autobiography:

"'First Bloody Marys, vodka and French 75. A repose before a nap at 4:30. They indulge in a time-honored custom, a cocktail fit for the mood of a pleasant captain's goodbye dinner. In the distance a calliope is releasing strains of forgotten melodies, a calumnious act to perform as promised in a fateful meeting in his conscious of the early morning. Today is the day. A canonical hour to be revered.'"

That sounded vaguely ominous, of course, but the flowery prose spoke in a voice that was not Frisbee's, and was likely plagiarized.

Dennis continued reading:

"'The shocking realization a startling battle of his wits. When, how, where? The dull day only heightens conviction, giving false strength a happy, very hearty drink to ease the senses and induce a purple cast over a sky of blue.'"

The next line Dennis read (I saw it nowhere in my copy of the manuscript) sent an electric shock through my system – the bolt of lightning I had been fearing:

"'Tonight she must die.'"

I went rigid.

Frisbee had translated all his shorthand for me. Had he overlooked these four appalling words?

Dennis turned to the witness, and trumpet-tongued his final, scripted question: "That is the real ending, isn't it, Mr. Frisbee?"

Frisbee looked at the page Dennis had read from. "No, sir, it's not. Your shorthand transcribing is not correct either."

I looked at my own copy. After the phrase, "a canonical hour to be revered," appeared four shorthand symbols: a "p" with a long stem, a minute "6," a horizontal line with a downward hook at the end, and what looked like a "9" with a long tail:

While I scrambled through my files searching for Frisbee's shorthand transcription of this passage, Dennis asked:

"Is it Gray's method of shorthand, sir?"

"Gregg's . . . Gregg."

"I'm sorry?"

"Gregg, G-R-E-G-G, Gregg, yes."

"Well, I defer, sir, to your expertise with respect to the shorthand, and I am referring you to page 220, and you can tell us, sir, in your own words, what that one portion in the body of the third paragraph says, as you see it."

Frisbee studied it. And studied it. And studied it.

And studied it.

An intense and horrible silence enveloped the courtroom.

Frisbee seemed in a state akin to comatose, as if hypnotized by the four little shorthand forms.

I finally found the transcription he had typed out for me. It made absolutely no sense: "A canonical hour to be revered (with or either) (most, impossible, also I think mistake, or must) entire."

I couldn't help him; I felt chained to my chair. Perhaps a minute passed, perhaps two.

Answer the goddamn question, I screamed silently.

He seemed to have broken into a sweat, guilt dripping from his brow.

Finally the judge's quiet voice broke the spell of silence.

"Mr. Frisbee, are you trying to transcribe that shorthand?"

Frisbee finally looked up from the page. "Well, they made a mistake in one, two, three, four words, your lordship. I would probably have to write them out to show . . ."

The rest of his response was all verbal gibberish to me: "This says 'daily,' 'S-E-E' or 'S-E-A' . . . 'miss' . . . 'must' . . . not 'must,' 'mistake,' and that last form would be 'entire' or 'entry.' If it were the word that the gentleman used it would be just opposite and it would not be open . . . it wouldn't be open in the way that it is, and it's on a slant. 'D,' meaning 'day,' would be a straighter line, and this is on an angle, which means 'entry' . . . 'enter.'" As he concluded this meaningless gabble his voice dropped.

Justice McKenzie turned to Dennis: "Where is the transcription of this? You read through it as if it were written and clear. Where is the transcript?"

That question should never have been asked, and Dennis's answer constituted a most damaging form of hearsay:

"Yes, I did, my lord. The transcription was obtained from a business college here in Victoria."

While Dennis might have been entitled to call as a witness a shorthand expert from that college, he was not permitted to give the evidence himself. It was too late to object; I would raise the issue later in the absence of the jury.

The judge asked Frisbee, "Now Mr. Frisbee, are you telling the court what the shorthand means after the word 'revered'?"

"Yes, sir."

"What does it mean?"

"I have 'daily.'"

"'I have daily'?"

"No, I'm sorry, sir. The first word is 'daily.'"

"'Daily.'"

"'S-E-A, S-E-E, miss or mistake.'"

"'Miss or mistake'?"

"'Entry' or 'entire.'"

"Can you make some sense out of that for us?"

"I am referring to a mistake in my daily entry in my journal," Frisbee said, an explanation which I thought odd, perhaps made up on the spot. "See mistake in daily entry," was, I guess, what he was now claiming he had written, but his evidence, as against Dennis's straightforward translation of the shorthand, seemed hopelessly contrived and unlikely.

"It has nothing to do then, in your evidence, with Mrs. Barnett's death?" said Dennis.

"None of this has any interest, as far as I know, in Mrs. Barnett's death."

Dennis thanked the court and sat down.

Frisbee seemed shaken, confused. What had the jury, I wondered, made of all this? I sensed they now felt disappointed in Frisbee, doubted his honesty. Frisbee had seemed to be, at best, discombobulated, and at worst confabulating. Dennis's next move, in rebuttal, would be to produce his shorthand expert to prove the phrase really read, "Tonight she must die."

I, too, must have looked as if I had died as I stood to ask some questions in re-examination.

I produced his own transcription of the phrase, and tendered it as an exhibit. It must have further baffled the jury.

I referred him to his use of the word "canonical."

"I don't know what that word means," he said.

"Do you know where you got it from?"

"Out of a book."

"There is a word in the previous sentence, calumnious. Do you know what that means?"

"No, sir." He'd also got that rounded, vowel-strewn word from a book. Its meaning, slanderous, didn't quite fit the text.

To try to limit the damage and shore up our breached defense, I seized on another passage from the ending of his manuscript: "'In passing she told me we would be going to England in April for her birthday and we would look for a suitable flat in Mayfair. This had all the earmarks of interrupting my personal mode of life. As it was we would be away for Christmas on this ship and it looked to me as if this might be the beginning of the end! I'd like to retire with Dan soon.'"

"What is that about?" I asked.

"Well, for years the Barnetts had been talking about taking a flat in London. It never materialized when Philip was alive, but she was starting to think about taking an apartment in London."

That would have interrupted his life with Dan. The "beginning of the end" meant Dan and he would be parting company.

"'She commented, "I love these French 75s, they will be the death of me yet."'" Now, where does that expression come from?"

"Well, she said that for years, she loved them so much."

"Why did you put that in the ending of the book?"

"Just for interest to a reader."

"And then you say on the next page, 'We retired and I thought of the many questions that Dan would ask; dreams and fantasies came into my mind. Maybe she would hire Dan also.'"

"Yes, that was probably a thought in my mind."

"'Would not please him, he loves Muriel, but from a distance. She had already given him a ticket to visit Jerry in Australia.'"

She had in fact talked to a travel agent about sending Dan to Australia for Christmas, he said. This was confirmed by an entry in Frisbee's Daily Journal: on the last page, he had written, "January 2, Dan due L.A."

The fantasy part of his ending, about an intruder stealing into the room and beating Muriel with a champagne bottle, was included in his book, he said, "to make an interesting ending that would appeal to any reader."

Other passages, he said, were lifted from popular books he had read: "'The first gaze is all-encompassing, a swift inventory at the most; he seems to be grinning like a gargoyle.'"

"I wrote it out of a book," Frisbee said.

The next passage: "'He is turning toward me – what is he reaching for? I feel myself levitating, my spirit spiraling me up to his mobile body, and I look down to see my body as if in a dream . . . was he now me?'"

"Just making a readable ending for the climax."

"'The face I loved is battered and bruised. Her blue eyes almost distinctly divorced . . .' Where is all that from?"

"That is the style that Mr. King . . . right out of one of his horror books."

"Stephen King?"

"Yes."

"Is he one of your favorite authors?"

"Not really, but we had very few books that were passed around, and he seemed to be a popular one in the jail, so I read most of his books."

I quoted another sentence: "'My head is aching, as I look down I feel a sensation of a great vacuum transposes my body once again. I somehow become a horrible monster, a call for help.'"

Again adapted from a book.

Indeed, contained among the many pages of manuscript were

photostat copies of pages from books he had read and not yet plagiarized in his memoirs.

His motive in composing the manuscript was simple financial gain. "Mr. Barnett always told me I should write a story," he said. "He thought I lived a very interesting life."

I concluded: "Now in the autobiographical parts of this manuscript, is there one single reference to any act of violence on your part?"

"No, sir."

"And have you ever committed an act of violence in your life?"

"No, I never have."

"By the way, prior to this matter coming before the court had you ever seen a psychiatrist for therapy?"

"No, sir, I never have."

I sat.

"That's all, Mr. Frisbee," said the judge.

That's all, Mr. Frisbee, I thought.

Today he had died.

Chapter 39

UP TO THE MOMENT OF HIS FALL, UNTIL THOSE LONG AGONIZING seconds of silence as Frisbee stared with an expression of dismay and pain at those four shorthand symbols, he had won the day. Now the game was lost – or would be, I knew, when Dennis called his expert shorthand witness.

I trudged wearily down to the courthouse cells, where an apprehensive Frisbee received me, that truant schoolboy look again upon his face: the strap this time, Robert, maybe expulsion. I pleaded with him to make sense out of his mangled shorthand. He struggled over the passage for several seconds, shaking his head in dismay, looking up at me with pleading eyes.

I asked: "Are you sure it couldn't mean, 'Tonight she must die'?"

"I don't think so," he said softly.

He was lying to me; I had lost much faith in him. How could he not read his own shorthand? But in truth, many other shorthand notations from both his manuscript and his travel diary were incomprehensible to him.

As I left the cells one of the sheriff's officers handed me a few of my paperbacks which I'd earlier promised to sign for his friends as Christmas gifts. Then he asked me:

"Going to write one about this, Mr. Deverell?"

"Not on your life."

At my desk, I read through the manuscript once again: what other horrors were contained in this document?

He'd recorded obscene phrases from fellow inmates in the

homosexual wing, quotes not likely to impress a jury of his more prudish peers:

"If the farts don't kill you the fists will . . . Yeah, man, I would not even piss up your ass if your guts were on fire . . . I just could not sit there and masturbate a typewriter."

A jury might forgive him for these, might understand that a writer must do his research where and when he can. But . . . "Tonight she must die . . ."?

I spent a ruined night of worry. How could Frisbee have been so stupid as to announce his awful intentions in his manuscript? How could I, his lawyer, successfully defend him if I myself were beset with doubts about his innocence?

Murder, He Wrote.

How could you do this to me, Robert?

I heard Dennis's accusing voice: "That's the real ending, isn't it, Mr. Frisbee?"

It wasn't. I found the real ending written elsewhere:

"Just a fermented fruit. Kaput."

◇   ◇   ◇

On the next morning, Wednesday, December 17, *The Times-Colonist* blared the grisly news from the front page: "'Tonight She Must Die,' Frisbee Wrote," the headline pronounced, a phrase that crown counsel Dennis Murray "read to a crowded Victoria courtroom Tuesday from a manuscript entitled 'A Demented Parasite.'"

"'Today is the day . . . Tonight she must die,'" proclaimed the lead paragraph of the *Province* story. "These are the words that Robert Frisbee jotted down as part of a novel he wrote while awaiting trial."

The media had reached its verdict.

Although not quite unanimously. In the *Sun*, Larry Still had buried the episode in the final paragraphs. That wasn't going to sell newspapers, I thought, his ignoring the lurid yellow stuff, merely offering an honest account of Frisbee's testimony. I asked him why.

He wasn't sure. He just had a "feeling."

A feeling?

"Something doesn't seem quite right to me."

Could Dennis have got the translation wrong? Surely the assistant deputy Attorney-General would not make an uncalculated error of such gravity.

Roxanne Helme, a bright young lawyer then taking articles with the firm, was given the task of tracking down a person knowledgeable about Gregg shorthand. She phoned various business schools and soon discovered that shorthand, though not a lost art, was much less practised in these days of the office dictaphone. Not that there weren't experts and tutors in the field: but these were trained in the Pitman school, the method of shorthand commonly in use in Canada. The Gregg system, very much different, was in general use in the U.S. Where had Dennis found *his* expert?

In the meantime, we dispiritedly returned to court to try to pick up the pieces. At 9:00 that morning, we showed up with our two psychiatrists in tow.

Dennis Murray asked that court be resumed in the absence of the jury, then gave blunt forewarning that if our expert evidence did not sufficiently raise the issue of automatism he would ask the judge to withdraw that defense from the jury. And he threatened us that he would then ask that the jury be allowed to consider a verdict of insanity:

"I just want for the record to be sure that my learned friends are aware that they, in calling their evidence, are running that risk."

"The cases make it clear that we are running that risk," Jeff Green replied. He knew the law; he was impatient at being lectured to.

"I don't think there is any question about it," said Justice McKenzie.

We had ventured forth upon a perilous sortie from which there was no retreat. If automatism went to the jury, we clearly faced the threat of a finding that Frisbee committed the act of murder while suffering a disease of the mind – and a special verdict of not guilty by reason of insanity would follow from that. The result would be tantamount to a life sentence for Frisbee in a chamber of horrors: the Riverview Hospital's unit for the criminally insane.

We had always known that the specter of an insanity verdict lurked behind an automatism defense. Frisbee had assured us that he was willing to take the gamble between a possible complete acquittal and incarceration for his remaining years in a snake pit. Among venomous criminal psychotics.

Jeff, in his turn, gave warning he would be opposing any Crown application to call rebuttal evidence. The issue of automatism was one for the Crown to negative during its own case, not during rebuttal. The usual rule in criminal trials is that the Crown, given notice of the defenses to be relied on, must not lie in the weeds until all the defense evidence is in and then spring new evidence upon the defense. The Crown is entitled to call only evidence that rebuts matters which it could not have anticipated arising.

The lines having been drawn, Jeff asked that the jury be recalled and that Dr. Fred Rosenthal take the stand.

A handsome, amiable gentleman of middle years, Dr. Rosenthal is a respected scholar of the mind, with a Ph.D. in educational and clinical psychology from Stanford and Berkeley and an M.D. from Stanford. Since 1977, he has maintained a private practice in San Francisco but also, generously, provides twelve hours a week of service to the free clinics of that city's community mental health system.

V. Roy Lefcourt had retained him shortly after Frisbee's arrest, and Rosenthal had interviewed the accused over the course of four days in October 1985, then ordered some psychological testing.

Jeff wasted no time: "In your interviews with Mr. Frisbee, did you form any opinion as to whether he was being truthful with you?"

"My opinion was that Mr. Frisbee was being truthful, and was trying as much as he could to tell me what he remembered, giving me the material in a fairly straightforward manner."

"Having seen Mr. Frisbee on those four occasions, did you form an opinion as to whether Mr. Frisbee, functioning normally, was capable of killing Mrs. Barnett?"

"I did form an opinion, yes."

"What was your opinion?"

"My opinion was that Mr. Frisbee would not have been able to kill anyone in his normal state of mind."

Frisbee's amnesia?

"I remember being concerned with that question and I did reach an opinion, and I felt that the amnesia was genuine."

The likely explanation for it was that it was alcohol-induced – in the standard parlance: a blackout.

Rosenthal embellished upon that, then gave expert evidence upon the effects of alcohol on the human body, and, after adding up Frisbee's August 19 drinks (from morning Bloody Marys to evening French 75s), calculated his blood alcohol reading at 6:30 that evening as being in excess of .24 milliliters of alcohol per one hundred milliliters of blood, indicating significant intoxication.

(Indeed significant, thrice the figure of .08 which The Criminal Code of Canada decrees as the amount of alcohol determining an impairment of one's ability to drive.)

What effect, he was asked, would twenty milligrams of Librium have on that level of intoxication?

The effect would be intensified. "In very general terms, if you are taking Librium with alcohol it's as if you were drinking more, and that's the simplest way of looking at it."

How deep a sleep would be induced? Jeff asked.

"Initially at least he would go into a fairly heavy sleep, a semi-stuporous kind of sleep."

"Would it be like knocking himself out?"

"Yes."

Advised that Frisbee had come to while in the bathroom, he said the need to urinate could easily have served as a stimulus, possibly painful, to wake him.

"The other thing that occurs with sedatives like Librium is that you get a loss of control, that is the conscious control that you often use to modify or monitor behavior is somehow lost, and a person becomes more erratic and irrational and impulsive."

He agreed with Dr. Solomon that severe emotional shock or stress can reduce the external symptoms of intoxication, "and a person can at least superficially appear that he is not as intoxicated as he really is."

Jeff dealt with the decidedly tricky matter of whether wiping blood from the bottles of scotch and wine was consistent with Frisbee being in an altered state of consciousness.

"I don't think it's inconsistent with the state of mind that I have described, in that a person can engage in complex behavior in a state of intoxication, and even with a blackout going on or beginning. There is the well-known example of people who drink heavily at parties, somehow get home, and the next morning have no memory of how they got home, whether they drove the car, or where the car is. That sort of behavior is very consistent with this sort of blackout state of mind."

"Finally, doctor, if Mr. Frisbee killed Mrs. Barnett, is it your opinion that he did so while in a fully conscious state of mind?"

"My opinion is that he was not in a fully conscious state of mind; he was in a state of impaired consciousness induced by the alcohol and Librium."

Much of Dennis's cross-examination was directed to a suggestion that Frisbee, an experienced drinker, tolerated alcohol better than a non-user. Rosenthal agreed there is such a thing as tolerance to alcohol, "but once a person gets beyond a certain age, as body functions start to deteriorate, the tolerance may not be as good as it was, say, ten years before."

"A tolerance to alcohol transposes over to a tolerance to Librium, doesn't it?"

"I don't think that necessarily is true."

The witness parried Dennis's suggestions that the alcohol and Librium would merely tend to reduce Frisbee's inhibitions.

Dennis asked him whether he had taken into account the Crown's evidence of motives to kill.

"Even if there were a motive, psychologically I don't believe Mr. Frisbee, in his normal state of mind, could commit this kind of killing."

Dennis completed a cross-examination that was surprisingly brief. He announced he had a meeting in Vancouver that evening with the Benchers of the Law Society, and wished to catch the 4:00 p.m. helicopter flight.

The judge again expressed some worry about our timing: "I don't know what this does, if anything, with our target. Is the target getting further away from us or what?"

I said Dr. Tyhurst, our last witness, would be called this afternoon, would be finished by noon the next day, Thursday.

That meant, I silently hoped, that we were still on schedule. But for what? I seriously doubted that Rosenthal and Tyhurst could now recoup our losses.

Tonight she must die . . .

I returned to the office.

Roxanne had tracked down an expert in Gregg shorthand. In the office I met with Joan Dellert, an instructor of legal secretaries at a Victoria business school.

Chapter 40

WHEN I RETURNED TO COURT IT WAS ALREADY IN SESSION. IT WAS
Jeff Green's show in any event. Starring Dr. James Tyhurst.

A word about Jim Tyhurst. He is not exactly the darling of the
courts. Or at least of certain judges (those of less liberal view),
and I have heard one or two of them audibly groan when his name
is mentioned as a probable witness.

Even less favorably disposed to him are prosecutors and police
officers, loyal guard dogs of the law who ill-manneredly snarl and
snap when they scent his presence.

This is because he is an effective witness for the defense. And
because he enjoys forensic combat.

He doesn't have much time for the dull wits of the legal
profession – or of his own, for that matter – and if he possesses
any flaw it's a calm arrogance born of sure confidence in his cause
of the moment. There's also, unfortunately, a side of him that
wants to be a lawyer, and in that regard he caused Jeff a few
problems, urging as he did that we make ours a test case for an
expanded doctrine of automatism that would wend its way to the
Supreme Court of Canada and ultimately bring essential reform
to an illiberal law.

Our duty was, we explained, to get poor Mr. Frisbee off. We
were not retained to serve as a law reform commission.

Jim built up a zest for the Frisbee defense such that I have never
observed in him during the dozens of trials in which I have either
employed him as defense counsel or, while on retainer to the
Attorney-General, cross-examined him (the effect is akin to beating one's head against a brick wall). Quite often, after court, he

would show up in our offices, a great fire constantly raging in the bowl of his pipe, and spiritedly debate our strategies for defending the soul of innocence who was our client. Manifestly innocent was Frisbee. Mentally and emotionally incapable of a conscious murder.

It was not the prospect of a comfortable fee as a forensic witness that ignited his ardor for Frisbee's defense. Jim works at legal aid rates, too, for all manner of mentally confused street people and down-and-outers.

In his early sixties, slender, tall, remarkably handsome (try to picture the late actor George Sanders), his voice resonant and firm. He was literate and compassionate (although he often tried not to let this latter quality show in court; experts aren't supposed to have feelings).

His credentials were as imposing as the man. A graduate in medicine and psychiatry from McGill in Montreal. A fellow of the American Association for the Advancement of Science. A life fellow of the American Psychiatric Association. A fellow of the Center for Advanced Study in the Behavioral Sciences at Stanford (one of only two Canadians privileged to have been invited). A stint as assistant professor at Cornell. As associate professor at McGill. As senior psychiatrist at the Royal Victoria Hospital in Montreal. As head of psychiatry at Vancouver's Shaughnessy Hospital. As head of the Department of Psychiatry at the University of British Columbia.

One thing more: in earlier years his closest friend was Justice McKenzie.

Their friendship, he told us, had been profound and confiding.

In later years they drew apart – in ways, he implied, that were difficult. There were political reasons, I gathered: he felt Lloyd McKenzie had drifted from liberal roots toward the safer precincts of the center; Jim had stayed in the field of action, in the more parlous arenas to the left. He told us they had quarreled over this.

And now? Jim wasn't sure. He thought there might have been a recent mending, a repair; the cement of their friendship had been strong.

When we told Dennis Murray we would be using Jim Tyhurst he wearily sang the standard refrain of prosecutors – the guy confuses juries into giving bad verdicts; the judges don't like him; you're asking for trouble. But Dennis wasn't aware of the history between Tyhurst and McKenzie. No doubt if he had been, he might not have been so rude when Jeff rose to address the court that afternoon:

"I tender Dr. Tyhurst, my lord, as an expert in the field of psychiatry."

"Mr. Murray?" the judge said.

"And, my lord, I for the record admit that he is a psychiatrist."

Usually, opposing counsel will simply admit the qualifications of a qualified expert, avoiding the necessity of a hearing before the judge to determine his capacity to give opinion evidence. (Generally speaking, only experts may voice opinions as opposed to facts.)

"I take it my learned friend is requiring me to go through the mechanics of qualifying Dr. Tyhurst as an expert?" Jeff said.

"No," said Dennis, "I accept he is a psychiatrist and as any psychiatrist would be, able to express an opinion of some kind." This cool derision was of course for the benefit of the jury, who would know that Dennis held our witness in dim regard. (Dennis's attitude outraged Jeff, who fumed after court recessed.)

The judge simply said, "Thank you."

Jeff decided to run him through some of his qualifications anyway, then sought some detail about his area of special research interest:

"The study of behavior of individuals and groups under severe stress, sudden change, combat as well as civilian experience." He had begun work in that field after the Second World War, among veterans and returning P.O.W.'s from the Pacific theater.

Like Rosenthal, Tyhurst had satisfied himself that Frisbee's amnesia was real. He was truthful, "insofar as he could be; he had some problems with his recollection and was also somewhat bewildered by some details."

A scientist in human behavior doesn't recklessly jump to such conclusions. He employs tested devices, cross-examines subjects to seek variance and consistency of story, watches their demeanor: "their behavior, their style, their conversation, the amount of eye contact and how that eye contact is managed; restlessness at certain points of the interview, constraint."

He checks his source's story against other facts. For instance, it was significant that in Frisbee's manuscript he described the murder weapon as being a champagne bottle. He had deduced that from erroneous newspaper accounts of the murder: this was an important indication that his amnesia was genuine.

Jim Tyhurst's work with Frisbee was, I later learned, intensely therapeutic for Frisbee. Initially terrified of Tyhurst (or of the self he had never looked at), Frisbee had, by the fourth day of Tyhurst's interviews, come to see the doctor as somewhat of a god figure, omniscient, all-knowing.

He later told us that Tyhurst had finally helped him understand his beginnings in the Dion household in West Springfield, Mass.

His ambivalence of feeling about his father – those conflicting emotions of admiration and fear, love and hate – were, Tyhurst told the jury, "very significant in Frisbee's history, a major factor in his personality development and subsequent sexual adjustment. It's of interest to me, for example, that subsequently most of his male relationships were persons of some twenty years older at least."

As for Frisbee's despairing and fearful mother, so often physically abused by her husband:

"She may have projected expectations of injury onto Robert, which became the focus for obsessive concern and overanxious, restrictive, overprotective behavior." These feelings were created when Frisbee was a small child, helpless, unable to do more than respond to the environment of his parents – and of his older brother, who introduced him to homosexuality, and imposed it on him.

As a result of these early molding forces, Frisbee developed a dependency trait, one which Tyhurst described as morbid and pathological. Persons suffering this disorder are unwilling to make demands on those they depend on for fear of jeopardizing their relationship and being forced to rely on themselves. Associated with this neurotic dependency is an element of masochism, a term that Krafft-Ebing introduced to the world of behavior science, describing it as involving an unusually intense dependence on the love-object: "sexual bondage."

Quoting the late Dr. Karen Horney of New York, a leading expert in the field of neurotic dependency, he described masochism as essentially a "'striving towards the relinquishment of self, toward the goal of oblivion, of getting rid of self with all its conflicts and its limitations.'"

A person suffering from a morbid dependency syndrome, she wrote, "'feels that he is as incapable of living without the presence of another person as he is incapable of living without oxygen. Without ever realizing it, and mostly in contrast to his conscious modesty and humility, his expectations are parasitic in character. The world is considered as more-or-less unreliable, cold, begrudging, vindictive; and to feel helpless and dependent on such a potentially hostile world is equal to feeling defenseless in the midst of danger.'"

Frisbee, said Dr. Tyhurst, had constructed from his chaotic background and the unresolved ambivalences of his early family situation a persona by which most people knew him and liked him. "In effect, he was his own construct, and it is interesting in this regard that he frequently refers to himself in the third person."

He had constructed a personality, a character for himself – "because there was no character, so to speak, given him in his relationships."

Part of this self-created personality came from powerful identification with heroes (or heroines) from romantic and historical novels. "Such a construct is fine as long as it works, but it has a certain fragile character to it" – and the personality thus created is precariously integrated.

In talking with Frisbee, Tyhurst said, it often became difficult to tell whether what he said expressed his real feelings and attitudes, which he had for so long and for the most part repressed, or whether he was speaking as his "construct personality," saying what he felt he should say. In constructing this personality, in maintaining it, he denied any negative feelings he may have had. This he had done most of his life.

Frisbee, he said, had never been comfortable with the homosexual stereotype – "the extrovert, the bitchiness, sell my body for five dollars type," to use Frisbee's recorded words. He sought security, stability, set limits to his own behavior. In many respects he was a very conforming and conventional character. Like most people, he had never examined his situation very much: "he just lived it."

Hopefully without doing violence to Dr. Tyhurst's description of the human forces that worked upon Frisbee, let me summarize his views:

While Frisbee's male relationships satisfied his needs for being dominated, at the same time he met the needs of those who dominated him: Dwight Frisbee, Dan Kazakes, Philip Barnett. They needed Frisbee as much as he needed them, and through them he was able to find a place in society, a niche that would otherwise have been denied to him.

The love-resentment ambivalence he felt for his father was echoed in the sentiments he felt for Philip Barnett. Frisbee admired Philip as an intelligent man of superior accomplishments and wealth, yet held a view of him (developed largely in retrospect) as verbally sadistic, as demanding his time and service without regard. But even when describing this side of Barnett, Frisbee showed no angry feelings: repressing them completely – at considerable cost – for fear of rejection and loss of dependence.

Frisbee was desolated by Philip's death, but because he was thrust immediately into Muriel's social whirl he lacked a normal opportunity to grieve. Grieving is essential to all who suffer great loss, and the failure of it unhealthy, and Frisbee suffered a significant clinical depression – which regrettably was not diagnosed. Preoccupied with his sorrow, he withdrew his attention from the world and suffered a serious loss of short-term memory. For the next seven or eight months Frisbee retained only some islands of memory and suffered significant periods of amnesia.

What feelings of resentment he held toward Mrs. Barnett, for her incessant demands upon him, were fleeting and immediately suppressed. In effect, he swallowed them (along with a great deal of alcohol), and only recently, following his long incarceration, had he begun to develop some insight into them – an understanding still quite incomplete.

As to Frisbee's state of mind at the time of Mrs. Barnett's murder, Dr. Tyhurst concurred with Dr. Rosenthal that if Frisbee killed her it was more probable than not that he did so in a state of altered consciousness, such that his behavior was not voluntary. He was incapable of conscious deliberation and planning or forming an intent.

This state of mind was brought about by a combination of factors, but the precipitating causes were alcohol and Librium intoxication and what Tyhurst described as "the context," the particular situation in which Frisbee found himself in his relationship with Mrs. Barnett at the time of her death.

On the Alaska trip, Tyhurst said, "Mrs. Barnett was not only being quite enveloping and overwhelming, but she was also talking of the future, and describing how they would spend six months in London and six months back in the United States." That would involve increasing separation from Daniel Kazakes. Frisbee found he was unable to extricate himself from these plans, and at the same time unable to deal with his feelings and confront her.

"He was under increasing pressure, in my opinion, from this, but was not consciously aware of the strain on him, because he would suppress the negative feelings, and a sudden eruption, if you like, of feelings can occur under different kinds of circumstances."

Such an eruption can occur following a sudden and immediate stress, an event which overwhelms the individual and produces untoward response, or can occur as the end point of a long process of strain. A person may attempt to resist but finally cannot, and at a particular moment disintegration occurs – in the same way psychologically as if there had been a single, sudden, and violent psychological blow: "like a snapping of a rubber band that's been stretched, rather than suddenly broken."

That, by the way, was the issue that Dr. Tyhurst hoped would work its way to the highest courts of Canada and would expand the concept of automatism. However, the defense of non-insane automatism has heretofore been restricted by Canadian courts of appeal to sleepwalking crimes or instances in which a person is rendered unconscious – though still physically active – by a physical blow to the head or the ingestion of drugs (being unaware of their effects on the mind), and does not encompass cases of psychological trauma.

I had felt – at least until Dennis's cross-examination of Frisbee – that the analogy of a rubber band stretched taut over many months, maybe years, then finally snapping, might best explain the sudden blind explosion of rage on the part of Frisbee, assuming he was the actor in Mrs. Barnett's murder. However likely that was the compelling factor, it offered no defense in Canadian law, which, tied and bound to precedent, trudges along at its own pace, far to the rear of our fast-growing knowledge of human psychology.

Jeff asked him: "Is it your opinion that this state of altered consciousness that you've postulated would have occurred without the alcohol and the Librium?"

"Unlikely, very unlikely."

That hopefully kept us within the bounds of the present law of automatism.

Tyhurst described the act of wiping the bottles – assuming Frisbee did so – as apparently purposeless behavior. It didn't make sense: under the circumstances there was nowhere he was going to go.

"If the suggestion is that he was removing fingerprints, then it was a relatively senseless act under the cirumstances. It is most probable that this occurred during the period of automatic behavior."

As to Frisbee's level of impairment, Tyhurst calculated his blood-alcohol reading on the evening of August 19 to be as low as .19 or as high as .26, and said a person at such a level would be disoriented and mentally confused but not yet stuporous. The ingestion of Librium would have taken Frisbee into a realm between confusion and stupor.

We had one more rabbit to pull from the hat. A little furry creature called somnambulism.

Sleepwalking is the more common term. Cases in which violent acts are committed in the course of a deep sleep are extremely rare but are recorded in the reports, and the courts assign them to the category of non-insane automatism defenses.

Such a defense succeeded recently in Ontario, and the story is chronicled in a book by June Callwood, *The Sleepwalker*.

Frankly, we had only the skimpiest framework on which to hang a murder-while-sleepwalking defense, maybe enough to persuade Justice McKenzie to allow it to go to the jury, in addition to the defense of alcohol- and drug-induced automatism. During my examination-in-chief of Frisbee in court I had asked him if during his early years he had any episodes of sleepwalking.

"I had just two that I know of; I can't say what age I was. One, I tried to walk off the back porch balcony, and another one, mother found me at the front door trying to get out." She woke him up on each occasion.

Frisbee had also told Tyhurst of an occasion of sleepwalking in the San Francisco jail when he woke up in the wrong bunk.

On August 19, Frisbee would have been in a deep sleep as a result of the effect of alcohol and Librium, Tyhurst told the court.

"If he had been asleep from the time he lay down until the time he woke up to go to the bathroom, how could he possibly have killed Mrs. Barnett?" Jeff asked.

Tyhurst referred to a form of sleep-related automatic behavior, different from somnambulism, which he called "sleep drunkenness."

"There have been a number of clinical descriptions of persons engaging in various kinds of assaultive and other behavior during a period of sleep drunkenness." He could not rule out the possibility that Frisbee had committed a violent act while either sleepwalking or in a state of sleep drunkenness.

"It's not common but it does happen." Usually at night, usually in a bedroom.

"Who is usually the victim?"

"Well, a person close to, or the spouse."

I asked that Dr. Tyhurst be stood down before cross-examination so that Joan Dellert, our shorthand expert, could be heard: her father had recently passed away, and his funeral was scheduled that afternoon.

Chapter 41

"MY LORD, I WILL BE SEEKING TO QUALIFY MRS. DELLERT AS AN expert in the field of shorthand writing known as the Gregg method."

"I have no difficulty with that whatsoever, my lord," said Dennis Murray.

"Thank you," said the judge.

For many years a legal secretary, now a teacher at Victoria's Executive Secretarial College and at Camosum regional college, Dellert had worked with the Gregg system for between twenty and twenty-five years.

I asked her to interpret a sample shorthand sentence from the ending of Frisbee's manuscript.

"I would do the sentence: 'She takes a nap first and then he makes' – the next word is actually 'neither,' and I would put 'another' – 'another drink for himself.'"

The judge stopped her: "I am sorry, but I don't get the transposition from 'neither' to 'another.'"

"If I were making sense of it, that's the word I would put in."

"Sometimes you have to make sense within the context of the sentence you are trying to read?" I asked.

"Yes."

I then referred her to the symbols after the longhand phrase, "A canonical hour to be revered."

"We heard two days ago Mr. Murray put to a witness that those words were, 'Tonight she must die.' Can those symbols in any possible way be construed as meaning that?"

"No."

A long, sweet pause between questions.

"Now, let us go through those symbols one by one. The first symbol represents what word?"

"'Today.'"

"Is the symbol for 'tonight' different?"

"Very different."

"Okay, and then there is, looks like a little '6' there? Are you able to say what that is?"

"It's a little '6.'"

"And is the symbol for 'she' different from that?"

"Yes."

"And the third symbol?"

"It stands for 'must.'"

"And the last symbol?"

"I have no idea."

"Does it resemble any other symbol in your experience?"

"Yes. It could possibly be the word 'lie.'"

"What about 'write'?"

"It could be 'write.'"

"Could it mean 'die'?"

"No."

"All right. Now, how much time did you spend puzzling over that phrase when you were in my office?"

"Oh, three or four hours."

She had looked at other examples of his shorthand. Some of it was reasonably good, some of it didn't make sense.

Dennis complained that Dellert's voice had fallen.

I asked her to speak up. "I don't want my friend to miss any of this," I said.

She had brought with her a book entitled, *Gregg Shorthand Manual Simplified*.

I tendered copies of some of the pages as exhibits. The jury was able to see that the symbol for "die," a kind of "p" with a long horizontal slant, was remarkably unlike the symbol contained in the manuscript, which resembled a curlicue "9".

"Now, Mrs. Dellert, if you were asked to interpret that phrase, what would be the best thing you could come up with?"

"Today something must something."

"Is a reasonable interpretation, 'Today something must write'?"

"It could be."

"In your experience," I asked, "do persons who write short-hand commonly make notes to themselves during the course of such writings?"

"Yes."

I then had her write out the phrase, in Gregg shorthand, "Tonight she must die," and beneath that, "Today he must write." I tendered it as an exhibit. They were markedly similar.

I thanked her.

"Mr. Murray?" said the judge.

There was not much Dennis could do. He put his best face on, asked her a series of general questions, and for what it was worth had her agree that in the array of possibilities, "Today she must lie" was one of the phrases that, in context, could make sense.

And that was that.

As Dellert left the stand, I was in a state of buoyant, delicious joy, complicated only by a sense that I had failed to keep faith with my client, that in my heart I had forsaken him, abandoned him to his accusers. No more. I would redouble my efforts to save this innocent fellow from the cruel mercies of the enemy.

I suspected the foulest of play on the part of the Crown. After the jury left the room, Jeff and I, with umbrage, took the Crown to task for its underhanded tactics, its malicious attempt to hide a bomb – dud though it was – in the luggage of the defense, to put damaging and patently false words in the mouth of the accused. Dennis's earlier bold assertion before the jury that his "transcription was obtained from a business college here in Victoria," was, I felt, so unfair, so blameworthy that it demanded the judge consider the ordering of a mistrial. Crown counsel's conduct – and I chose my words carefully – had departed a far distance from accepted ethical standards.

Dennis entered a vigorous plea of not guilty. The business school transcription that he received, he insisted, was in fact, "Today she must die."

"In my question to the accused I inadvertently said, 'Tonight she must die,' and for that I apologize. But I can assure your

313

lordship that there was no great design in it, and at the end of the day I don't think it makes very much difference." He was at a loss to understand how he had done anything improper.

In fact he was prepared to produce in rebuttal his shorthand expert to testify that in the "context" of the whole of Frisbee's writings, the otherwise meaningless sentence could somehow be taken as reading "Tonight she must die." The judge refused to allow him to do so, but seemed unwilling to cast blame on crown counsel: "I certainly cannot attribute to him any willful interpretation to mislead."

The false road that the trial had followed consumed the rest of that Thursday. Tyhurst's cross-examination was still to come.

We were in time trouble.

The Times-Colonist, having emblazoned across its front page Dennis's false interpretation of Frisbee's shorthand, buried Dellert's evidence in its back pages, near the end of its reporting of Tyhurst's testimony. *The Province* ignored her evidence.

Larry Still's account in *The Vancouver Sun*, however, bore the head: "'She must die' not in notes, expert says."

"Told you I thought there was something fishy," he said to me later.

Chapter 42

BY LARRY STILL, SUN STAFF REPORTER

Victoria – The prospect of sequestering a B.C. Supreme Court jury over the Christmas holidays did not sit well Friday with the judge trying Robert Frisbee on a charge of first-degree murder.

So Frisbee, a dapper male secretary with a taste for champagne and caviar, will be spending the festive period in a cell at Wilkinson Road, his long-term fate still undecided.

We tried. Counsel had been invited into the judge's inner sanctum, his chambers, and there Jeff and I pleaded to be allowed to wrap up the trial in three days, in the desperate hope we could still win a Christmas gift for Frisbee.

But it was not to be. Justice McKenzie felt that as matters stood the case would be going to the jury on Christmas Eve and they would be locked up during the great Christian feast day. Nor were we able to obtain a consensus to conclude the trial between Christmas and New Year's. The favored option was to start up again on Monday, January 5 – a two-week break in the action, a time during which jurors would be placed under immense pressure from family and friends to discuss the case.

In the end, Justice McKenzie put the matter to the jury, offering a choice between a ruined Christmas and a January 5 recommencement: the former option, he said, "imposes on you and on me a kind of pressure that you shouldn't be under."

He asked them to retire and talk it over.

The foreman returned a few minutes later with the expected

315

verdict. The jury wished to hear the rest of the evidence, then adjourn until the new year.

Another sudden reversal of fortune during this roller-coaster trial. For the first time in my experience, if not in the annals of law, a jury had been allowed to determine court procedure.

Earlier, during the conference in chambers, Justice McKenzie mentioned in passing that he and Jim Tyhurst had been long-time and close friends.

Dennis suffered a mild loss of aplomb, and was shaking his head as we returned to the courtroom. He turned to Jeff and said, "I didn't know that. Did you?"

Jeff smiled his most brittle smile. Yes, he did seem to recall Jim Tyhurst having mentioned it. (Later, during argument over rebuttal evidence, Justice McKenzie made a comment that must further have nonplussed Dennis, describing Dr. Tyhurst's evidence as having been drawn from "his extensive and distinguished experience.")

Observing that the wind was blowing in a new direction, Dennis announced to us that he didn't think Tyhurst was such a bad fellow after all. He was careful not to attempt to malign Tyhurst during his cross-examination, and did commendable work in limiting the force of his evidence.

He didn't take the psychiatrist head on, instead attacked the foundations of his opinions: Tyhurst's belief in the accused's credibility. Dennis correctly felt that if the doctor had erred in his conclusion that Frisbee was telling the truth, there was not much framework upon which to hang the defense of automatism.

"Would you agree with me, sir, that a critical part of the whole process of forming an opinion is the accuracy of your assessment of Mr. Frisbee's credibility?"

"Yes."

"And you don't suggest, do you, that the twelve members of the jury would be ineffective at making that kind of assessment?"

This was a timeworn but often effective device to appeal to the jury's pride. Few lay people doubt their ability to see through others' lies, and often they resent being instructed as to matters which they regard as involving a simple exercise of common sense.

Jeff objected to the question as being argumentative. The judge asked Dennis to recast it.

"Do you suggest that you are better at it than the jury would be?"

Tyhurst trod carefully: "I have had thirty years of training in understanding the dynamics of people's behavior. It is likely that my opinions on those matters might possess a degree of expert understanding that might not be available to the average citizen. In that respect I would think that they might profit from comments I make."

"But you don't suggest for a moment that they might differ from you."

"I make no suggestion of that sort."

Dennis continued to play to the jury: "One advantage that they have is they have heard all the evidence sworn in that box you are sitting in."

Tyhurst agreed with him.

Dennis also scored points by drawing the jury's attention to the fact that Tyhurst had also interviewed Kazakes – and found him to be truthful as well. Dennis felt, with cause, that the jury would not necessarily share that view.

"With Mr. Kazakes I felt at times that he was perhaps somewhat protective of Mr. Frisbee, but I confronted him a couple of times on those matters and satisfied myself in the main he was telling the truth."

"You were satisfied that you got the straight goods?"

"Yes."

"And at the end of the day neither of them emerged as deceitful?"

"No."

Dennis brought out that Frisbee had not been open with Tyhurst regarding his pilfering from Mrs. Barnett's checking account.

"I did not have an opportunity to raise it with him because it had not come up at the time that I saw him."

That example of Frisbee's failure to be candid with Tyhurst hurt us, I think, although Tyhurst did his best: "Mr. Frisbee was depressed and not functioning well during much of this period."

Dennis may have believed that Tyhurst's hypothesis about Frisbee's "construct personality" argued a false side to the man:

317

"What you hear from the construct isn't necessarily the real Mr. Frisbee?"

Tyhurst was having none of that: "Oh, yes it is. It is the real Mr. Frisbee insofar as he knows himself. I want to make it clear that when I am using the word 'construct' that I am not using it in any sense that it is consciously constructed."

Dennis wasn't on confident footing here, and turned to the issue of automatism. He wanted to know more about the concept of "purposeless behavior."

There followed an absorbing *mise-en-scène*, a kind of verbal Punch and Judy show starring Dennis as the murderer and, to his obvious discomfort, assistant prosecutor Ernie Quantz as the victim.

Asking Tyhurst to assume he, Dennis, had drunk a sufficient quantity to black out and suffer amnesia – "Say that Mr. Quantz is in the room with me and I bash him over the head with something, and I kill him, would you be testifying here today that was done in a state of automatic behavior?"

"Perhaps he could use me," Jeff said.

"Now we are talking," Dennis said, with a not altogether reassuring smile.

"I would like to get to know you a bit better to understand whether there was an unconscious motive," Tyhurst answered.

Dennis continued his hypothetical assault on Ernie for a few minutes, and, after the court took the morning break, went at it again.

"If I bash Mr. Quantz over the head and I killed him, would you be here testifying that because I didn't remember it the next day I wasn't aware of what I was doing?"

"I would be testifying it was possible you were in a state of automatic behavior. But I would want to know a good deal more about it than that."

I assume Ernie felt relieved that Dennis's illustration wasn't more graphic.

After Dennis concluded with Tyhurst, the judge took over – with a lengthy series of questions relating to his assessment of Frisbee's credibility. Justice McKenzie was clearly concerned about the matter, and I feared the effect of his questions was to alert the jury to that fact.

Whether out of academic interest or for some other reason I couldn't divine, Justice McKenzie asked Tyhurst about individuals' behavior under hypnosis. "Surely the hypnotist cannot induce the subject to do something that is totally foreign to his nature?"

"No, that's not entirely true," said Tyhurst. "Some persons who are very discerning of weaknesses in other persons' personalities are able to split them by strong suggestion or hypnosis."

Asked if there were any questions arising from that, Jeff dared the court's wrath and earned a Purple Star for our side – his question arose from absolutely nothing that came before, and was outrageously leading: "One of the facts that were provided to you was that in San Francisco Mr. Frisbee voluntarily agreed to take a lie detector test when asked by the police?"

Oh, how desperately we had wanted to get that utterly improper evidence before the jury. (Lie detector evidence is simply not admissible in Canadian courts.) The suddenness of the question must have caught Dennis by surprise, because before he had a chance to object, Tyhurst calmly said, "Yes, that's true."

Jeff sat. "Thank you."

A long silence.

"No questions, Mr. Murray?" said the judge.

Dennis seemed to think about it. "Well, questions come to mind, but it is dangerous territory."

"The comment about the lie detector didn't arise from my questions," the judge said. We could tell he was put out.

"No, I think I should leave it alone," Dennis said.

And Dr. Tyhurst was excused.

After some hours of argument about whether the Crown was entitled to call rebuttal evidence, Justice McKenzie held against us: Crown witnesses would get the last word on the issues of automatism and drunkenness. We expected, on Monday, to hear evidence from a Crown psychiatrist, doubtless someone from its well-trained stable of debunkers of defenses.

Under no time constraints now, we decided to call another witness, a navigation expert we had been keeping in reserve.

Master mariner Neil Keeper seemed too boyish-looking, too young to own all the certificates the walls of his office are adorned with: among them certificates for foreign-going vessels, electronic navigation, and marine emergency, obtained variously in Scotland, Norway, and Canada. His career experience included serving as third, second, and ultimately first officer on ocean-going vessels in the North Sea, the Middle East, the East Coast of Canada, and the Arctic Ocean.

We weren't seeking certainty from his evidence; we were seeking doubt: a reasonable doubt as to whether the ship was in Canadian waters at about 6:45 p.m. on August 19.

Captain Keeper had examined the records of both the ship's bridge and the U.S. Coast Guard's onshore tracking system – from its maritime traffic control center – and found an inexplicable variance between the two as to the location of the *Viking Star* at critical times.

His evidence, though technical and lengthy, can be sufficiently summarized: apparent errors were made by bridge officers of the *Viking Star* in taking her bearings as she departed Victoria through the Strait of Juan de Fuca, and a vast host of possible circumstances could have resulted in those errors being compounded, causing the vessel to drift from the outbound traffic lane (the Canadian side) across the international boundary to the inbound traffic lane on the U.S. side.

For instance, the vessel made a change in position at about the time of the murder which, because a vessel of that size takes some minutes to respond, could have caused it to cross the border before completing its turn. "It's like driving a car on a very wet road; the car is going to skid around the corners."

A one-knot flood tide was in effect at the time, which could have compounded the error, pulling the vessel farther south. Add to that errors in compass readings, the fact the ship was on auto pilot, the fact that her officers had used floating aids to take radar fixes (an "extremely bad practice"), and Captain Keeper was unable to conclude that the ship was in Canadian waters at the critical time.

"I would say it is very sloppy navigating that has occurred in this instance," said Keeper.

"Could you say with any certainty that the vessel was never in American waters during that time period?" I asked.

"No, I couldn't."

"In your opinion is there any way of knowing exactly where that vessel was between the radar fixes at 6:34 p.m. and 6:47 p.m.?"

"From the conflicting information I have seen, no."

The officers on the ship's bridge really couldn't know where they were at the time, he said.

Ernie Quantz asked him if he had ever navigated a ship through the Strait of Juan de Fuca. He replied he had twice taken the Vancouver weather ship through it.

"If you were navigating the *Royal Viking Star* on the 19th of August you would not be able to tell us whether you stayed in the correct traffic lane?"

"Well, I have had occasion where I have wandered out of a traffic lane and gone where I wasn't supposed to be." A vessel traffic lane isn't demarked like a highway, with a white line down the middle, he said.

But, he admitted, he would probably, if navigating the *Viking Star*, have maintained the vessel in her correct lane. That satisfied Ernie, and the case was adjourned until after the weekend to hear the Crown's rebuttal witnesses.

Chapter 43

IMPAIRED DRIVING IS PROBABLY THE MOST COMMONLY CON-
tested criminal offense in Canada, and the Crown employs a raft
of specialists who interpret breathalyzer readings and testify as to
the effect of alcohol on the human body. Behind a façade of
rigorous scientific honesty, they often tend to paint a hopelessly
sodden picture of a drinker-behind-the-wheel, but when intoxication is a defense they may be expected to switch intellectual gears,
minimizing the effects of drink.

Jeffrey Caughlin, a young pharmacist employed by the RCMP's
Vancouver crime laboratory, and a frequent commuter to many
courts, was the expert called by the Crown on Monday, December
22, to rebut drunkenness. Jeff Green had faced him across a
courtroom many times but had never heard him give evidence
about the effects of Librium, an area in which Ernie Quantz
successfully qualified him as an expert.

The gist of his evidence was that at 6:30 p.m. Frisbee's probable
breathalyzer reading, given the drinks he'd had, would range from
.14 to .235 per cent.

But because he was an alcoholic, his body would better tolerate
drink; the rate of metabolism of alcohol (normally it burns away
at a rate of .015 per cent per hour) would likely be .02 per cent.
Therefore his reading would probably be at lower end, close to .13.
At such a level of insobriety a person's behavior becomes more
impulsive or reckless but one is not highly intoxicated. The added
twenty milligrams of Librium would cause "at worst a mild sedative effect."

Jeff in cross-examination accused Caughlin of skewing his figures; the witness had posited a higher rate of elimination of alcohol than would likely be the case.

"Some long-term alcoholics develop what is known as a reverse tolerance for alcohol, don't they?"

"What can happen is that the metabolism of alcohol may drop suddenly because of a diseased liver. It does happen, yes."

Jeff put to him the case of a person who had been drinking heavily for twenty years, then quit cold turkey for two and a half months, and gradually started up again.

"I would agree that in general the tolerance would fall off."

Jeff put other facts to him. Reverse tolerance. Alcohol consumed the night before and not yet eliminated. He got him up to .305.

Caughlin agreed that the average social drinker at that stage would be not quite stuporous but very heavily intoxicated.

He also agreed that alcoholics learn to appear less intoxicated than they are.

"They practise walking in a different way?"

"Yes, that's one of the factors."

"They probably avoid using certain words which are more likely to be slurred than others?"

"Yes."

"They have certain methods of picking things up so as not to appear to be uncoordinated?"

"Yes."

Jeff knew he had Caughlin in a bind. He had no choice but to give these answers: he had often done so in impaired cases when explaining why a driver's physical symptoms didn't seem as severe as would be warranted by his breathalyzer reading.

A rush of adrenalin, Caughlin conceded, would temporarily reduce the physical symptoms of intoxication.

Caughlin's claim that Librium would at worst involve only a mild sedative effect was not borne out in the medical literature, Jeff suggested. The witness had to agree his expertise was confined to what he himself had read in texts and journals.

"One of the adverse effects that can occur with Librium is drowsiness, am I right?"

"Yes."

"And one of them is dizziness?"

"Yes."

"One of them is weakness?"

"Yes."

"One of them is fatigue?"

"Yes."

"One of them is lethargy?"

"Yes."

"One of them is disorientation?"

"Possibly, yes."

"And one is retrograde amnesia?"

"That . . . I would agree."

"And one is depression?"

"It can occur."

"And one is psycho-motor agitation?"

"Rare."

"But nevertheless a known side effect of Librium?"

"Sure, yes, I would agree."

"One of them is sleep disturbance?"

"Yes, that's quite common."

"One of them is mental confusion?"

"Possible, yes. Most of these things do not occur very often."

"No, they are just considered sufficiently important for the pharmaceutical manufacturer to warn physicians they might happen, right?"

Caughlin was forced to concede that was so.

Still he maintained the additive effect would be minimal.

"You haven't examined the accused in this case, have you?"

"No, I have not."

"To determine what his rate of absorption or elimination of alcohol is?"

"No, I haven't."

"And you haven't done any experiments with him to determine what effect Librium has on him when he is drinking?"

"No, I have not."

"And you don't know whether he is a person who has liver damage or not?"

"No, I do not."

All in all, not bad.

Ernie Quantz asked in re-examination how damaged a person's liver would have to be to significantly reduce the elimination rate of alcohol.

Extensively damaged, said Caughlin. "Effectively one would have to be experiencing symptoms of liver disease. One would likely have abdominal pains, jaundice."

This smacked to Jeff as involving an area outside Caughlin's expertise and he won permission to ask a last question:

"Are you competent to give evidence on liver disease and the effects of liver disease on human beings?"

"No," he replied, "I'm not."

◊   ◊   ◊

The psychiatric witness the Crown originally intended to call – a professional unmasker of malingerers – had begged off because of a prior commitment, and we greeted the Crown's substitute choice with some relief.

Dr. Alistair Murray is a respected Victoria psychiatrist not infrequently employed as forensic expert. Jeff had so used him, in fact. Like the Crown's other psychiatric witness, Dr. Solomon, he was not unfriendly to the defense, nor was his evidence of much aid to the Crown. Called to court by Dennis to fill the shoes of the absent Dr. Pause, who presumably would have been a more compliant Crown witness, Dr. Murray was remarkably open and self-effacing.

"First of all, are you an academic in your field, sir?"

"No, not at all. I work in the trenches. I would liken myself to, perhaps, counsel here, compared to a law professor."

"You have a practice of your own, do you?"

"Yes, I have a private practice in Victoria. I also work part-time at the University of Victoria, seeing undergraduates, and I do a small amount of forensic work."

Dennis asked him about the effects of alcohol and Librium in combination, and may have been taken aback by his response, which went beyond anything we had so far heard from other experts. Dr. Murray said the effect was not merely additive but

325

"synergistic": they act together to produce a more powerful effect than the actual sum of their parts would cause.

The effect of that opinion upon our intoxication defense was equally synergistic, and clearly deflated Jeffrey Caughlin's decrial of the effects of Librium.

Could Librium cause hallucinations? Dennis asked.

Dr. Murray had never seen an instance of that, but it was a theoretical possibility, given a big enough dose or an idiosyncratic response.

Sleepwalking? It undoubtedly occurs, said the good doctor. "There is no question that a sleepwalking person will perform complex acts of which he or she is subsequently unaware."

Only upon the issue of automatism did the witness give succor to the Crown. It was apparent that Dr. Murray was no great fan of the concept of automatic behavior. Occurrences were rare, he said. One weighty psychiatric text devoted less than one page out of two thousand to the condition. And the standard diagnostic manual of the American Psychiatric Association did not even list automatism in its index, although it spoke of "dissociative disorders" which were characterized by similar symptoms. Dissociation is considered by the courts to be a disease of the mind. To this point in the trial the Crown had offered little evidence to buttress an argument that Frisbee was insane at the time of the offense, but now Dr. Murray's evidence raised the awful threat of an insanity verdict. We thought such a result highly unlikely . . . but juries are rarely predictable.

In cross, Jeff used the doctor to rebuild, after Caughlin's attempted razing of it, the argument that Frisbee's cirrhosis had reduced his tolerance to alcohol. The liver is a giant factory, said Murray, which metabolizes significant amounts of alcohol. If the liver is impaired there will be more alcohol in the brain. "In general terms, somebody with an impaired liver is more susceptible to the effects of alcohol on the body."

Jeff had him reiterate his evidence of the synergistic effect of alcohol and Librium, then asked:

"And of course when you get into the higher levels of alcohol concentration in a human being and link those with even small doses of Librium, it can't be ruled out that there might be some surprising or unusual effects?"

"No, it can't be ruled out. I would think that it would be possible, but not probable."

Possible was just fine. Possible gives rise to a reasonable doubt.

Jeff Green knew Dr. Murray had high regard for Jim Tyhurst and saw an opportunity to bolster our chief forensic witness's evidence.

He asked if Dr. Murray was aware of Tyhurst's credentials and professional experience.

"Dr. Tyhurst is a well-known psychiatrist. He is a respected professor. He still is and for many years was an examiner for professional qualifications." In other words, he was one of the psychiatric elite who pass on the post-doctoral training of others before admitting them into the profession. "Certainly I am aware that he is a man of standing."

Dr. Murray agreed he had not examined Frisbee. "I wouldn't be so foolish as to express an opinion without examining a person."

Nor had he read a transcript of Tyhurst's evidence or his report.

"So you are basically not here to contradict anything he said in his evidence or his report, are you?"

"No, I'm not."

Dennis in re-examination hoped to blunt the impact of Dr. Murray's laudation of Tyhurst:

"What about his reputation around the issue of his views on automatic behavior?"

It was a central area of Tyhurst's expertise. Dr. Murray had even referred to him a criminal case that involved automatism, advising the accused's counsel he would be better served by consulting Dr. Tyhurst.

"What do you mean by that?"

"I mean two things. First of all, Dr. Tyhurst is an academic professor and he probably ... not probably, he no doubt has wider knowledge of the literature than I do." Dr. Murray carefully chose his words: "And Dr. Tyhurst is probably more sympathetic to the concept than I am, and therefore he might be more ready to consider the diagnosis."

"And throughout the province, he's the first name that comes to mind when considering if someone will testify as to automatism?" asked Dennis.

"He's the first one that comes to my mind."

"Thank you," said Dennis.

"Now, does that conclude the rebuttal evidence?" said Justice McKenzie.

"It does, my lord."

And we adjourned until January 5, 1987.

Chapter 44

JEFF, HIS MAIN TASKS COMPLETED, WENT TO A BEACH IN MEXICO for Christmas. I stayed home and prepared my address to the jury.

It was as bleak a Christmas season as I can remember, clammy and cold, gray by day, dark by late afternoon. Escaping from the gloom of the office, I took work home. We had ordered daily transcripts of the evidence and I buried myself in the words of DeLuca and Dearnaley, of Raszl and Rosenthal, of Kolb and Kazakes and Klotz and Keeper, the wisdom of Solomon and the other men of the mind. Synergistic effects, dependency syndromes, nautical miles, feelies in pink bathrooms.

I gorged myself on this barely palatable Christmas stew. Someone with a misplaced sense of humor had presented me with a bottle of Famous Grouse whiskey for Christmas (very good), and I recklessly worked my way into it, a heady catalyst for a clogged and wearied brain. I soon found myself, as Philip Barnett once had, light-headed and lost in Disneyland. A Disneyland of pretend tears and blood spatter, vibes and levitations, sadism and masochism. Concordes, caviar, and canapés. Calliopes, canonical hours, calumnious acts, and confabulation. The preacher chap and the sailor chap and the chap in the movie house wandered by, paid their compliments, wandered out. Then to Trader Vic's for lunch. M.C.B. to the hairdresser's. Go to the doctor another day; today I am out of it, so to say. A drink a day keeps the shrink away. Shout the ship.

Tipsily pondering the whats and whys and hows, the meaning of justice, of innocence, of guilt (and why not life while I'm at it?), I demanded to know: Did you do it, Robert? Did you smash

329

in the skull of that frolicsome fluttering butterfly? Did all your accumulated acid, all that bile and spleen you choked down over the months and the years, that you swallowed, suppressed, did it all ignite within you, explode into a raging conflagration of evil, blood, and terror?

Or did you just want to inherit a fortune?

Have you lied to me? Have I been a fool to believe in you? Have you been offering me manure from Taurus the bull?

Please, simply tell me you didn't do it. Tell me the truth about that jewel thief . . .

I talked to his ghost. (You've done this yourself, Robert. Didn't you talk to the ghost of Dr. Barnett; didn't you ask him: Why? Why? Didn't you tell me you couldn't understand?)

Make me believe.

His manuscript screamed back at me: "I am in jail, accused of a nefarious crime, and awaiting trial for murder! They are accusing me of murdering dear Muriel! . . . The how and where I do not fathom."

He accused me of being a waverer, a man of confection. If he'd wanted to murder Muriel, could he not simply have poisoned her ritual morning Bloody Mary? Her Moët, her martini, her French 75? Would he murder her with the butler at the unlocked door? With Jeannette and Eva down the hall?

Don't you understand? he cried. I loved her.

I was ashamed. I apologized. Crisis of faith, soon conquered.

Robert was innocent. In a nutshell.

Shouldn't be trying him at all. Should put the ship's helmsman in the dock, the guy who murdered the whale. Or Dennis Murray for threatening to beat in the head of Ernie Quantz, right in the courtroom . . .

Mr. Frisbee. Mr. Freezie. Mr. Freebie? Chauffeur, chambermaid, court jester, house poodle, lover, and slave. Faithful always to the motto of his high school: "Industry, Integrity, and Honesty." Majorette, choir girl, ballroom dancer. Connoisseur of chocolate truffles and King's Delights. The mad knitter. Sleepwalking fearer of the nail-biting night. Dreamer of cliffs and nightmare abysses. Hater of carrots.

Now just a queen in the gilded cages of the P.C.U. at Wilkie. The cirrhotic Robert William Dion Frisbee.

Your liver may not have long to live, Robert. Not if you go back to the bottle after we spring you. Back to Dan Kazakes's alcoholic bosom.

Think you can survive it?

Or will freedom kill you? Will an acquittal be your death sentence?

Could we win the battle for your freedom and lose the war for your life? *C'est la guerre* . . .

◊   ◊   ◊

Frisbee must have known I needed cheering. He sent me a card.

Not a Christmas card, nothing so banal and unFrisbeeish as that. Part of a panel torn from the comic section of a newspaper: a picture of the ageless tow-headed cartoon rascal, Dennis the Menace.

With it a note: "Dear Mr. Deverell: Mrs. Barnett always commented on the fact I share a pet hate with Dennis – hatred of carrots – to the point that most hostesses in S.F. did not serve Robert carrots when he came to dinner. Seems there is another Dennis on my horizon I can associate with . . ."

In the cartoon, Dennis is standing at an open door, looking in. Frisbee has color-penciled a long lawyer's robe over his shirt and pants. One of Dennis the Menace's nemeses is a bespectacled girl called Margaret who, holding pen and notepad, is holding the door open for him. Frisbee has given her navy trousers, mauve shirt, red tie. She bears a certain resemblance to Frisbee.

She is saying to Dennis the Menace: "Come in! I'm writing my autobiography!"

On Christmas Eve I sent Rhonda, our receptionist, to the candy store to fetch a box of fancy chocolates, and she and I went to Wilkinson Road.

The officers at reception said no. Chocolate was contraband. Can only give money.

331

Yes, they realized it was Christmas. Sorry. Regulations.

I took my appeal to the office of the deputy warden on duty. He was a paragon. (Also, he'd read some of my books.) He said if I were to slip the chocolates in my briefcase, proceed to the Protective Custody Unit, surreptitiously turn them over to Frisbee (so the other prisoners couldn't see this dastardly deed being done) a blind eye would be unofficially turned.

In the unit's common room, I wished Frisbee a happy Christmas and bade him take a seat. I slipped him the chocolates under the table.

December 26

Dear Mr. Deverell:

Thanks to you and the office for my delicious contraband. Much appreciated it, and I eat it under covers at night. I have been much sought after since all the notorious nouveau riche life style I have led has become common knowledge. Even the guards come up to me and ask ME how to spell simple words like somnambulism – what fools men are to rely on my nodding acquaintance with a dictionary! Webster also came from Massachusetts, but any comparison ends there.

I gave a bash for the kids. Served Coke (the drinking kind), smoked oysters, smoked clams, crackers, Gruyère. It was a surprise and they all came! Sort of a captive guest list.

We who had TV turned them on to Christmas carols and it was all very merry. Some devil went around getting signatures on a Christmas card and they gave that to me. Made up little stockings with candy cigarets and, of course, fruit.

Hope you had a merry Christmas and the New Year brings nothing but good things for you.

Sincerely,

Robert

I remained haunted by imagined pictures of jurors with loosened tongues and listening ears at office and New Year's parties. How could they *not* talk about the case with their sworn buddies, their lovers, their dear moms and dads? The judge of course had warned them not to, but surely he had asked the humanly impossible. There was nothing we could do about it – no appeal lay from his lordship's order for the long adjournment.

In my worst imaginings I heard well-meaning confidants urging on my jurors their own opinions of the case, garnered from television and *The Times-Colonist*, from headlines like "'Tonight She Must Die, Frisbee Wrote.'"

Or self-styled experts-in-law voicing the conventional canard that the courtroom is only a stage where is played the lawyer's game, sly shysters trying to trick ordinary, gullible folk into freeing their crooked clients.

The fag wouldn't have been charged in the first place if he hadn't been guilty. The police know what they're doing; you probably haven't seen half of their evidence. I know. I used to be a cop.

Yeah, and what about that case I read where this guy gets off a charge of murdering his wife, then goes out and shoots his mother-in-law?

Hard to blame the old faggot, though. Twenty million dollars, that's what I heard the will was worth.

Of course it's possible all the jury did was relax and read. Novels of the courtroom, for instance, novels written by . . . well, me. Did they squeal with delight when they found a copy of *Needles* or *High Crimes* in their stockings? I can't be sure, but when they returned to courtroom duty, five days into the new year, several jurors brought copies of my thrillers with them. They wanted me to sign them.

A couple of the sheriffs entrusted with seeing to the care and comfort of the jury urged me to do this favor for their charges. They would act as go-betweens, run the books like contraband from the jury room, and present them to me for signing during breaks or after the daily adjournment.

I was leery. Could signing books not be seen as a kind of gift-offering, a subtle form of undue influence?

I created a convenient if uncomfortable fiction: As far as I know, I told the sheriffs, you're giving me your own copies to sign. Bring out the books; I will ask no questions.

"Interesting they want you to sign them *before* the verdict," one of the sheriffs said.

I signed a few that first day. On the following morning I was presented with a dozen more. Signed those for the sheriffs, too.

The jurors and I maintained our conspiracy of silence about the books, even during our chats in the elevator (about the weather, of course, or the latest 5-1 loss by the Vancouver Canucks). They were in a good mood, no hangovers, no calamities involving overcooked turkeys. They smiled at me.

It all felt a little strange. And, in a way, ominous.

Chapter 45

WHEN PROCEEDINGS RESUMED AT 10:33 A.M., JANUARY 5, 1987, Justice McKenzie said, "Well, I am off to a good start, I wrote 1987. Yes, gentlemen?"

Dennis advised him that several issues of law were alive and had to be dealt with. The jury was excused until the next day. There was no pressure on us now, no time-clock: it had ticked well past Christmas anyway, into the harsh winter reality of January.

Dennis had also got a nice present, from his boss.

"Mr. Murray," said the judge, "I should note that I observe that you are accoutred somewhat differently today, in silk rather than the stuff which you formerly wore. It's a great honor to be appointed Queen's Counsel. I congratulate you. It's, I think, a particularly heart-warming thing that it occurs at this season of the year."

"Thank you, my lord."

"Congratulations," said the judge.

Jeff and I took no part in the ceremony, remained seated in our lowly robes of stuff.

We'd seen the Attorney-General's New Year's honors list in the newspaper. Dennis had donned silk. He was now entitled to put the initials "Q.C." on his business card. In the Province of British Columbia, appointment as Queen's Counsel is an honor reposed by the Attorney-General upon politically well-connected or otherwise deserving lawyers. Not only is it a great honor, it lets you jump up your fees.

Jeff rose to make the first argument:

"My lord, it's our submission, if I may say so in a nutshell,

335

there is no evidence in this case to go to the jury of either planning or deliberation. . . . "

We were asking him to withdraw first-degree murder from the jury. Not that we felt there was much chance the jury would convict on that most serious of the charges. Second-degree murder maybe, manslaughter maybe, a total acquittal maybe, but not the kind of murder that puts a person behind bars, without parole, for a minimum of twenty-five years. We did not see our jury as willing to do that to Frisbee.

We knew juries not in agreement will tend to compromise. If some want to convict an accused armed robber and others want to acquit, they may find him guilty of theft. If some see the accused as a cold-hearted murderer and others want to send him home to his wife and kids, they may agree on manslaughter. We did not want this jury compromising on a verdict of second-degree murder.

First-degree murder must be planned and deliberate, says the Criminal Code. Those two adjectives have been defined, refined, and underlined by the highest court in the land. "Deliberate," says the Supreme Court of Canada, means much more than intentional. It means what the *Oxford* says it means: "not hasty in decision; slow in deciding; considered, not impulsive." "Planned," the courts hold, presupposes a calculated scheme or design which has been carefully thought out.

Murder may be planned but not deliberate. Or deliberate and not planned. It must be both to be murder in the first degree.

Jeff submitted there was evidence of neither to go to the jury. The chaotic circumstances of the murder belied a calculated scheme, implied an impulsive act, one not slowly but hastily decided. The weapon was the first thing that came to hand, a bottle; the door was unlocked; the butler scheduled to arrive, a date planned with the Biegerts for the captain's party that evening.

Dennis couldn't have agreed less. It was open for the jury, he said, to conclude that Frisbee's thinking was this: "I'll wait for Mrs. Barnett to die and then slide in the codicil, because I can't wait for her to die any more because she's going to have a new will when I come back."

But Justice McKenzie reminded him that Frisbee believed he couldn't benefit from her death – because the codicil drawn up in the summer of 1985 (naming Frisbee as co-executor) had the effect of reviving the original will and wiping out the earlier codicil of October 1984. "The two and a half million dollars had gone out the window, had it not?"

I liked this question. Had our judge accepted our version?

Justice McKenzie apparently felt Frisbee had substantial grounds for believing the October codicil had been destroyed. "It's a very nice question for the probate court to decide whether or not there was a wipeout of that intermediate codicil."

Dennis decided to steer a different course: Frisbee's resentment toward Mrs. Barnett caused him to plan her murder.

"Mr. Barnett didn't ask very much of Robert Frisbee, he asked three-hour lunches at Jack's, World Trade Club, not a heck of a lot of work. Mrs. Barnett was a different kettle of fish. No entry to the sort of big-time lunches at the World Trade Club, at Jack's, and et cetera."

"Why do you say that?" said the judge. "He still had lunches at Jack's. Is it clear that his entry to the World Trade Club was cut off by Philip Barnett's death?"

"Not cut off. What I'm trying to represent here, my lord, is a different kind of world. It's a world of lunches with Mrs. Barnett, tea parties, that kind of effort."

The court: "I don't think we had any tea parties."

Jeff Green: "Not one tea party, my lord."

Court: "No tea parties."

Jeff: "No milk and cookies either."

Court: "There were ceremonies but not tea ceremonies."

Our judge was in a good mood.

Dennis said, "The essence of it is, to use his own words, he was more a chambermaid than he had been before." Moreover, matters of motive and of planning and deliberation were issues of fact for the jury. The jury's right to decide on the facts was sacrosanct.

In the end, Justice McKenzie once again disappointed us:

"This is a remarkable case in more ways than one. It has the appearance altogether more of a work of fiction than of fact in many respects. Argument could rage on for a very long time as to whether the background events are solid enough so the jury can make findings of fact. I have arrived at the conclusion that there is sufficient solidity in the web of circumstantial evidence which could result in findings of planning and deliberation. The question of first-degree murder will be one which is submitted to the jury. I make no comment as to how high or low the quality of evidence is."

When a judge says he makes no comment, he is actually making comment, and obviously Justice McKenzie thought the evidence of planning and deliberation skimpy. Still, he did not propose to invade the territory of the jury or limit its range of options.

In the afternoon it was Dennis's turn. He asked the judge to withdraw non-insane automatism from the jury. There was not the kind of evidence here that would get this defense off the ground. We weren't even in the "automatism ballpark."

Justice McKenzie reminded him that this morning he had been arguing that the jury has a sacrosanct right to determine all issues of fact. "It seems to me that you are operating out of two sides of your mouth."

It was not, Dennis said ruefully, an uncommon problem.

Automatism would go to the jury, the judge ruled. "The charge to the jury will leave open the option – the limited option – of somnambulism, and the possibility of founding a verdict of acquittal based on non-insane automatism arising from the ingestion of a combination of alcohol, in a strong dosage, and Librium. I will have to insist that the jury give the accused the benefit of every doubt and that if they are wavering between a verdict of greater gravity or a verdict of lesser gravity, that to give him the benefit of the doubt means giving him the lesser of the two verdicts."

Jeff and I greeted that decision with unadulterated relief. Our evidence – particularly as to sleepwalking – was marginal, almost tenuous. But the judge ruled that the issue of insanity had been raised by our automatism plea and he was now bound to put that to the jury, too.

So the jury was to be served up with the entire fruit salad – five verdicts would be open: not guilty, manslaughter, second-degree, first-degree, insanity.

But there was one other possibility: that the jury could not find unanimity. If twelve persons cannot agree on a verdict the jury, not the accused, is hung. A new trial must be ordered and a new jury struck. The cost to the accused would be punitive, of course, but a case as complex as this would not easily be reconstituted by the Crown, which might cut its losses and drop all charges through a stay of proceedings. It often happens.

Dennis had one other item on his menu: a complaint about our back-door evidence of the polygraph test Frisbee offered to take. Justice McKenzie said since these tests are inadmissible in Canada he would tell the jury to ignore anything they heard about it from the witness stand. The jury, he said, "are the lie detectors."

Jeff urged the judge to tell the jury to erase from their consideration Dennis's claim that an expert read "Tonight she must die" from Frisbee's shorthand.

Dennis said: "Well, I entirely agree, and I intended to tell them that."

That seemed to satisfy the judge.

A final matter: "We would appreciate it," said Jeff, "if you would admonish the jury with respect to the press coverage of this case," particularly with regard to the "Tonight She Must Die" headline in *The Times-Colonist*. Mrs. Dellert's evidence was not the subject of a headline and "indeed was buried in a story somewhere in close proximity to the classified ads, and that is a matter that was not only annoying but of some concern to us."

The judge said he would deal with it.

Chapter 46

THE NEXT MORNING, JANUARY 6, I GAVE MY FINAL ADDRESS TO the jury.

I feel now that I was over-prepared. It was too filled with fact, too organized, too empty of emotion, too dry. Better if I had winged it, if it had come from the heart not the head. Better if I simply shouted the ship.

I have never understood why it should be so, but under a provision of the Criminal Code of Canada, when the defense calls witnesses, the prosecutor is entitled to address the jury last. He can impugn anything defense counsel says and make the wildest of allegations without fear of contradiction, because the defense has no right of reply. So I began by telling our jury that I had no idea what Dennis would say to them, and had to blindly anticipate his arguments.

"He may try to lift a phrase or two from the manuscript, and say, 'This proves his state of mind.' Well, Mr. Frisbee in writing that manuscript is entitled to his fantasies and Mr. Murray at the counsel table is entitled to his fantasies. You are not entitled to any fantasies in the jury room."

The notes excerpted here from my speech hopefully do not give too flagrant a sense of its windiness. I was on my feet for three and a half hours, and made multiple ports of call.

The location of the ship: "We have a Norwegian vessel, the deceased an American, the accused an American; not a single Canadian is involved in this case. God knows how many hundreds of thousands of dollars were spent on it, and we are not even sure where the ship was, and if the prosecution suddenly is sure now that on August 19 of 1985 that the vessel was in Canadian waters, what was Robert Frisbee doing in the American court system for a year?"

Obviously a mistake had been made. What that proved was that prosecutors could make mistakes, tragic mistakes. Mistakes which had already cost the accused a year of his life in penal institutions.

I didn't belabor that issue, nor did I spend much time with the Crown's threadbare evidence of first-degree murder: "I think you will have little difficulty with it," I said. I naturally wanted to lever the jury's attention toward verdicts better grounded in the evidence: second-degree murder, manslaughter, acquittal.

As to motive: "At the outset of this case until now the Crown has stuck like a bulldog to this theory that somehow Robert Frisbee bamboozled Mrs. Barnett to sign over two-thirds of her estate and made out a couple of big checks and killed her. What happens in prosecutions is this – and I have prosecuted a bunch of murders – you get tunnel vision. You have a body, you have someone in the same suite, you ask around, you look for papers and you come up with a codicil and she has never shown it to anyone. You say, 'Aha, there is the answer; look no further,' don't look for other rational explanations. You get a fixation, and you come up with all sorts of plausible but mostly implausible theories to back that up. You just can't bring yourself to accept that you could be wrong."

Lawyer Ted Kolb: "You saw him on the witness stand; remember him – he was a very strong and persuasive man and it would be hard to face Mr. Kolb with the fact you want to change your will, to reduce significantly the gift to his alma mater, and Mrs. Barnett is not the kind of person to face up to people and tell them unpleasant news."

The big checks: "Why does Bob Frisbee have them on his person on the 21st of August when he is arrested by the police?" The fact he held onto them showed an innocent mind. The $300,000 check couldn't even be cashed.

Her reasons for the $100,000 gift to Kazakes: he and Mrs. Barnett were close; he was rather like Mrs. Barnett's strange son-in-law. In her diaries were dozens of references to social outings with the man.

341

"But I suspect a warmth of friendship wasn't the only reason. I have a theory about all this, and it's based on the evidence, and I urge you to listen to it, and I think it's the most logical explanation for these checks. The payments to Dan and his son were probably meant as a kind of payoff. She was getting older, had had one apparent bout with cancer, she wanted Bob Frisbee close, she wanted more of his time." Moving him to an apartment down the street and taking an apartment in London would draw him away from Dan Kazakes. The payment to Kazakes was guilt money, and so was the $300,000 to Frisbee.

"So here's the problem the accused was in; he was mesmerized by all the jewelry and champagne and caviar, the fancy clothes, and San Francisco high society. He was drawn to that world and yet he was torn because he was drawn to another world and that was a home life with good old, not so bright Dan Kazakes, just a funny old dreamer that Bob Frisbee had a thirty-two-year relationship with."

A guilt payment was typical of her indirect approach. "Here's $100,000, buy a business." That was her way; she couldn't be direct with Kazakes and just say, "I want to take your lover with me to London for six months, and too bad."

The pilfered trust account: "It's like a kid going to the cookie jar when you are talking about $90,000 trips to Europe, $16,000 suites on a cruise ship, Concorde flights to London, and I have no doubt that if Bob Frisbee had been able to bring himself to speak to Mrs. Barnett about it, she would have said, 'Here, there is more.'

"But maybe the more important point is this: this is a sword that cuts both ways, and the way it cuts most severely is right through the heart of the Crown's case, because if he was stealing from her account the only way that would ever be discovered is if she died and the estate went into the hands of an executor."

Why was blood found smeared on not one but two bottles? And it was important to note that no one from the ship noticed that either of the bottles seemed to have been washed. It was only later, when the ship docked, that police drew that conclusion.

"I have to submit there was some sloppy police work going on there in San Francisco. Why were a lot of these items not seized?

This towel that was in the bathroom, where is that, and the other towels and pieces of clothing that were found at the scene? The champagne bottle that was half full? The little piccolo bottle that was in the basket, the various glasses, the tumbler that Bob Frisbee was drinking from, why weren't they seized and why weren't they lab tested? How many people came into that room after August 19 before the ship docked?

"Very, very sloppy work, in my submission, and as a result of that Bob Frisbee was kept in the jail in San Francisco for a year before he was brought to Canada, a year and a half taken away from the life of a man who may be totally innocent."

I related the evidence of Frisbee's good character.

"Now with that background let us look at Robert Frisbee's evidence, and on the witness stand I am suggesting he came across as a straightforward, fully honest person who didn't quibble. There were a couple of very long, grueling days on the witness stand. I think one was from 9:00 in the morning until 5:45. There was nothing he hid, and very much that he gave. I know a jury of honest, caring Canadians is not going to hold it against Robert Frisbee that God made him a homosexual or that he succumbed to the blandishments of older persons when he was a young boy, twelve and thirteen and fourteen. These are men who use children, and I suspect that many of us would rather see some of them in the prisoner's dock than their victim who is here today.

"His whole personality argues against the possibility that he could consciously have committed a murder. He is a daydreamer, a person who is really unable to confront others with distressing news or ask for a raise. He is a man plagued by not knowing, not remembering, desperately trying to reconstruct the events of the night of August 19; making notes, making more notes, trying to bring it back."

She had instructed Frisbee to tip the waiters, and he did so with the last of the money he had with him. "He doesn't sound from that like a man who is consumed by greed."

The manuscript: "Mr. Murray dragged from it every sexual innuendo and peccadillo he could find, every little bit of spicy writing, and paraded it in front of us here, and at the end of that long, long cross-examination, at the end of the day, with a flourish

343

he attempted to transcribe a passage in this manuscript in short-hand, and he did so incorrectly, and he did so in an attempt to damage my client, and I say he overstepped the bounds of fairness by a country mile in doing so.

"Well, Mr. Frisbee couldn't read that phrase. You remember that long, long tense few minutes when he studied it and studied it and tried to make sense of it, and it turns out that even a short-hand expert who teaches the art wasn't able to transcribe that phrase clearly." Her best effort was not even close to the transcription offered by the Crown.

I then read to the jury those doleful passages he had written about his first days in the San Francisco jail.

"Now that is not fiction; it is the plaintive cry of a lonely, bewildered man in jail. 'They are accusing me of murdering dear Muriel. The how and where I do not fathom . . .'"

I dealt with the psychiatric evidence, and said:

"Okay just let me before concluding with the medical business make some reference to a possible verdict of not guilty by reason of insanity. We are not asking for such a verdict. Quite frankly we are no more interested in the accused being sent to a mental institution at the pleasure of the Lieutenant-Governor, for however long that might be and it might be forever, than we are interested in having him convicted for murder for which he may be sentenced to a life in prison."

The possibility of a third-party killer: "You have Mrs. Barnett around the ship flashing her jewelry; it doesn't take much to postulate a theory that Robert Frisbee, in an altered state of consciousness or otherwise, or just very, very drunk, could have been in the living room of that suite or in one of the washrooms, found the attacker there, an intruder, and he fled and that Robert Frisbee suffered a traumatic amnesia. I suppose the point is, can you take a chance? Can you be satisfied beyond a reasonable doubt that he killed her? It is a very, very difficult step to take and you have to be very, very sure. It's a dangerous and wrong one if you have a reasonable doubt.

"So you add to that, automatism from whatever source, and you add alcohol and Librium, and you put it all together, and I suggest there is doubt upon doubt upon doubt. You must give the benefit of any of those doubts to the accused. So I am going to ask you with your verdict to end the nightmare that Bob Frisbee has been enduring for the last year and a half in the jails of two countries, and ask you to send him back home to live out the balance of his life in peace. And I am going to ask you to tell this court and tell Bob Frisbee and tell the world that a Canadian jury is a fair jury and a compassionate jury . . . and I am going to thank you."

My address had gone too long, had devoured more than half the day. The judge asked Dennis how he felt about starting in mid-afternoon. "I am prepared to roll," he said.

The judge wasn't, he implied, so Dennis said, "I wonder if your lordship would be inclined to put the question to the jury as to what their pleasure is." This, I thought, was getting ridiculous.

"How do you feel," asked the judge, "would you prefer to have a fresh start tomorrow?"

The jury left the room; came back. This time they weren't unanimous.

The foreman said, "We are divided but the majority feel we would prefer to hear Mr. Murray tomorrow."

The judge complimented them on a wise decision.

I thought: If they were divided on this issue, how would they ever achieve unanimity on one of the several verdicts?

I felt a wave of disappointment in myself as the court recessed for the night. The preparation of that turgid speech had ruined my Christmas, and in my delivery of it I had sounded like a humor-less, hectoring preacher at his pulpit. The jury seemed unmoved; they wanted passion, not analysis.

But Frisbee was in my corner, my loyal second. Unable as usual to express himself orally, he handed me a note: "You were terrific."

And in the morning came a letter:

"I was happy I did not have to sit in judgment and make the decision you asked for – I would have been spellbound once again. I do not have enough adjectives in my vocabulary to describe my feeling of admiration I have for you, Mr. Green, and your entire staff in their efforts to assist me in this unhappy event. That admiration will only increase – if I can transcribe my goddamn shorthand notes!"

Chapter 47

DENNIS'S SPEECH THE NEXT MORNING WAS IMMEASURABLY more effective than mine. A folksy, modest, man-of-the-people speech, a gosh-and-golly cornucopia of colloquialism. The jury ate it up.

It was easy, he told them, to become lost in tiny details of evidence. Yes, there were bits and pieces missing, "but there are a whole bunch of bits and pieces that kind of go clunk, clunk, clunk, and at the end it fits the big picture."

He warned the jury that at some point they were going to suffer information overload; fog might threaten to becloud the big picture. "You're going to go, what I describe when I'm talking with friends as, gaga." At that point they should pull over to the side of the road, wait for the fog to clear away, then carry on.

With that preliminary advice out of the way, Dennis launched into the attack, recalling Frisbee's history of leeching money from his many mentors, his bitter disappointment at being left out of Philip's will, his resentment toward Muriel, his deceitful codicil.

"Here, suddenly, seventy-two hours after she's out of hospital he pops up with what I describe as a whippy-up phony codicil providing a series of gifts on the first page which are cover, they're peanuts, and a gift on the second page which is two-thirds of the estate to Robert Frisbee."

Dennis never made clear his current theory of how the whippy-up phony codicil came to be signed by her: she simply was "not addressing her mind to that codicil."

It was then spirited away, "and Mr. Kazakes – and I will get to him later – he knows all about it as well. It's been spirited away, and the idea is when Muriel Barnett dies, we slide in the codicil into the personal papers, and when the estate is probated we get to say Mrs. Barnett was a real generous person towards us, she gave us all these checks and, oh, by the way, she gave me, Robert Frisbee, two-thirds of the estate. She is going through a very generous phase now. And that generous phase was, bingo, $100,000 over here to Mr. Kazakes to buy a store, and $300,000 over here to me for buying an apartment or some such thing, and $20,000 to Jerry Kazakes."

The big checks were a cover, an attempt to portray Mrs. Barnett as having become the soul of generosity. "With the greatest respect to Mr. Deverell who has so ably and honestly and fairly defended this case, I urge you not to find the checks are something called guilt money."

(Mr. Deverell, he insisted on reminding them, had acted with great skill and absolutely properly. This was in deft contrast to my own indictment of Dennis Murray's tactics as being less than scrupulous. Deverell, like Brutus, was an honorable man.)

But the real bad guy in all of this was Dan Kazakes. "Perhaps he ought to be sitting right there beside Mr. Frisbee, but sometimes things don't work out the way they ought to. Suffice it to say Mr. Kazakes is into this issue up to his ears. He knows exactly without a shadow of a doubt that something is going to happen to Mrs. Barnett; she is going to die during the course of that trip to Alaska."

The cad had even tried to filch Mrs. Barnett's furs. "I mean, talk about greed. I mean we are at the point where Mr. Frisbee has stolen more than $10,000. He's got $2.5 million coming because Mrs. Barnett's going to die on that trip, and they're going to get the furs as well." His voice throbbed with indignation at the Machiavellian plots devised by this arthritic old drunk, the guiding hand, the masterminding mystagogue. Who with his special powers had somehow been able to levitate from the grasp of police authorities.

"He tries to distance himself once the gig is up. He tries to distance himself from everything that might look bad." He had denied knowing anything about the codicil after it was signed, yet told Janet Wilkins the codicil was in the security box. "'Oh, by the way, it's in the security box.' Why is he lying about that? If this codicil is so legit, so tickety-boo, why not, Mr. Kazakes, just come here and testify, 'Oh, yeah, it's in the security box and I knew that and dadit-dadit-diddo.'"

He reminded them of the Kazakes video. "Use your common sense to consider Mr. Kazakes's evidence. When I'm asking him questions, he's either lying or it's like pulling teeth. But when he's cross-examined by my friend Mr. Deverell – again I cannot say enough about the extent to which Mr. Deverell did everything entirely properly – and he asks him a question in cross-examination like 'What time is it?' you get an array of the whole calendar."

The jury shouldn't put any stock, he said, in Frisbee's claim to amnesia. "One of the fundamental things you have to keep in mind is that one of the best hiding places for someone who is accused of a crime is to be able to say, bingo, from that point I don't remember, and bango, from that point I do – and guess what's in the middle."

Frisbee had tried to bingo and bango not only the jury with his lies, but the psychiatrists as well.

"I don't for a moment suggest that Dr. Tyhurst was being dishonest." Tyhurst's opinion was "kind of big and mushy and not very helpful at the center of this case. Sometimes you look at witnesses, if you ask a short question you get four pages of answer, and Dr. Solomon was the same."

Frisbee had used his consumption of alcohol and Librium as another convenient hiding place. "But as the bricks fall into place, the places to hide get smaller and smaller and smaller, and the places to hide include, 'I don't have a memory,' but they also include, 'Oh, oh, this is a force over which I didn't have any control, I took alcohol and Librium and I didn't know what those would be like.'" The effect of Librium was like taking another drink – "it's not like you're taking angel dust or LSD or some crazy drug. You're not talking about something that will take you to Mars."

Let's face it, those Libriums and French 75s were downed by Frisbee only to get his courage up to commit the evil act.

Well, what really happened in that stateroom? Dennis had his own theory:

"It wasn't that he forgot that Michael Michael came every day about 6:45 with canapés; it was that he *banked* on the fact.

"You don't throw her overboard. Robert Frisbee would never in a million years grab Mrs. Barnett while she is awake, conscious, looking at him, pick her up, and try to throw her overboard. First of all, it's not the way he is. He couldn't face her and do that. Second, it would be a dumb thing to try to do on a cruise ship with the possibility that someone could see him.

"What did he have as an ace in the hole? What he had is that Mrs. Barnett had a history of falling. He's got to make this look like a natural death because a murder death is not going to work. Mrs. Barnett goes to sleep. His plan is that he is going to hit her over the head with a bottle and make it look like a fall. The only thing that will work is a perfectly placed and perfectly executed one blow to the head that, yes, crushes her skull, and then put her in a position leaning over the bed. When Michael Michael comes to the door, I go to the door, 'Oh, hi, I'll just get Mrs. Barnett up.' I walk into the room, I turn around and Michael Michael is there as my witness, and I go, 'Ah, she's dead; she must have fallen.' And that's the plan and it goes bad.

"You have to wonder to yourself why there are two bottles in this case. We know that it doesn't make sense that he walks into the bedroom with two bottles in his hand getting ready to do the dastardly deed.

"He walks into the bedroom with one bottle in his hand and it's the Demestica bottle. He hits her once. He's of the impression that it's been enough. He leaves the room to have a drink to calm his nerves and to begin the process of wiping that bottle, and he hears a sound. Mrs. Barnett is still conscious. I don't know exactly how it would have worked, but she has regained consciousness."

I sat there listening to this highly speculative scenario with awe and wonder. Not one hint of evidence to support it – admissible or otherwise. (But were the jury wondering: does he know something we don't? Something those crazy rules of evidence kept us from hearing?)

"He comes in, he takes the first thing at hand as he comes by, a scotch bottle, and now we have got two bottles involved. Now it's total panic. He takes that scotch bottle, and what he does at that point in time is not measured with nicety at all. His mind is so bunged up that there is no way he is going to make it work, but in the back of his mind the vestiges of the plan are still there.

"Now he's in the bathroom; he's wiping off the scotch bottle. Now what do I do? So it's, 'Wait a minute,' I will get the bloody robe off, I will finish the washing of the scotch bottle. It took forty-five seconds to get to the door. Something's going on in that forty-five seconds. I will tell you what's going on: the finishing of the washing of the scotch bottle, casting off the robe, throwing on your tuxedo pants, opening the door to Michael Michael and carrying on with the vestiges, and saying, 'Oh, Lord, she's dead, she must have fallen,' kind of thing."

I watched to my horror as a couple of jurors nodded. Dennis had filled in the gaps, had recited some plausible non-evidence that would answer all their questions. In full, majestic flow, in an eager torrent of conjecture, crown counsel had made a brutally convincing case out of air.

Frisbee's manuscript provided the final, telling proof of his guilt. In an exercise that vaguely reminded me of an English teacher dissecting a Milton ode, he picked Frisbee's ending apart, line by line.

"'She his nemesis floats by under the guise of joy': Well, in my respectful submission, Mrs. Barnett was his nemesis.

"'The dark silhouettes over your shoulder are here in the guise of fortune-tellers guiding your hand for the final thrust. . . .' You will recall that I asked Mr. Frisbee about Mr. Kazakes's view of himself as a medium. Mr. Frisbee's answer, quick as a bunny, was, 'He's not a fortune-teller.' Well, a fortune-teller guiding his hand is Mr. Kazakes.

"'The final thrust that says goodbye to the past; it's what's going to happen now that gets a nod of approval . . .' The nod of approval from who, ladies and gentlemen?

"'A calumnious act to perform as promised. . . .' Perform as promised to who?

"'Today is the day. A canonical hour to be revealed. . . .' And we are into the shorthand issue. If you want, ladies and gentlemen, I urge you to find that the shorthand says, 'Let's have a peanut butter sandwich.'"

Was this the promised warning to the jury to ignore his own mis-translation? Peanut butter sandwich?

"I don't care what the shorthand says, quite frankly. I don't want you to get hung up because his lordship asked me a question during my cross-examination of Mr. Frisbee, and I don't want anything here to be unfair in that connection." His statement to the court that he got his transcription from "a lady who is a teacher of shorthand" was not evidence.

What he reluctantly gave with one hand, he snatched back with the other: "In my respectful submission it's quite likely something like, 'Today she must lie,' 'Today she must die,' because it entirely fits in the context of the page."

I winced. A calumnious act had been here performed. Something must be said to the judge about this.

He picked out more phrases from the manuscript's ending:

"'The shocking realization, a startling battle of his wits. When, how, where?' The days are getting shorter, there's only a couple left, it's got to get done, where am I going to do it, how am I going to do it; it's going to be a fall, how am I going to make it look like a fall?"

Frisbee's prose revealed the murderer in the man. Mrs. Barnett's writings, however, said something sweet and charming about the woman. He quoted from her diary her indigestible *Reader's Digest* "Recipe for Friendship." ("Take two heaping cups of patience, a dash of laughter," kind of thing.)

As to Frisbee's character, Dennis agreed that "if you look across the run of Mr. Frisbee's relationships, he's a real nice guy," although he had good reason to be when one considers that so many of those relationships were parasitic.

But at a point near the end of his address, Dennis said something that pleasantly bingoed me. He hinted that the planet wouldn't self-destruct if the jury convicted Frisbee only of second-degree murder:

"This is a case where if you are going to give the accused a break, what it's got to boil down to is if it's anything except first-degree murder, if you are going to give the accused a break, it's a second-degree murder break. But one has to keep in mind the rules of the game are that we go on the evidence, we don't go on the sympathy."

Never would a prosecutor so express himself unless he truly believed his chances for a first-degree murder conviction were marginal. Hearing such phrasing, any judge sitting without a jury would know an almost formal concession had been made – the words are a courtroom code, an invitation to acquit upon the most serious charge.

But would the code be broken by the jury – or would they merely divine in Dennis a large and generous spirit?

No, surely they would understand what he was asking of them. Suddenly Dennis seemed like a real nice guy.

He concluded: "I urge you to give the accused the benefit of every reasonable doubt that there is, and that's fundamental to our system of justice and nobody in this room believes in it more strongly than I do. But I also ask you to be fair to the facts."

A real nice guy. The prospect of a first-degree verdict had receded to the dim, distant horizon. Unless the judge rehabilitated it in his instructions to the jury.

Justice McKenzie waited only until Dennis sat down, then began to address the jury.

At the Captain's party with charming chit chat. we tour this small English paradise. We must return by 4:30. As indeed we do — what madam declares madam makes decisions quickly as her new title of President gets results. First Bloody Mary's. Vodka & Fu 75

First a repose before a nap at 4:30 they indulge in a time honored customs — dressing cocktails — only the best with Don Perigone & Stolichnaya Vodka. A cocktail fit for the mood of a pleasant Captain & good bye dinner In the distance the calliope is releasing a strings of forgotten melodies a Calliumnios act to perform as promised in a faithful meeting in his conscious of the early morning. Today is the DAY.

A canonical hour to be revered 1.6 → I The shocking realization a startling battle of his wits. When how where. The dull day only heightens conviction giving a false strength. a happy (5. very hearty drink to ease senses + endure a purple cast over a sky of blue. One could be happy always. she S. a first S o o S n ! o

A page from Robert Frisbee's self-styled memoir, containing incriminating phrases the Crown would seize upon at trial.

The following are photos taken by the San Francisco police inside the suite which Robert Frisbee and Muriel Barnett shared on the *Royal Viking Star*, as it was the evening of the murder. Above is the living-room area, facing the entrance of the bedroom.

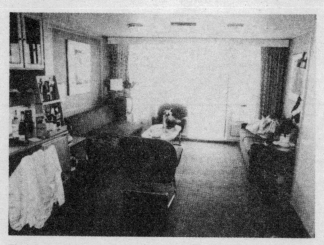

The balcony doors at the end of the living room; the well-stocked bar and Robert Frisbee's white shirt on the left.

The bed, nearest the window, on which Muriel Barnett was murdered while sleeping; Robert Frisbee's bed as it was when he got up from his nap.

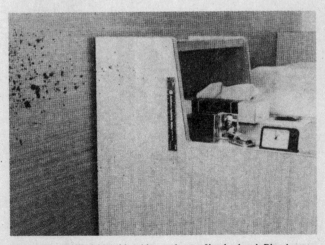

Muriel Barnett's bedside table with two photos of her husband. Blood spatter can be seen on the headboard.

This blood-smeared towel on the floor of the suite's bathroom would prove damaging to the defense.

Next to Frisbee's portable bar can be seen bottles of Demestica wine, Moët champagne uncorked, and the blood-smeared label on the alleged murder weapon–a bottle of Famous Grouse whiskey. In the foreground is the invitation to the captain's farewell party and Frisbee's bowtie, silk handkerchief, and ruffled sleeve garter.

The controversial checks made out and signed by Robert Frisbee on Muriel Barnett's account.

Defense attorney William Deverell. (Tamara Deverell)

Crown prosecuting attorney Dennis Murray. (Jeff Barber/INFocus)

Robert Frisbee in May 1991. (Brian Gray)

Chapter 48

A JUDGE'S CHARGE INSTRUCTS AS TO THE APPLICABLE LAW AND
relates the evidence to it. The task is never easy, although usually a
judge's instruction on the law (known as "the standard charge") is
simply read from prepared text: the time-proven language that
describes such concepts of reasonable doubt and presumption of
innocence and the various technical elements of the offenses. The
case was complex, but Justice McKenzie had had the benefit –
which judges are rarely allowed to enjoy – of a long interlude to
prepare himself. I expected him to complete his charge that afternoon, January 7. Following that the jury would be taken out and
counsel would address the court, making "exceptions" to the
charge. The judge might recall the jury for redirection. They
would then retire to make their decision.

Justice McKenzie began: "In his opening to you, Mr. Foreman
and ladies and gentlemen of the jury, which is some time ago, Mr.
Deverell said that this is not a whodunit, as Mr. Murray has
suggested in his address to you. It *is* a whodunit, as well as a
wheredunit, a whendunit, and a whydunit."

Not a salutary beginning, I thought. I minded not so much
being contradicted as the judge employing the dangerous analogy
of a whodunit, suggesting as it did some duty on the jury's part to
act the detective, to seek out the murderer. Their duty was not to
decide whodunit but whether the Crown had proved beyond a
reasonable doubt that the accused dunit.

He told them they were to consider only facts proven and not
consider "graphic, attention-getting" newspaper headlines. Then

he commenced the standard charge on the law, referring to bits and pieces of evidence as he did so.

Regrettably, his instructions were peppered with phrases that implied a partisan view of the case:

"When you get right down to it, you only have the accused's word for it that he suffered a total lack of recall . . ." "You decide whether it is at all reasonable that he would be innocent of the realization of the combined effect upon him of the drink and the Librium. . . ." "You might consider that the reasons for his use of Librium are not consistent. . . ." "Consider whether this writing could ever be a saleable product, or that it was ever intended as such. Consider whether passages are claimed to be fiction because they could be embarrassing if accepted as fact."

As to Frisbee's stated belief that he thought the October 1984 codicil was void: "I don't know that you would want to regard Mr. Frisbee in matters of probate as being an average lay person. He had a considerable acquaintance in a variety of ways with probate matters." The judge had earlier remarked, in the jury's absence, that the validity of the codicil involved a difficult question of law; now he was implying that Frisbee should have known it had never been invalidated.

I was becoming distinctly uncomfortable. This was, putting it at its mildest, not a charge favoring the defense.

By day's end, the judge had not finished. But, he said, because counsel had already related the evidence in detail, "what I'm going to try and do is try to limit my review of the evidence as much as I possibly can." He anticipated he would be through promptly the next morning.

When charging a jury upon the evidence, most judges undress it to the bones, slice off the meat, and serve it up in chewable relevant morsels. Their duty is to put facts in context, isolate the issues, relate evidence to the law. To simplify and paint clear pictures.

I believe Justice McKenzie began with full intentions of doing this, but perhaps we had erred in ordering daily transcripts. The next morning, January 8, the judge began reading from them.

And reading. And reading. Examinations and cross-examinations. Michael Michael. Jeannette Helan. Eva Falk. Dr. Hansson. He raised his eyes only occasionally from the transcripts, often to point out contradictions in the defense evidence.

We took a twenty-minute break at 11:40. I looked at Jeff. Jeff looked at me. "Maybe he thinks we're winning," he said. "And maybe he thinks that's wrong." Yes. Maybe he was trying to level the playing field to avoid an acquittal.

At noon, the judge began reading the transcripts of the doctors who had attended on Mrs. Barnett and Frisbee. Dr. Raszl. Dr. Goldstein. Questions verbatim, answers verbatim. His side comments became fewer and fewer. Any attempt to relate the evidence to the issues before the jury was abandoned.

"Well, it is 1:45." The jury looked woozy. The judge seemed a little depressed himself. It was as if he had mired himself in a process from which there was no climbing back.

We reconvened at 2:45. More verbatim transcript. Matters relevant and matters that didn't matter. Every word of testimony, every chap and sir and nutshell. Dr. Don Carlos Musser. Connie DeLuca. Millie Dearnaley. Ted Kolb. Dan Kazakes. Dr. Solomon, every pause, every blemish in his sentences. Dr. Rosenthal.

Several jurors appeared to have withdrawn into a state of automatism.

At 4:30, he looked up and said, somewhat hoarsely, "We'll take a break."

Justice McKenzie went to his chambers to consider his options, to seek some detour from a journey that seemed without end.

At 4:47 he came back: "I don't propose, ladies and gentlemen, to review the psychiatric evidence any further. So far as Dr. Tyhurst is concerned, he has prepared this fifty-page report, and it's all here as an exhibit. The views as expressed by Dr. Murray, I think, are firmly lodged in your heads. I don't plan to canvass the evidence of the blood-alcohol experts or the blood-spatter expert, and I don't propose to canvass the evidence of Mr. Frisbee."

The judge had run out of gas before reaching the defense's filling station.

Hey, just a minute, I wanted to shout. What about *us*?

The judge said he would ask counsel if they had any comments, then complete his charge on the morrow. "And very shortly there-after I hope the matter can be in your hands."

The jury lurched from the courtroom. Justice McKenzie didn't want to hear counsels' objections now; he merely wanted to know how extensive they would be. Jeff and I assembled a hurried list: perceived errors in his instructions on burden of proof, unanimity of verdict, automatism, drunkenness, the theory of the defense, and (said I with the greatest of respect), "Your lordship did, with the greatest of respect, editorialize to the jury on some aspects of the evidence, and I want to ask your lordship to recharge the jury in some of those areas."

"Mr. Murray?"

Dennis naturally wasn't going to be heard to complain much. "Every charge to a jury results in a shopping list from either side that says, 'Gee, I sure wish he would have said that.'" But heck, he wasn't going to bother the court with any such picayune griev-ances. His list was a short one: some comment, if it wouldn't be too much trouble, about the lie detector business and a reminder to the jury that Frisbee had never been tried or acquitted in the United States.

"I intended to do both those things," said the judge.

"That's it for me, my lord," Dennis said cheerfully.

The arguments would be heard the next day, January 9, at 9:00 a.m. The jury, sighed the judge, had a hard day.

"It's been a very long day," I sourly agreed.

He brought them back, assured them he'd be ready for them at 10:00 in the morning.

Jeff and I, still stunned at this strangest of charges to the jury, worked past midnight compiling our exceptions, composing our arguments, photostating our cases.

Our shopping list comprised some two dozen matters of judi-cial misfeasance and nonfeasance, as well as Dennis's failure to clear the air over the Crown's distortion of Frisbee's shorthand, not to mention the judge's total failure to review the evidence of that forgotten soul, Robert William Dion Frisbee. Having read word for word the evidence of almost all the Crown witnesses, his ignoring the accused's version seemed (I said with respect) a little unfair.

The judge was, as most trial judges are, protective of his charge, and we scuffled with him over it until late into the morning. He refused to make further comment on the Crown's mistranslation of the shorthand, but recharged the jury upon several of the matters we raised and both the issues Dennis was concerned about. (They were, of course, to disregard Frisbee's offer to take a polygraph test.) He gave them a few key passages from Frisbee's evidence, reminded them of the burden of proof, cautioned them to avoid becoming a hung jury through stubbornness, recited the five verdicts open to them, told them to deliberate until they reached a verdict, and asked the sheriff to take them to lunch.

And we waited.

Chapter 49

AND WE WAITED.

The tension counsel suffer while a jury struggles over its verdict is not unlike that endured by a parent awaiting the results of a first child's birth, listening for the cry. Something between that and, say, waiting for missiles to strike, hearing them whine through the clouds.

I have seen strong men, dignified men in robes, turn into whimpering imbeciles while a jury is out.

A jury works long hours, morning, afternoon, evening, and at night will be sequestered in a hotel, isolated from contamination by others, by the media. There is nothing to do while one waits for them. One paces a lot. It's possible to get in a good ten miles in the course of a day.

From time to time we hovered near the jury-room door. All was quiet within. No raised voices. Was that good, bad, indifferent?

Many reporters hung about, too. And many of the devotees of live soap opera, the folks from the gallery, kept vigil with us.

One of them asked me: "Going to turn this into a piece of fiction, Mr. Deverell?"

"No," I said. "Fiction has to be believable."

In the less formal times of old, it was common during The Long Wait for a judge to invite counsel into chambers to share a bottle. That is a ceremony fraught with peril, for if the judge is over-generous with his Chivas, counsel have been known to become quite drunk, hiccupping and gabble-garbling their way through the sentence submission.

I can recall – only too vividly – the aftermath of one such bibulous session: at a trial several years ago a particularly slow jury was escorted back to the courtroom to be admonished by the judge for taking too long. We all, counsel and jurors alike, watched with alarm as our Supreme Court judge, in a state somewhere between confusion and stupor, staggered into the courtroom, tried to maneuver up the steps to the bench, then fell flat on his face. He finally made it to the bench, though, and gave an incoherent pep talk to the jury which confused them into acquitting.

Jeff and I thought we should carry on the tradition that Friday evening, but in the more sedate surroundings of a fine restaurant, and we invited Justice and Mrs. McKenzie (out of politeness, of course, not to soften him up for sentencing) to join all counsel and spouses for dinner. The jury, we felt, wouldn't be back for at least a couple of days, given the mass of reports and transcripts they had to plod through.

Justice McKenzie said he'd be delighted. Dennis and Ernie offered to share the cost, but we would have none of it. We reserved a table at Chauney's Restaurant, the same decorous eating house at which sneaky Frisbee had pretended his vodka was Perrier on August 19, some seventeen months ago.

Reservations at Chauney's were for 7:30. At 6:45 the jury sent a message asking for some help with the evidence. We hastened back to court.

"Your message to me," said the judge, "was, 'Can we have Mr. Kolb's evidence reread regarding the new will due to be signed on completion of the cruise to Alaska?'"

I felt a little queasy pang of fear. They wanted not Frisbee's explanations but the Crown's accusations. They wanted the evidence of one of the Crown's champion witnesses.

The judge read the appropriate evidence of Ted Kolb, and said, "And that, I think, comprehends everything relating to the new will, so we will –"

The foreman interrupted: "Just a question for clarification, my lord."

"Yes."

"Is there any reference to the executor of that will?"

Why would they be asking that?

The judge said there was no evidence from Mr. Kolb as to who would be executors for the new will.

"Thank you, my lord."

The judge had suggested we might put the jury to bed early this night. We had agreed. No point in having our nosh at Chauney's interrupted by the inconvenience of a verdict just as the joint of lamb arrives. "As chance would have it," he said, "it is just 7:00. We will call it a day and you can have your dinner and you will get back to it tomorrow at 9:00."

Chauney's gave us their best table. We were nine: my wife, Tekla, and I; Jeff and his partner, Barbara; Ernie and his wife; Mr. Justice and Mrs. McKenzie. Only Dennis was without escort; his wife had been ill.

When we ordered pre-dinner drinks Dennis asked for a French 75.

He announced he was going to see if you could actually get drunk on a couple of those things.

French 75s were not on the menu. It took Dennis some time to explain to the waiter what he wanted. Three ounces of vodka in a tall glass, throw in ice cubes, fill with five ounces or more of champagne.

Dennis was in a very good mood.

I was not. I was, as Michael Michael might have put it, a little sadded. I did not like those questions the jury had asked, questions about Mrs. Barnett's new will. Were they obeying the judge's counsel to seek whodunit and whydunit, reasons to point the finger at Frisbee?

But I had to make conversation. I asked Mrs. McKenzie if she had been following the trial.

"Yes, and I'm afraid I'm not a supporter of your cause."

I wasn't sure which of my several causes she had in mind.

The cause was Frisbee. Mrs. McKenzie had not only been following the trial, she'd been watching it from the gallery. I didn't remember her there, but apparently she'd been in daily attendance.

I don't imagine anyone has ever accused Mrs. McKenzie of

being shy about expressing her views – to her mind Frisbee was guilty as sin. Courage failed me before I could ask her if her husband shared this conviction.

Justice McKenzie guessed the jury would be out a few days. If they came back late, it was his guess they would probably do so with a compromise verdict reached after long and heated debate: most likely manslaughter. If they come back quickly, he thought, the result would more likely be first-degree murder or a complete acquittal.

At some point over wine and the entrées Jeff became emboldened enough to ask the judge what verdict he would render if sitting without a jury.

"Toss-up between manslaughter and second-degree murder," said our judge. "If backed to the wall I'd go with manslaughter."

That gave me some cheer, although I thought he'd done his best to instruct the jury for murder.

Well into his second French 75, Dennis was becoming noticeably voluble, and I winced as several indiscreet expressions of the four-letter variety tripped loudly and recklessly from his tongue.

After a while he got up and wandered around the table, boisterous, pumped up, gregarious, profane, and perhaps a little unsteady. "Very merry," as Frisbee would put it. Not once, though, did he come close to beating anyone over the head with a bottle. Not even Ernie. I guess he made his point, although in fairness he should have popped a couple of caps of Librium.

I'm not sure if he had an amnesia the next morning. Having observed the disapproving look on Mrs. McKenzie's face, I would hope he did.

At some point in the evening, Dennis let Jeff and me know that if the jury returned hung there would be no retrial. The Crown simply couldn't afford to reassemble the case.

That was news that made the heart soar. A hung jury would bring Frisbee's nightmare to an end. It would amount to an acquittal.

The next morning our hangovers made the vigil even more oppressive.

A little piece of you dies whenever you do a major trial.
Waiting, waiting.

Waiting for that electric moment of pain or exultation.

In my novel *The Dance of Shiva*, I had tried to describe that moment – in the voice of the young idealist and civil rights lawyer who was the story's narrator:

"There is no lower a low than losing a verdict. It is what makes the practise of law so bloody, so hard on the psyche. A few straight losses and suddenly you are suffering from a siege mentality, judges and prosecutors coming at you with fifty-millimeter cannon fire.

"But winning – ah, that is a different thing. There is no higher a high than winning. Only those who have practised criminal law – and I do not include the three-piece-suit pansies from the uptown firms who stick their toes in the water timidly once in a while – can ever know the almost narcotic rush you get when you walk out of that courtroom, your heart pounding blood to a flushed face, the words of the judge – 'I must regretfully find that the Crown has not made out its case' – ringing like gongs in your ears, the client babbling happily behind you, the prosecutor left sulking at the table. If it's a big case, the kick can be almost orgasmic."

Dream on, says our hero softly to himself.

But probably the strain was even worse for the jury. From time to time, voices were loudly raised from the jury room, though words could not be made out.

Several years ago I defended a lateral handoff from my partner David Gibbons, a case of rape. (David loftily claimed a moral stance – he could not defend a rape case in which the defense was consent; also he was tied up with another trial. I believed a person's right to a defense was paramount, so I had to take his client.) The accused, of unblemished record, had got himself involved with a very angry young woman. She was caught up in some serious lies during cross-examination, but a few of the jurors, including the foreman, seemed bound for conviction, and there had obviously been much sharp debate in the jury room.

When the foreman was asked for the verdict, he said: "Guilty." A storm of protest broke from the jury's ranks and the foreman quickly amended: "Oh, sorry, I mean not guilty."

I wouldn't be surprised if my client developed a neurotic fear of encounters with the opposite sex as a result of that.

A jury trial is a lottery. One never knows. Twelve persons mixing five verdicts can stir up an unsafe, fickle brew.

A lot depends on the human chemistry of the men and women serving. One firm and persuasive juror can swing eleven doubters to his or her side. Many jurors will bend to the strongest breeze. For the sensitive, the experience can be traumatic. And there is no one who can later give a juror therapy because it is a criminal offense in Canada – it's not so in the U.S. – to reveal to anyone the nature of a jury's deliberations even after the fact.

At 2:00 that afternoon of January 10, our jury told the sheriff they had a verdict.

I could feel my heart pummeling my ribs.

I was at the office when a sheriff's officer phoned, and I ran outside, into the misty gloom of a cold January Saturday, across to the courthouse, buttoning my vest and tying my bib.

An eerie, preternatural quiet enshrouded Courtroom D, brittle with tension and dank with human sweat.

Frisbee was in the dock – pale, passive, morbidly dependent Robert Frisbee. Dan Kazakes was not in the box as Dennis had wished, but his ghost hovered there, smelling of old gin, teeth clanking like chains, the weird sister, a witch of Cawdor Castle.

Double, double, toil and trouble.

Kazakes's ghost dissolved into the ether as Justice McKenzie strode to the bench.

"Would you bring the jury in, please?"

The jury arrived in solemn procession, a few of them red-faced and sorrowful, others smug with victory. Not one of them looked me in the eye.

I couldn't look at Frisbee.

"Madame Registrar," said the judge.

She rose: "Members of the jury, have you reached a verdict?"

"Yes, we have, my lord," said the foreman.

"What is your verdict, Mr. Foreman?" she said.

"Guilty as charged, my lord," said the foreman.

Guilty of first-degree murder.

The registrar recited the ancient language: "Members of the jury, harken to the verdict as the court doth record it; you find the prisoner Robert William Dion Frisbee guilty as charged. This is your verdict, so say you all. Please stand to confirm your verdict."

They all stood.

PART THREE

Post-trial

Chapter 50

GUILTY AS CHARGED.

I was incredulous, numb.

I slid weakly back into my chair. The room stirred and hummed around me.

"Would you stand, Mr. Frisbee, please," said Justice McKenzie.

He fluttered to his feet. "Oh, yes, sir, pardon me."

"Do you have anything to say, Mr. Frisbee?"

"Oh, not a word, your lordship, not a word." Words wispily twittered. Sorry to have been such a bother. Anything you desire, I will be happy to comply with. Castration.

Justice McKenzie cut the anguish short, sentencing him immediately:

"This is a most pathetic occasion for any person to face, and I am sure you are aware of the consequences of the jury's verdict. The Code makes it mandatory for me to pronounce upon you, which I do, the sentence of imprisonment for life without eligibility for parole until you have served twenty-five years of that sentence. That really is all that I can say to you, Mr. Frisbee. I'm not going to moralize on an occasion like this."

He thanked the jury, then said: "I should not let the occasion go by without also commending counsel for what I regard as professional work of the highest caliber. Counsel, every one of them, I thought did a superlative job."

I guess he was trying to soften the sting. I did not share his view. I had failed.

Jeff and I couldn't face the media wolves at the courtroom door.

The sheriffs took pity on us, brought us down in the prisoners' elevator, to the cells.

We had a few moments alone with Frisbee in the visiting room. I guess we conversed, but I remember nothing of it. Traumatic amnesia.

I do remember Jeff embracing Frisbee. I understand I did that, too.

We walked from the cells and waved goodbye to wan, weary, forsaken Robert Frisbee.

A part of me did die. All that time and money and work and pain . . . and now having to endure the terrible knowledge we had condemned Frisbee to spend his waning years behind bars, to a deathbed in a cell, because we had counseled him to refuse the Crown's original offer of a plea to second-degree murder.

I swore I would never take another trial.

First-degree murder . . . it's reserved for hit men, terrorists, serial killers, thrill killers, chainsaw murderers. Animals like the infamous Clifford Olson, who had roamed the Fraser Valley in search of children to murder (eleven of them) and was serving a similar sentence of twenty-five years without parole.

If only I had discovered that damnable manuscript. Burned it, shredded it, buried it, fed its pages to the fish in the Strait of Juan de Fuca. Was Frisbee (literally, as it were) the author of his own misfortune? "Tonight she must die" . . . I would never know the jury's thoughts, but Frisbee's exhibition of toiling agony on the witness stand as he sought to read the peanut-butter-sandwich shorthand – had that been our rooftop edge, our nightmare precipice, our fall?

Or had the script been written on a ouija board by the psychic Greek Svengali, a telekinetic guiding of the hand for the final thrust that says goodbye . . .

But I blamed not Kazakes, not Frisbee, not the Crown, not the judge, not the jury. I blamed myself. I should not have rushed the trial, should have abandoned hopes for a Christmas verdict. I should have raised a hue and cry over the Crown's mean attack on Frisbee's character. Our shotgun approach had been wrong; we should have concentrated our firepower on manslaughter, fought with passion not facts . . . I should have referred poor Frisbee to more able senior counsel.

Somehow we got to the office. I hid from the reporters banging at the door. Jeff was stronger than I; he dealt with them, sending them on their way with promises of appeals.

THE VANCOUVER SUN, January 11, 1987
Frisbee's Lover Gets Life in Sun
By Larry Still,
Sun Staff Reporter

VICTORIA – As a pale and shaken Robert Frisbee, 59, stumbled from a courtroom here to begin serving a life term for first-degree murder, his lover was sunning himself in Palm Springs.

Daniel Kazakes, 65, said by a prosecutor to be "up to his ears" in a plot to kill wealthy San Francisco socialite Muriel Barnett, 80, is unlikely to join Frisbee behind bars.

"We have strong suspicions concerning his role but there is insufficient evidence to take proceedings against him," prosecutor Dennis Murray told *The Vancouver Sun* in interview after the trial.

Asked if he felt any sympathy for Frisbee, Murray said he was struck by the "pathetic nature of the man" during sentencing, but added: "One has to keep in mind the death of Muriel Barnett."

Frisbee, dressed in a dark blue suit, blue shirt, and maroon tie, appeared stunned by the decision.

Justice McKenzie, showing compassion to a man who will likely spend the rest of his life in prison, told Frisbee he had no choice but to pronounce the severest sentence in Canadian law.

The media couldn't get enough of it. For days after the trial, new angles were sought, new informants were quoted.

"Crime pays," announced *The Province* three days later. "Just ask convicted murderer Robert Frisbee. The 59-year-old homosexual will get $250,000 U.S. from the estate of the woman he bludgeoned to death. A San Francisco judge has signed an order awarding Frisbee the cash . . ."

The *Sun* followed up with an interview with Ted Kolb about the bequest for more than a third of a million Canadian dollars.

Frisbee wouldn't have to pay taxes on it, he said, but added, "I think a good portion will go to Mr. Deverell and Mr. Green."

"Slain Woman's Money Used to Pay Lawyer's Bill," trumpeted *The Province*.

Our firm invested the bulk of the funds for Frisbee in safe securities. (Despite this, he kept dipping into these funds, making large donations to his favorite charity, the Reverend Dan Kazakes, who quickly drank the monies away.) We were unable to comment to the press about our fees – a matter of client privilege – and as a result it was widely speculated that Frisbee had been left only with spare change in his pockets. (Several years later one of the trial-watchers told me: "I hear you got the whole two-fifty.")

On Thursday, January 15, Larry Still wrote:

"Frisbee's lawyers filed an appeal Wednesday against his conviction. No date has been set. Defense lawyer Jeffrey Green said there are fifteen grounds of appeal cited."

I emerged a couple of times from my black funk to mumble a few words into a microphone, but the weight of despair had me bent and sour, churlish to friends and cynical about our justice system.

But Frisbee brightened quickly, and with a certain majesty of spirit became an unlikely tower of strength. The day after his conviction, on January 11, he wrote:

Dear Mr. Deverell:

It seems I have been a big disappointment to my fellow man in here – they are all much more depressed than Robert! Dark clouds loom over the portals of Unit I. But I am not in a state of acute, demonstrative dementia. Robert is okay, Mr. Deverell, do not worry about him . . . he has always been able to adjust, and this is one more plateau. Definitely not in a giving up state of mind.

The guards are watching me rather carefully . . . two came last night after I locked my door. No suicide – with what? Robert can't even get AIDS!

Soooo, we pulled a foxy one on the press yesterday afternoon. The driver warned me the reporters would be waiting for me when I came out of the garage, and he was upset anyway, so he took a different route, he came out of the garage across the way from where they were all standing with flashbulbs awhirl while we sped away unnoticed!

I have not felt like talking to anyone ... did call Dan and of course he is upset beyond reason, as his psychic powers had me escaping to Palm Springs.

When you see or talk to Dr. Tyhurst pass on my thoughts and feeling of gratitude ... would love to talk to him some day and see just what it is that makes Robert tick ... he has me on the right track of self-analysis, if there is such a thing.

Bye and thanks again for everything.

Bob

Chapter 51

Dear Mr. Deverell:

Was awakened this a.m. with squeals of delight from a roomie – your attorney is on TV. That is why you looked so dapper yesterday with carefully chosen shirt and suit! You devil, you did not tell me. You were great as always.

Have a good trip to Costa Rica.

Bob

I fled to the sun, sand, and birdsong of Quepos, Costa Rica, my winter home. I healed slowly. I returned to my word processor and plunged myself into fantasy's oblivion. Stolen songs, dreams of glory, and gifts of love; drugs, sex, and rock and roll: *Platinum Blues*. Its author shunned violence, was surprised at his gently comic tone. It was as if I had had enough of blood.

Frisbee kept letters pouring into the office. A month after the trial he was transferred to the federal penitentiary at Kent in the Fraser Valley, a maximum security dead end for the condemned. Where mass murderer Clifford Olson once was jailed.

February 14

As you can see, I made it to Kent.

How is Robert? I don't know right now, but I am giving him plenty of space (one thing he does not have here . . . from the bed to the washbasin is a matter of six steps, and to this desk about three in a northerly direction). My roommate is as big as a Minotaur; we do have to dodge around one another.

Informed I am in a unit of P.C. devoted to WIMPY inmates.

Robert is popular! Not for his scintillating personality you are so familiar with . . . his color TV and typewriter are the culprits.

My roommate seems a compatible soul, and no problem of lack of communication . . . he prefers to talk to himself. He does have a penchant for early morning cartoons I will have to put a restraining order on.

The Minotaur became less and less a compatible soul as the weeks wore on. Twenty-one years old, a multiple murderer, one day he decided to deal with Frisbee's complaints about his insatiable appetite for the morning cartoons by raping him. He met minor but terrified resistance, so he did it again. Again and again.

Terrorized to the limits of sanity, Frisbee endured several months of physical hell.

"They wanted to put the fruit with the nut so they could make a fruitcake," he told me later.

Officials at Kent seemed to think they deserved each other – or thought Frisbee was expendable; they could find no one else to live with the young psychopath.

Frisbee was at Kent for four months until John Conroy, a prison rights lawyer we retained, won his transfer to the comparatively serene surroundings of Mountain Prison, a medium-security jail for protective custody inmates.

May 5

Look who's sixty! Mrs. B. always said, "Don't count them, Robert, enjoy them." And I am content in my new digs – solitude at last, no noisy clanging doors and loudspeakers droning on day and night. This is a more or less respectable senior citizens' encampment. Every day brings a pleasant surprise! A walk in the garden to breathe fresh air!

Through everyone's successful efforts Robert was transferred from that Whore's Horror, and much happier at Mountain. The mental abuse I was able to cope with, but the physical abuse would eventually have turned me into a vegetable. Don't know anything about karate, but aren't they supposed to take off their shoes before kicking one in the stomach?

◇   ◇   ◇

The appeal should have been heard by the fall of 1987, but delays occurred, the appeal books having to be reworked several times by the official court reporters. In the end the eight volumes of appeal books – transcripts of all the evidence, copies of the seventy-plus paper exhibits – ran to 1,400 pages. Our factum, the outline of our legal arguments, was originally seventy-five pages long, then was honed to fifty-seven.

Aside from my work for Frisbee, I took no more trials, and immersed myself in my novel, finishing *Platinum Blues* for publication in 1988 and writing several screenplays.

Frisbee was patient. Accept and carry on – that was his philosophy.

On November 14, 1987, he wrote: "THEY WANT TO ARREST ME!"

A police officer had come calling with a warrant for his arrest and deportation (to take effect after twenty-five years). We told him not to worry about it.

Winter arrived and settled in and grudgingly withdrew and still no appeal date could be set. A summer passed, and another winter.

Every month, though, new delights for our forbearing, stoical client. His letter of February 8, 1989:

"We had a storm! Personally relished and enjoyed the snow. The picturesque scenery in the mountains was lovely and I was luckily able to contentedly sit, knit, and watch the blizzard tumble down outside picture windows."

He had a job now at Mountain Prison as law librarian. Soon he was put in charge of the music library, too. Ultimately he became senior librarian. Working his way up.

He made friends there, among them an eighty-two-year-old priest serving time for his pedophilic sins. Ninety per cent of Mountain prisoners are sex offenders, segregated there to deny them the adventure of being tormented by the bullies down the road at Kent. The non-sex offenders included a couple of former jail guards.

Finally, the Court of Appeal date was set – for the first few days of the week of January 9, 1989. The court would have a wide array of choices: it could dismiss the appeal altogether and let the first-degree murder conviction stand; it could substitute another verdict such as manslaughter; it could order a new trial.

Dennis Murray and Ernie Quantz would not be acting for the Crown; they'd handed it to Richard Peck, assisted by Carolyn Bouck. Richard was friend and fellow courtroom combatant of long standing, unprepossessing, self-assured, a vigorous volunteer among bar organizations, and treading a career path to the bench.

He told Jeff and me he was doubtful whether our grounds would hold up – although he clearly felt that Frisbee had been given too rough a ride by the jury (and, in his tough cross-examination, by Dennis Murray). But juries are entitled to their unwise decisions, and whether we would succeed depended upon the British Columbia Court of Appeal being convinced a serious error in law had been made: a misdirection by the judge to the jury, as an example, or a wrong ruling upon one of our many points of law and jurisdiction.

In B.C., a hearing in the appeal court – before a panel of three of its judges – can be just as dicey a gamble as a trial before a jury: much depends on the chance of the draw. A few are liberal, many more are stern upholders of the unbending right.

Our three-man coram was, I suppose, somewhere down the middle. Mr. Justice John Taggart was a long-serving veteran, courteous and pleasant to appear before. Mr. Justice William Esson had come from the civil side of trial practice, and was sharp and tough. Mr. Justice Sam Toy I knew well – he had been a criminal lawyer of keen talent and swift wit, and although most of his work had been for the Crown side he was always a fair player. While a Supreme Court judge he had gained a reputation as meting out rugged sentences, but he knew a reasonable doubt when he saw one.

Wrote Larry Still: "Author William Deverell, switching to his alternate role of criminal defense counsel, related Monday a real-life drama in which the characters might have stepped from the pages of one of his own novels."

The appeal was hardly as much fun as Larry's lead implied. It was unkind, rigorous work. Justice Esson was the court's trigger man, and put Jeff and me through some difficult dance steps. Justice Toy took turns in working us over from the other side of the bench (although he, too, took umbrage at the Crown's treatment of Frisbee on the stand). Many of our grounds they demolished quickly; others had obviously set them thinking.

Richard Peck, too, probably had to work a little harder than he expected to, but he knew how to back-step and dodge, and kept his balance. At the end, he seemed content to abide whatever result would follow.

The appeal lasted four days. Justice Esson seemed clearly against us; Justice Toy was perhaps a little more supportive. Justice Taggart offered no clues. The court reserved judgment on about ten grounds. And again we waited.

Judgment came down on April 11. Seventy-seven pages. It was written by Justice Esson. The other two judges concurred.

Justice Esson dealt painstakingly with our pre-trial complaints about errors of law and jurisdiction, but dismissed each in turn. As to the facts, he held that the defenses of automatism and drunkenness were not grounded in adequate fact to allow the appeal, despite clear errors in the judge's charge.

But he was not pleased with the manner in which the offense of first-degree murder was placed before the jury.

"There were weaknesses in that aspect of the Crown case and there was much in the circumstances of the killing which could create a basis for doubting that it was planned and deliberate." Skeptical comment by the trial judge about Frisbee's testimony had undermined the defense's position in a way that was damaging.

"Some of the other aspects of the evidence relied upon by the Crown in proof of planning provided rather doubtful support." The checks for $100,000 and $300,000, for instance, which would have more than exhausted Mrs. Barnett's account. "Why would Frisbee have written an uncashable $300,000 check to himself, thus adding to a suspicious trail of paper which could do him no good after the death of Mrs. Barnett?

"Then there is that matter of the circumstances of the killing. Why would Frisbee choose to carry out this carefully made plan in a manner so messy, and at a time when he knew that crew members were near the suite and would shortly be entering it?"

The Crown's theory that Frisbee had built up a resentment toward Mrs. Barnett could have provided a motive for planned murder, "but it could also have played a part in building up a great anger which, with no plan, caused an emotional explosion."

Justice McKenzie's charge failed to separate the issue of intent to kill from the issue of planning and deliberation, and his failure to emphasize aspects of the evidence which could create doubt about planning and deliberation "was a significant non-direction amounting to misdirection."

He concluded: "I would substitute a conviction for second-degree murder for that of first-degree murder, and request counsel to arrange a date to deal with the question of parole eligibility."

My feelings were confused. I was relieved that Frisbee might live to freedom. I was disappointed that our court took what I felt was a wrong view of the evidence and denied our most formidable arguments.

But our efforts had borne fruit, and Frisbee accepted and carried on.

Dear William,

Enjoying relatively good health, walking around in a disillusionary manner. Am not and never will be "jail smart" so find myself alone once again. Outside the norm, looking in . . .

There are good feelings here on the grounds and I get waves and arms of greeting from across the camp . . . The guilt and remorse will always be present with the thought that a person I loved dearly is no longer here. But with the stigmatism of premeditation (premedication???) has been removed. I cannot imagine myself planning such an obscene act.

There remained a chance the Court of Appeal might order Frisbee to spend anything from ten to twenty-five years before parole, but Richard Peck promised he would not seek more than ten.

On June 29, 1989, the court reassembled and sentenced Robert Frisbee to the minimum detention.

We made a last-gasp application to the court of final resort but received word on August 31, 1989, that the Supreme Court of Canada would not entertain an appeal.

So it ends . . .

A few years have softened the bite of loss, but I still feel a strong sense that the quality of mercy failed to droppeth as the gentle rain from heaven upon the soul of Robert Frisbee. "Injustice," said H.L. Mencken, "is relatively easy to bear; what stings is justice." But all criminal lawyers have won cases they had no right to win, and there's balance there of a kind. Our lumbering, stumbling system of justice works well enough nine times out of ten.

But it's not much nurture to you, is it, Robert, to be number ten?

The story has too bittersweet an ending for my taste, but it's a story.

Might make a good book.

Epilogue

Ferndale, B.C.

DEAR MR. DEVERELL,

Good news! As you see, I have a new hometown. Yes, Robert has just been transferred from Mountain Prison to Ferndale Institution. Must not call it a jail – it's an INSTITUTION. Like marriage? Anyway, a little closer to Vancouver and to civilization. (Is there civilization in Vancouver?) But no gates, no walls. No rooftops, no precipices. Minimum security.

I can walk right out onto the road if I want. But don't worry, I won't. I'd only get lost looking for the nearest bar. (Just joking.) And believe it or not there's a nine-hole golf course here! Not that I would ever use it . . . too many memories of Philip, driving him around in that ridiculous cart, chasing his silly little balls.

I live a solitary life here in my own private room. Not exactly a villa, but no bars, no views of razor wire or guard towers out my window. And I'm making new friends. There's quite a mix of people here. Some are just kids, but some are more my age (an immature sixty-four). There are interesting people, teachers, priests, professionals, men of letters, people who if you met them on the street, you'd think they're very nice. Normal like me. (Another joke.)

Guess what? I'm going to be a student!

I'm going to study sociology. So many kids with problems here. It's the first step to try to understand them. And maybe I'll follow up with some studies in psychoanalysis, because if I get to know myself better I might learn to understand others. I want to help people, Mr. Deverell, I want to give what I never received.

The kids in here, if they could just have some kind of stepping stone . . .

I go to mass on Sundays these days, by the way. Wear a chain with a cross around my neck. I never really gave up religion, you see, I just got careless.

What else? Still knitting away. Cowichan sweaters, no less. Some of the Native kids at Mountain taught me how. Oh, yes, and I've taken up Native bead work. (Doing something weird, as you might expect of Robert, making Christmas ornaments from Indian beads.)

So I don't get bored, Mr. Deverell, and I don't get depressed.

But I still doubt and I still worry. I feel questions nibbling away like mice at my brain, at the edges of my memory. Did I murder dear Muriel? Did all that resentment eat at my bowels just like the cancer ate at hers? Was it love I felt, or was it fear or was it hate? Or all of those? I guess I'll never know where the love stopped and the anger began.

You always ask when you visit me: Has it come back? Do I remember anything? Has that broken-down calliope in my brain released any strains of forgotten melodies?

I know you want to know how it ended, for your book. You want to know if Robert did the unendurable deed. With a conscious, cold-blooded, mindless mind, I would like to give you a catchy ending for your book, but THERE IS NO MEMORY. Just a hole where memory should be, a black hole in the galaxy sucking up the past.

So . . . the hands knit fast, the brain knits slow. But it does knit. A few threads here and there. I TRY to remember, Mr. Deverell, I try. Last month I asked a psychologist at Mountain if hypnosis could help me remember. He said, "Why do you want to remember?"

I didn't know how to answer that. I guess I just want to know. I'm not afraid of knowing. Dr. Tyhurst taught me not to be afraid of the dark. I see more of my roots now, because he taught me how to dig for them. So, once in a while I do pull a thread from the long-ago past, my childhood, my father's anger, or my mother's tears. Sometimes I recall another tear of my own, for Dr. Barnett . . . or the migraine of despair when he abandoned me.

And other memories have begun to pop up, of more recent vintage. (Demestica '85? Vin Ordinaire de Viking Star? Vin Extraordinaire!)

One of them has to do with the odd behavior of M.C.B. on the famous cruise . . . parading around the suite in that black, provocative, ludicrous negligee she had bought especially for the trip. "Don't you love it, Robert?" she cooed. "Philip would never let me wear a thing like this." And her smile. So saccharine. (Impressed? I looked it up: "cloyingly sweet.")

Then there was the morning – I think we were sailing south by then – that The Bride woke up in a pout. I asked her why. Seems I had not kissed her goodnight when I tucked her in.

And so when the next night rolled around I did proper lip service as I tucked her in. And, well . . . the return of kiss, let us say, was a little out of the ordinary, not anywhere to be found within my limited anthology (is that word right?) of heterosexual amour. A *meaningful* kiss, with parted lips, and wet! Wet with a kind of terrible invitation. I remember pulling away, so frightened.

Anyway, I went to bed, filled with unease . . .

I think that was the night before the fateful day. "Today is the day." Remember that?

I think I've come up with one more memory of that last evening. As I lay down to rest with the French 75s and the Librium bubbling through my head, I somehow see Dan hovering over my bed, sour and impatient, as if I conjured him up, or maybe I was trying to levitate from the ship into the safety of his arms. Then blankness and darkness until the butler knocked.

I wish I had made it into the safety of Dan's arms. Now I never will.

I guess you heard, Mr. Deverell. Dan is dead.

Hard for me to comprehend that little sentence. Three little words. Dan is dead.

I can repeat it a thousand times a thousand times and the words still come out wrong, but Dan *is* dead, Dan is dead.

It's circled on my calendar. January 24, 1990. He was sixty-eight.

It was Mr. Conroy who told me – the lawyer you hired for me to get me out of the House of Horrors, and who rescued me from the Minotaur. He visited me with what he said was some bad news and some bad news. Dan had died in a nursing home in Palm Springs after two bouts of pneumonia. And he had died penniless, all the thousands of dollars that I had sent him spirited away (vodka spirits, not holy spirits), and our house trailer in Palm Springs in a terrible mess, not worth anything. Owned by the bank, anyway.

I guess I never quite got myself ready for the transmigration of poor Dan's psychic soul, but I knew all those cigarettes and drinks and the reckless sex would eventually demand their price. The decline really accelerated after I was arrested. "How could you do this to me, Robert?" That's what he said. Then after the trial, he just seemed to vanish into himself, into bones and flesh, into hopelessness, I guess. He only wrote me to plead for more money.

Pneumonia, they said. Did they mean AIDS? Dan always complained about discomfort in what he called "the dessert." But I don't believe the killer was AIDS. I think the killer was alcohol. Complicated by a broken heart. I believe he loved me. In his way.

But . . . Robert accepts and carries on.

So now, Mr. Deverell, with all my dreams of retirement with Dan stolen from me, I guess the future has to take new shape.

It will, it will. You see, Robert has become more assertive as he has carried on. He has *changed*, and is mildly astonished at the new 1991 version. Thank you, Dr. Tyhurst. I am not afraid now. No dreams of the edge. Thank you.

And thank you, judge and jury. Thank you, your Lady the Queen, your crown and dignity. Thank you, Inspector Klotz, and thank you, Dennis the Menace. Thank you all, all you instruments of change. Would Robert be alive except for you? Except for you, wouldn't I have returned to drink and Dan, and death with a bloated bleeding liver? Bob ill, Bob dead. Wow, end of trip.

I will be different when I come out, Mr. Deverell. I've never been alone before, never on my own. But I can do it. I don't need the protection of others any more. Anyway, there aren't many men left older than Robert. And all the kids . . . well, they treat me like a kindly grandma. My taste doesn't lie in that direction anyway. Never did.

I am going to continue with Alcoholics Anonymous. No Dan to hold me back. (He always said the only way he could handle those A.A. meetings was to get drunk first.) I have no choice but to shun the evil drink forever – considering the shape my liver is in.

Okay, enough of that, enough liverish musings. More cheerful news. In a little over a year from now, by August of 1992, Robert will be eligible for day parole. And then I'll be able to take those classes in sociology. And if I'm good, maybe full parole by 1995. I could get admitted into a half-way house. Maybe Harbour House, the place the Salvation Army runs in Vancouver. And maybe they'll let me help some of the poor kids with AIDS. That's really what I want to do.

I keep wondering, how will people treat me on the outside? Of course one has to worry. You put that Q for Queer up on your forehead, and they think you have only one thing on your mind. PERVERSION. Kinky drag queen fag.

Well, Robert could care less what people think. He's going to be his own person.

And maybe one day Robert will remember, maybe he will remember.

Bob

A Final Note

But Robert Frisbee will never remember . . . in this lifetime.

Shortly before this book went to press at the end of July 1991, Frisbee's lawyer, John Conroy, telephoned me with tragic news. Frisbee had been taken to Mission Hospital, near Ferndale Institution. He was diagnosed as terminally ill, with cirrhosis and liver cancer, his survival likely measured in weeks only.

John immediately began strenuous efforts to obtain a prerogative of mercy, allowing Frisbee to return to the States to be with his sister. He even obtained a letter from Dennis Murray in support, but the Attorney-General of British Columbia declined to add his voice. The last official word we received was that members of a special committee of the federal cabinet, who would have to pass on the application, would be unable to interrupt their schedules to meet and make the order in timely fashion.

Upon receiving the news of Frisbee's illness, I made a visit to the hospital, where I found him wan, wasted, but still alert – and able to joke about whether he would have time to prepare his own final codicil. I held my sadness within and laughed with him.

I remember that one of Frisbee's letters to me had ended thus:

"Not sure I am ready to face the all-forgiving Lord – is He ready for Robert?"

I pray He is. The great all-forgiving Jurist proclaimed a final Judgment Day, from which there will be no adjournment, no appeal, no parole. But perhaps there will be peace.

Robert Dion Frisbee died in his sleep on July 21, 1991.

William Deverell
North Pender Island, B.C.
July 25, 1991